◼◼◼◼◼◼◼◼◼

*Earth & Sky*

# Earth
# &
# Sky

*Visions of the Cosmos*
*in Native American Folklore*

EDITED BY RAY A. WILLIAMSON
AND CLAIRE R. FARRER

UNIVERSITY OF NEW MEXICO PRESS
ALBUQUERQUE

Library of Congress Cataloging-in-Publication Data

Earth & Sky: visions of the cosmos in Native American folklore / edited by Ray A.
  Williamson and Claire R. Farrer.
         p.      cm.
  Includes bibliographical references and index.
  ISBN 0−8263−1317−5
  1. Indians of North America—Astronomy.
  2. Indians of North America—Religion and mythology.
  3. Indians of North America—Folklore.
  I. Williamson, Ray A., 1938−
  II. Farrer, Claire R.
  III. Title: Earth and sky.
  E98.A88E18   1992
  398.26—dc20
  91−43268
  CIP

# Contents

■■■■■■■■■

*Earth & Sky*

## How to Write a Poem about the Sky

*for the students of the Bethel Middle
School, Bethel, Alaska—Feb. 1975*

You see the sky now
colder than the frozen river
so dense and white
little birds
walk across it.

You see the sky now
but the earth
is lost in it
and there are no horizons.
It is all
a single breath.

You see the sky
but the earth is called
by the same name
     the moment
     the wind shifts
sun splits it open
and bluish membranes
push through slits of skin.

You see the sky

# 1

■■■■■■■■■

## *Introduction:*
## *The Animating Breath*

■■■■■■■■■

RAY A. WILLIAMSON AND CLAIRE R. FARRER

---

*You see the sky now*
*but the earth*
*is lost in it*
*and there are no horizons.*
*It is all*
*a single breath.*
　　　　　　　—Leslie Marmon Silko (1981 : 177)

Native American myths and tales of the sky have entertained and instructed non–Native Americans for well over a century. They also provide important insights into Native American worldviews. Yet, until recently, scholars of Native American traditions have often neglected the wisdom available from the study of these sources. Although Native Americans did not ignore the importance of the sun and moon, stars and planets in their lives, anthropologists and folklorists generally did. Astronomers, caught up in their pursuit of research on the structure and order of the observable, material universe, had not thought to look for underlying meaning in Native cultures. An imbalance resulted, weighted toward Euroamerican perceptions and philosophies. The present collection of articles, offered by scholars from the fields of anthropology, astronomy, English, folklore, and religion, attempts to correct this imbalance. It offers new insights into Native North American cultures by providing examples of the power of their folklore and mythology to construct alternatives to the prevailing scientific definitions of reality.

Silko's six lines from "How to Write a Poem About the Sky," eloquently express one recurring aspect of Native North Americans' vision of Earth and Sky—their inherent oneness. Although, for the purposes of speech, we may separate Earth and Sky, animals and humans, these categories are fundamentally "a single breath" in which, on one level at least, "there are no horizons." Generalizing about Native American philosophic world views has its dangers, because each tribe, indeed each group within the tribe, may well hold different views of the cosmos. Yet, as the articles in this book demonstrate, the notion of the essential oneness of the cosmos is widespread in native North American philosophy. Rocks, rivers, trees, animals, sea creatures, people, sun, moon, and stars are all related.

While it constitutes a whole, the cosmos is not static. These stories and their interpretations also show us the roles of supernatural beings and humans as mediators traveling along an ideational *axis mundi* between the two realms. Sky beings come down to the surface of the Earth and humans travel to the Sky. Yet the two realms and the two classes of beings are not mirror images of one another. An event in one realm potentiates, but does not legislate, an event in the other. Regular motion is the hallmark of the Sky realm, while Earth supports apparent stability that is always on the brink of breaking into chaos.

Most of the stories show celestial beings as manifestations of the sacred who intercede in human affairs, often in a beneficient way. For example, the stars may aid in healing, as among the Navajo (Haile 1947) and the Pawnee (Chamberlain 1982:45), or the sun may bring health and prosperity, as in the Pueblo tribes. Yet sky beings also show a dark side, as among the Chumash, who feared Sun's propensity to grab up the weak and unprotected as he swept through the sky. When Sun arrived back at his crystal home in the west, he and his daughters would pass them "through the fire two or three times and then eat them half cooked," (Blackburn 1975:93).

In these stories, the experiences of humans who travel to the sky provide useful lessons, for they are taken from vibrant oral traditions and derive their power from reflecting daily life. Unfortunately, the stories that appear in the following chapters, or are paraphrased within them, have a static quality forced upon them by the printed page rather than the dynamic immediacy they possess when narrated. To most native Americans, speech has a special status: words, especially those carrying cosmogenic or cosmological meaning, have a potency they generally lack in Euroamerican society. They are literally gifts from the gods, not the works of human beings. As N. Scott Momaday has explained (Momaday 1970:62), for the traditional Native American, language "is the dimension in which his existence is most fully accomplished. He does not create language but is himself created within it. In a real sense, his language is both the object and the instrument of his religious experience." Native American stories often carry the equivalent sort of sacred power that Christians impart to Christ's words at the Last Supper, and as such, these stories have the ability to impart precepts that sustain the tribal group.

In general, whether from the stars, the sun or moon, Native North Americans find laws and principles in the sky by which to live. This is understandable, for traditionally they have lived within a sustainable economy in which understanding and living by the rhythms of Sky and Earth were essential virtues. Cynics will point out that they had no choice—their technology would not allow otherwise. They had to heed the teachings inherent in celestial events in order to survive. Yet whether by choice or not, they made a virtue out of necessity. In attempting to maintain their lives within the strictures of a sustainable economy, Native North American groups learned important lessons about both Earth and Sky and their own place in the cosmos; such lessons give their stories a breath that provides aesthetic and daily inspiration.

## Naked-Eye Astronomy and the Calendar

Native American groups throughout the hemisphere were avid watchers of the sky, carefully noting the cyclic patterns inherent in the motions of the sun and moon, the stars and planets (Aveni 1977, 1989a; Williamson 1981). The demands of agriculture certainly drove some groups to develop a celestial calendar, as the signs of earthly behavior portending the change of seasons are uncertain, even chimerical. Watching the regular motions of the sky made possible more accurate timing of planting and harvesting activities. Indeed, scholars of Native American traditions early on documented agriculture's connection to the calendar. However, generally they have been slow to address the use of sky calendars among nonagricultural groups.

Recent scholarship has made substantial contributions to a deeper understanding of hunter–gatherer or hunter–forager societies by showing that these groups also developed highly sophisticated celestial calendars. Led in North America by the work of Hudson in records of the California tribes (Hudson and Underhay 1978; Hudson 1984), and extended by others (Benson and Hoskinson 1985), we are beginning to appreciate the extensive use these groups made of celestial calendars to guide food production and ritual activities. As Patencio (1943 : 113), a member of the Cahuilla tribe in California, noted:

> They studied the north star, how it turns about, and the seven stars [the Great Dipper] and the morning star—all this helped to know when to go and gather their food. The month that the road runner flies means certain things, and the habits of many animals all meant something to these older people who studied the signs of the sun and the moon and the stars and the animals.

Practical considerations related to food production most certainly aided the development of much sky watching. However, the calendar also served ritual, and the demands of ritual in their turn undoubtedly gave considerable impetus to the calendar's refinement. In general, an emphasis on high accuracy in a calendar seems to have been driven by ritual needs, rather than food production (Williamson 1984 : 316–18).

Whether by agriculturalists or hunters and gatherers—foragers, consistent observations of the celestial bodies provided Native North Americans greater power to participate fully in the rhythms of their environment. In many tribes, those who have maintained traditional practices still watch the sky in order to determine the appropriate times to plant, to gather wild foods, or to hold ceremonies.

Although many Native North Americans continue to observe the celestial sphere and keep alive the associated narratives, there are difficulties moving from Native to mainstream understandings. One of the primary impediments to interpreting the subtleties of sky-related mythology and folklore is the general lack of observational experience among scholars without special training in astronomy. Even many professional astronomers have little experience in contemplating the apparent motions of the heavens from the standpoint of a naked-eye observer. Yet in using naked-eye observation, daily, monthly, yearly, and even millennial changes in the patterns of Sky are readily visible. Such grand designs in Sky demand attention on Earth. The following sections summarize the primary celestial features a naked-eye observer would be able to note. Here, we have deliberately avoided explaining the causes of these phenomena from the standpoint of an omniscient observer in the solar system in order to focus attention on what can be observed.

## THE FIXED STARS

Our night skies, polluted as they often are by the scattered light of street lamps or by the gaseous products of vehicles and industry, generally make careful observations of the sky difficult indeed. Yet a reasonably dark, clear sky rewards the observer with a glorious spectacle—a canopy of thousands of points of light. Some of these form obviously ordered patterns; more do not, but instead appear spread at random—the result, according to both Navajo and Pueblo traditions, of being scattered by Coyote (Monroe and Williamson 1987).

Western astronomical tradition calls the stars "fixed" because, over a few generations at least, they seem to maintain their positions relative to one another. During any night, stars and planets can be seen to move from east to west through the sky, providing a convenient timing device. Indeed, the Klamath Indians of California watched the changing position of Orion to determine time in the winter (Spier 1930:218); the Cahuilla (Strong 1929:129) and Chumash (Hudson and Underhay 1978:119) set the times of nightly rituals by the stars. The Mescalero Apache watch any star or constellation in the south–southwest and, by noting its movement through the night sky against the backdrop of the horizon or of an artificial structure, determine the passage of time (Farrer 1991).

The positions of individual stars and their constellation patterns, as seen in relation to the horizon or to a stationary earthbound marker, also change from night to night in such a way that the constellations appear to rise a little earlier each night. In a twenty-four-hour solar period, the change in time of star rise is only four minutes, but over a month these small changes accumulate to equal a full two hours. For instance, at the summer solstice in mid-June, the Pleiades rise just before the light of dawn swallows them. Yet by mid-September they rise at midnight, and by mid-December they are readily visible in the eastern sky just after dark. Thus, when on each summer night the familiar western constellation Cygnus passes overhead, we can count on seeing Scorpio's sinuous pattern in the south. By contrast, the equally familiar constellations of Orion and Taurus are seen most readily in the winter sky, when they appear nearly overhead in December and January. Cygnus and Scorpio will have disappeared from view by November.

This small daily shift of the stellar background comes about because the sun's apparent daily journey around the earth is nearly four minutes shorter than the stars' journey, imparting to the sun the appearance of a small eastward shift each day. As the sun moves through the stellar background, stellar patterns that had been invisible in the sunlit sky become briefly visible in the first faint light of dawn before the rising sun overwhelms them. As the sun daily works its way further eastward, the stars appear to move higher in the sky each morning before dawn.

The first yearly appearance of a star or star pattern, in association with sunrise, is called an heliacal rise after the Greek term for sun, *helios,* and can be highly effective in setting a yearly calendar, because it marks a narrow range of days (depending on sky conditions and the visual acuity of the observer) in the yearly calendar (Fig. 1.1). Some Navajo medicine men, for example, watch for the heliacal rise of certain constellations to determine the beginning of each month. The first appearance of Old Man with Legs Spread (Corvus) marks the beginning of the Navajo month corresponding to November and the time to begin preparing for winter. When First Big One (part of Scorpio) is first visible after setting in the fall, December has arrived (O'Bryan 1956:16–17). Some Navajos have also used the heliacal setting of First Slender One (Orion) in the spring at Twilight as a signal that it is time to begin planting (Brewer 1950:136). In the Great Plains, the Pawnee watched for the first appearance of the pair of stars called the "Swimming Ducks" to tell them when they could start their spring Thunder Ritual (Chamberlain 1982:139).

The circumpolar constellations remain visible throughout the year in the Northern Hemisphere as they rotate about the pole star to form a special set of time markers. The brightest of these, the Big Dipper, seems to have been used throughout the Northern Hemisphere as a nightly timepiece and seasonal calendrical aid (Allen 1963:419–47). In North America, Navajo farmers, for example, employed their observations of the angular position of Revolving Male (the Big Dipper) around the pole to schedule planting times. When Revolving Male is standing straight up, at about 9:00 P.M. early in the spring, it is time to prepare the fields for planting. When, in May and early June, Revolving Male lies on his side, it is time to complete the planting of corn, beans, and squash (Brewer 1950:134). Likewise, the Zuni have used the position of the Seven Ones (the Big Dipper) to indicate when they should begin to plant corn in the spring (Cushing 1896:392). The Pomo used the position of the Big Dipper to schedule their fishing (Loeb 1926:228–29).

Careful observation through many generations leads to the realization that the stars, while steady and almost thoroughly predictable in the short term, change slowly over time. Although the pole star, Polaris, today lies less than a degree from the earth's geographic North Pole, at the beginning of the thirteenth century it was a full $7°$ away. This extremely slow movement, which is called *precession,* results from the continual wobble of the earth's orbital axis through the celestial sphere. Over a period of twenty-six thousand years, the position of the North Pole traces a wide circle through the stars, making it seem to the earth-bound observer that Polaris has

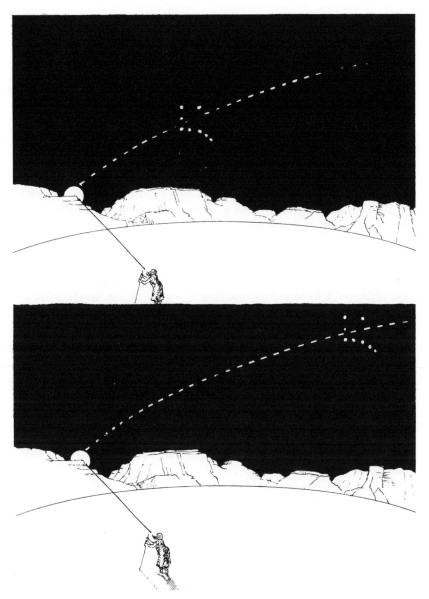

**Figure 1.1.** *Upper:* heliacal rise of a constellation. *Lower:* several weeks later. The first time in the year a star or star group is seen in the eastern predawn sky is termed "heliacal rise." Several weeks later, it will have moved farther west and can be seen for a longer period before dawn. The last time in the year it can be observed, just after sunset in the west, is termed heliacal set. (From Williamson 1984:50. Drawing by Snowden Hodges.)

moved away from the pole and back again. The constellations move with Polaris, causing a slight shift in heliacal rise-and-set periods over the years. For example, four thousand years ago, the Egyptians watched for the heliacal rise of the bright star Sirius as a signal that the summer solstice had arrived. Today, it doesn't rise heliacally until late July. Astronomer Eddy (1974) has postulated that the prehistoric builders of the Big Horn Medicine Wheel eight hundred years ago may have observed the heliacal rise of the bright star Aldebaran in late June to confirm that the summer solstice was drawing near. Today, Aldebaran makes its first appearance about a month later.

The Milky Way, a vast collection of stars that to the naked eye appears like a hazy band roughly 10° wide, cuts across the celestial sphere at an angle to the celestial equator. It is best seen on late summer evenings when it crosses nearly overhead in the Northern Hemisphere. In the Southern Hemisphere, where the Milky Way is brighter, and where several dark patches are particularly evident against the faint background, native groups have identified dark constellations (Urton 1981). In the Northern Hemisphere, the phenomenon is often thought of as a single entity and considered to be a path—whether one of flour, as among the Cherokee (Mooney 1900:259), or the path of the Dead, as among many California groups (Hudson 1984) and the Pawnee (Chamberlain 1982:112)—taken to reach the next world. It has little calendric significance, save to celebrate the arrival of summer and comfortable nights. One's ability to see the Milky Way is highly susceptible to atmospheric moisture and scattered ambient light and it is generally much more visible in isolated, desert regions. The Milky Way has been the subject of both folklore and myth in Native American tradition.

SUN

Unlike the stars, which over a period of years, at least, appear to follow the same circular track from one night to the next, the sun follows a complicated path. During the course of a year, it moves among the stellar background along a path astronomers call the ecliptic, as well as along the horizon. In contrast to the stars, when seen from a fixed location, the sun rises and sets at a different place each day. In the spring and fall, the daily change equals a full diameter of the sun, and the sun marches quickly along the horizon, apparently impatient to move either north or south, respectively. As the year approaches the summer or winter solstices, the sun's horizon movement slows gradually. Finally, at the solstices it comes to a halt and the sun reverses its yearly journey.

The sweep of the sun's journey along the horizon depends on the latitude. At the equator, its total motion is relatively limited, moving only 23.5° north and south of east. At a latitude of 36°, about the latitude of Greensboro, North Carolina, and Santa Fe, New Mexico, the angle has increased to 30° on either side of east. Thus, at this latitude, the total yearly swing of the sun equals a full one-third of the eastern horizon. Nine degrees further north, along a latitude line that falls nearly through Bangor, Maine, St. Paul, Minnesota, and Salem, Oregon, the sun swings through an arc that extends a total of 70° from north to south. The wide solar swings in the temperate zone make possible a calendar that relies on observations of sunrise and sunset against the backdrop of fixed horizon features (Fig. 1.1).

The winter solstice, especially, has retained a special status in the calendars of most peoples of the Northern Hemisphere because it marks the day on which the sun, which has been steadily moving south since the summer solstice, turns north again, promising spring and the world's renewal despite three or more months of cold weather ahead. The winter solstice is also the shortest day of the year, so the sun's reversal marks the approach of longer days, offering light and hope to the human psyche.

The slow, apparent motion of the sun along the horizon near the solstices from day to day makes it extremely difficult for an observer to determine the arrival of the solstice. Therefore, Pueblo observers, at least, would choose a place on the horizon where the sun rose or set days or even weeks prior to the solstice. Because, at those times, the sun's day-to-day motion is fast enough to detect daily differences, it was possible for them to "anticipate" the arrival of solstice (Zeilik 1987). Announcing the coming solstice well in advance also gave celebrants sufficient time to prepare for solstice rituals.

Although the equinoxes have been observed, they were less important than the solstices to most Native American groups, perhaps because the sun does not turn around but simply appears to move either north or south rather quickly, which accounts for the rapid change in the amount of daylight. At 36°N, for example, between the first of March and the equinox, the day lengthens by about one half-hour, whereas an equal period between June 1 and the summer solstice yields an increase of only four minutes. A corresponding rapid movement along the horizon from day to day means that unlike the times around the solstices, the sun advances daily by an angle nearly equal to its own diameter.

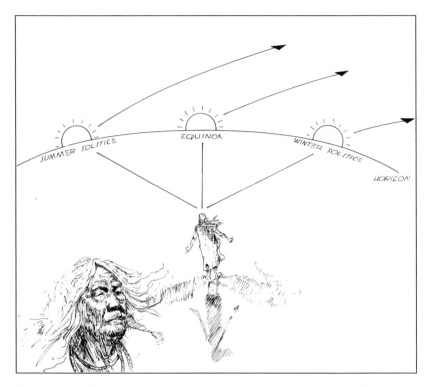

**Figure 1.2.**    Sunrise positions along the horizon throughout the year. Because the sun's apparent yearly orbit lies at an angle of 23.5° to the celestial equator, the sun's position changes from day to day. The sun appears to move slowly along the horizon from day to day near the solstices and nearly a diameter of the sun per day at the equinoxes. (From Williamson 1984:39. Drawing by Snowden Hodges.)

Evidence from archaeological sites throughout North America indicate that Native Americans have used the small change in position of sunrise and sunset for centuries to keep close track of the passage of time (Williamson 1984), especially by watching for the solstices, although other calendar dates, including the equinoxes, were probably also observed. Many groups who keep the traditional ways still watch the sun to set ritual and agricultural calendars. The southwest Pueblos (Fig. 1.3) still observe the sun regularly to set their agricultural and ritual calendars (McCluskey 1977; Zeilik 1989).

At the beginning of the century, Native American groups throughout California watched the sun for the arrival of the solstices and celebrated these events with considerable investment of time and effort (Hoskinson in

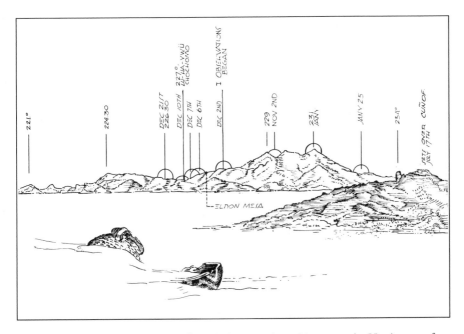

**Figure 1.3.** Hopi solar calendar. Horizons such as this one at the Hopi town of Awatovi allow the Pueblo Indians to determine the appropriate times for ceremony and for planting and harvesting. (From Williamson 1984:80–81. Drawing by Snowden Hodges; after Stephen 1936: map 5.)

press). To survive, nearly all of these groups depended on strategies of gathering, hunting, and fishing, rather than horticulture. As Broughton explains in this volume, observing the solstices and equinoxes is still important among the Ajumawi of northern California. The Mescalero Apache, who lived by hunting and gathering, also observe the solstices closely (Farrer 1986).

The sun's yearly apparent path affects the length of the day and of twilight, depending on the latitude. In the tropics, the sun appears to rise and set nearly vertically. Morning and evening twilight are consequently relatively short, lasting less than one half-hour. Throughout the year, day nearly equals night. In the middle latitudes, however, the sun appears to move along a path tilted with respect to the horizon, rising to the south and setting toward the north. Twilight accordingly lasts much longer; summer days are longer and winter ones shorter. At 36° north latitude, for example, midsummer twilight lasts just over a half-hour, and night is eight and one-half hours long. At 45°, twilight lengthens to over forty minutes, and the night is only seven hours long. At 60°, twilight is nearly two hours long and the sky never becomes fully dark.

The angle between the apparent path of the sun and the horizon, which grows ever smaller as one moves closer to the pole, nearly falls to zero above the Arctic Circle. Observed from the North Pole, the midsummer sun travels from left to right and parallel to the horizon in a twenty-four-hour extravaganza of light. Between the Arctic Circle (66.5°N) and the pole, the day–night phenomenon so familiar to dwellers at middle latitudes becomes instead a seasonal experience. Summer brings sunlight lasting twenty-four hours; winter brings nights that are twenty-four hours long. In the polar regions, for example, to see the sun at all on the winter solstice would require being at the Arctic Circle, where it would appear for a brief time to the south in the protracted twilight, then disappear from sight.

## MOON

As the second brightest object in the sky, and one that makes readily noticeable changes in form and position among the stars from night to night, the moon has been of considerable interest to every known cultural group. Moon's inconstant nature, its relationship with the sun, and the closeness of its monthly cycle to the menstrual period have made it the subject of myth and folklore for Native Americans, as well as for other groups throughout the world.

Moon's 29.5-day synodic cycle of renewal, fullness, and decline, which we commonly refer to as a lunar month, serve to make it a highly effective calendrical marker. The moon shines by the reflected light of the sun; when the moon is new and invisible to the naked eye, it stands beside or in front of the sun. It therefore rises and sets with the brighter body. Some Native American groups consider the lunar month to be twenty-eight days long, because the moon is invisible during one day of its synodic cycle.

The moon first appears as a thin crescent following the sun below the western horizon at sunset. The sun lights the western side of the moon resulting in cusps that face east, away from the sun. As the moon grows to fullness, it pulls progressively farther and farther away from its brighter companion and rises later and later each day. The growing light spreads slowly from west to east across the entire face. When fully lit, it stands opposite the sun, rising just after sunset and setting just after sunrise. During its decline from full to gibbous, and then to waning crescent, darkness spreads across the moon from west to east, as the moon again pulls nearer to the sun. A full twenty-nine days later, it finally disappears in the sun's glare as both again rise together.

The synodic lunar month is the basis of many calendars, including our familiar, twelve-month western calendar, which combines uneasily the yearly cycle of the sun and a month that is as close as possible in length to the lunar month (Aveni 1989b:chap. 3). Most Native American groups observed the phases of the moon to set a calendar. For example, late in the last century a lunar calendar was apparently in use throughout California (Hudson 1985:44), along with counting sticks and knotted cords, to keep track of the days. These Native American keepers of the calendar faced the same problem encountered by all peoples when they have attempted to reconcile the lunar calendar with the solar one—twelve periods of 29.5 days fall short of the 365.24 days of a tropical year by 11.24 days, or more than one-third of a lunar month. Thus, a year of twelve lunar months quickly falls short of a solar year. The Hopi, who keep both a solar and a lunar calendar, solve the problem by adding an additional month every three years or so (McCluskey 1977), a device to which other groups certainly resort. The Tolowa of northern California captured the problem of the extra fraction of the month in a story (Drucker 1937:240) in which it was said that there used to be fifteen moons. Coyote, who worried that this made the year too long, hid outside their sweathouse one day. When they came out, he managed to kill two of the fifteen, but only wounded a third by stabbing it in the rump, leaving the thirteenth moon partially disabled.

The moon's motions are much more complicated than the sun's. For example, during the course of a month, moonrise and moonset follow a pattern similar to the yearly course of the sun along the horizon. When the sun crosses the equator, which occurs at the equinoxes, the new moon rises with the sun, within a few degrees of the equator. Seven days later it rises near one of the solstice positions. When it turns full some fourteen days later, the moon will rise and set near the equator again. However, in the fall and winter, when the sun stays below the equator, the new moon rises near the sun but moves to the Northern Hemisphere by the time it turns full. If a full moon occurs near the winter solstice, it will travel a nightly path very similar to the summer solstice sun, high in the Northern Hemisphere and lighting the winter landscape in a striking and dramatic manner.

The moon also possesses a sidereal cycle, which depends on its position with respect to the stars. A sidereal month, which is measured from the time the moon passes a given position among the stars to the time it returns to the same place again, lasts 27⅓ days. No evidence exists that Native

North Americans paid any attention to this cycle, which is difficult to observe, as it requires watching the second passage of the moon by a star group when the moon is at a different phase of its synodic cycle. However, the Inca of Peru apparently observed it (Zuidema 1977 : 247−50).

Because the moon does not quite follow the ecliptic but appears to travel a course that extends both above and below the ecliptic by about five degrees, its extreme points of rise and set will fall both without and within the solstice extremes (Fig. 1.4). The cycle during which this occurs takes 18.6 years; deducing such a cycle requires extremely careful observations of moonrise and moonset. Predicting the beginning of the cycle requires observations and a long-term calendar. No doubt, Native American observers were capable of observing and predicting this cycle. However, evidence that they actually did so is currently lacking. For example, although several claims have been made that the Anasazi of Chaco Canyon

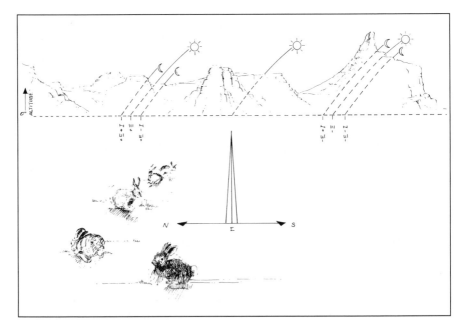

**Figure 1.4.** Moonrise throughout the 18.61–year lunar cycle. Because the moon's apparent monthly orbit is tilted to the sun's apparent orbit, during part of its cycle (+E+I and −E−I), the moon will rise or set outside the solstice points. Halfway through its full 18.61–year cycle (+E−I and −E+I), the moon will always rise or set within the solstice points. (From Williamson 1984 : 45. Drawing by Snowden Hodges.)

may have observed this cycle in prehistoric times, the available evidence is extremely weak (Carlson 1989; Zeilik 1989: 159–61).

## PLANETS

Because the planets are the brightest objects in the sky after the moon, they command particular attention. They must have been especially confusing to early peoples because they look nearly like bright stars, but follow highly complicated paths through the stellar background, most often moving east among the background of stars but sometimes in the opposite, or retrograde, direction toward the west. The early Mediterranean peoples named them for the most powerful gods in their pantheon. Accounting for the motions of the planets consumed early Babylonian and Greek astronomers, and, in Claudius Ptolemy's time (the first century A.D.), led to a mathematically complex theory to explain these wanderers of the sky.

The planets follow paths nearly along the ecliptic, but rather than completing that celestial circle in the course of a year they take different periods to do so. Venus and Mercury, which early Greek astronomers termed the inner planets, never stray too far away from the sun along the ecliptic. When they are visible, they always appear either as morning or evening stars. Mercury never reaches beyond $27°$ from the sun and is thus difficult to pick out in the sun's glare; Venus swings through a full $47°$ on either side of the sun. Because Venus is the brightest planet, it receives considerable notice even under modern, urban viewing conditions, especially when it appears near the waxing or waning crescent Moon. The careful observer who knows where to look can even pick out Venus in the daytime sky.

In Mesoamerica, Venus was watched intently for its cycles on either side of the sun. The Maya, for example, seem to have taken no interest in the other planets, but apparently they deliberately oriented the Governor's Palace at Uxmal, Yucatán, to Venus (Aveni 1980: 275–76). A line perpendicular to the eastern doorway on the Governor's Palace passes directly through the principal pyramid of Nohpat several kilometers distant and to the point on the horizon at which Venus rose when it was at its maximum southerly position about A.D. 800, when the Governor's Palace was constructed. The Mayans were interested in all phases of Venus's cycle, watching especially for its first eastern appearance, or heliacal rise, as it appeared briefly in the early morning twilight and then faded from view as the sun rose behind it. After making its first appearance, Venus remains in view for longer and longer periods each morning, finally reaching its greatest elongation from the sun when it rises about three hours ahead of the sun. From then on, Venus reverses its apparent motion and closes the gap with the sun. Nearly 263 days after first appearing in the predawn sky, Venus disappears again in the glare of the early morning sun, to reappear briefly more than seven weeks later as an evening star. For another 263 days it serves in that capacity before it once again disappears from sight against the sun's disk for about a week. Thus, the total cycle of Venus relative to the sun is nearly 584 days, a period that was of great importance to the Maya, probably because five Venus cycles ($5 \times 583.9 = 2,919.5$ days) nearly equals eight tropical years ($365.24 \times 8 = 2,921.9$ days); observations could therefore be used to measure the length of the year to considerable accuracy.

In contrast to Venus and Mercury, the visible outer planets—Mars, Jupiter, and Saturn—appear anywhere near or along the ecliptic, and disappear in the sun's glare only once in a synodic period. They are thus seen in the night sky at any position along the ecliptic. Like Venus, they also follow paths among the stars that can turn contrary (retrograde motion). The synodic period of Mars, its interval between successive heliacal risings, is about 780 days, but its passage among the stars, or sidereal period, takes 687 days. For Jupiter the synodic period is 399 days, and its sidereal period 4,333 days. Finally, Saturn's synodic period is 378 days and its sidereal period is 10,759 days.

Data on Native American observations of the planets are exceedingly sparse, no doubt the result, in part, of lack of knowledge on the part of the ethnographer about the motions of the planets. Many groups recognized morning and evening stars, but the available data seldom make clear whether they applied the designations "morning star" and "evening star" only to Venus or Mercury, which can be observed only in the morning or evening, or whether it also applied to other planets or to bright stars. For example, the Zuni certainly used observations of an eastern star or planet to time the beginning and ending of several ceremonies (Stevenson 1903). Yet as Young points out in her contribution to this volume, the available data suggest that they used any convenient starlike object that might appear in the early morning sky. Indeed, although Venus is brighter than the other planets, because their apparent orbits may take them near the sun either in the evening or in the morning, other planets might easily mimic Venus in those positions.

Among the California Indians, Venus was an important celestial object and was differentiated from the other planets (Hudson 1984). For some groups, morning and evening star was a single being, associated with Venus. Others, like the Pomo (Loeb 1926:228), considered the two as different, closely related beings. Chamberlain (1982:71–91) argues that the Skidi Pawnee observed both Mars and Venus to set the time of their Morning Star sacrifice and were well aware of the different motions of both. Indeed, he suggests that evidence from Skidi Pawnee mythology, particularly the Origin Myth (Curtis 1968:91–144), would support the inference that Mars served as the Pawnee Great Star, or Morning Star, and that Venus was understood as the Evening Star.

### IRREGULAR APPEARANCES

In addition to observing and charting the regular motions and appearances of celestial objects, Native American observers also watched for, and attempted to understand, the irregular occurrences of eclipses, meteors, and comets, as well as unusual atmospheric phenomena. Most groups took these appearances for portents, usually possessing negative connotations.

Solar and lunar eclipses are especially impressive appearances because both circumstances cause the sun and the moon to alter their appearance dramatically. A lunar eclipse, which can occur only at the full moon when the earth comes between the sun and the moon, begins as a slightly curved shadow starts to work it sway across the bright lunar surface. The progression from the first noticeable shadow to complete coverage takes about an hour, during which the surrounding landscape becomes darker as well. During the entire period of full shadow, the moon appears to take on a disturbing, deep blood-red color, which darkens as the shadow deepens, then lightens again as the darkest part of the shadow moves on. Finally, after a half-hour or so of full shadow, the reflected sunlight reappears on the opposite side of the moon and gradually enlightens the entire moon.

A total solar eclipse in many respects is more impressive. During the progression of the eclipse, the moon takes a progressively larger "bite" out of the sun, the sky darkens, and daylight takes on an eerie quality. Finally, the sun turns totally dark and the stars become visible. When the moon's disk totally covers the sun, a glowing white corona surrounds the moon. After eight minutes or less, the moon and sun begin to move apart again and a blindingly bright crescent sun reappears, obscuring the faint corona. During totality, diurnal animals often act as if night had fallen and prepare for sleep. Even outside the path of totality, daylight assumes an uncomfortable aspect.

The following moving description by Virginia Woolf (1953 : 111–12) captures the "feel" of a total solar eclipse on the Yorkshire moors in 1927:

Rapidly, very very quickly, all the colours faded; it became darker and darker as at the beginning of a violent storm; the light sank and sank; we kept saying this is the shadow; and we thought now it is over—this is the shadow; when suddenly the light went out. We had fallen. It was extinct. There was no colour. The earth was dead. That was the astonishing moment; and the next when as if a ball had rebounded the cloud took colour on itself again, only a sparky ethereal colour and so the light came back. I had very strongly the feeling as the light went out of some vast obeisance; something kneeling down and suddenly raised up when the colours came. They came back astonishingly lightly and quickly and beautifully in the valley and over the hills . . . It was like recovery. We had been much worse than we had expected. We had seen the world dead. This was within the power of nature.

On the average, four eclipses occur each year, as seen from somewhere in the world. A maximum of seven eclipses is possible (either five solar and two lunar or four solar and three lunar), and a minimum of two solar eclipses. However, because the three bodies need to be lined up just so to produce a total eclipse as seen from a given location, partial eclipses are much more common. Total solar eclipses are much more difficult to observe by chance than lunar eclipses, as the average path of totality on the earth for the former is only about 120 kilometers wide. Thus, the probability of witnessing a total solar eclipse from any arbitrary place on earth is one time in four hundred years. An individual who failed to witness a total solar eclipse during a lifetime might nevertheless see several total lunar eclipses because the shadow cast by the earth is much larger than the shadow cast by the moon.

Although no data exist to support the proposition that Native Americans were capable of, or interested in, predicting eclipses, they were certainly affected by them. Eclipses of the sun or moon were often considered as indicating an imbalance in the world that would lead to danger and death for the tribal group. The Tewa of the Rio Grande, for example, dreaded the eclipse of the sun and feared that Sun Father was displeased with them and was retiring to his house in the underworld (Stevenson n.d.). The Pawnee told a tale citing their fear "that when the time came for the world to end the Moon would turn red; that if the Moon should turn black it would be a sign that some great chief was to die" (Dorsey 1906 : 134–37).

Meteors and fireballs elicited interest among some Native American groups, as they considered them to be falling stars. For the Pawnee, meteorites, meteors that have fallen to earth, were the children of Tirawahat, their supreme being (Chamberlain 1982:44). They especially revered meteorites they found, and kept them wrapped in their medicine bundles. Observing the sky on nearly any clear night will reveal meteors streaking across the heavens at random. However, in August and November many thousands of meteors fill the sky over the course of a night as the Perseid and Leonid meteor showers respectively appear. These regular occurrences were noted by Native American observers.

### THE OBSERVABILITY OF CELESTIAL PHENOMENA

Discussions of naked-eye celestial phenomena rarely include considerations of their actual visibility under field conditions. Yet various atmospheric phenomena, as well as the capabilities of the human eye, will affect the observability of celestial objects, especially near the horizon (Minnaert 1954:31–73). Among the atmospheric effects that reduce celestial visibility are refraction, which can vary greatly according to the weather and the season (Schaeffer 1986); high-altitude cirrus clouds; and atmospheric moisture and dust. Such effects, for example, may vastly alter the ability of an observer to witness star rise or star set near the horizon. It can also reduce the visibility of extended objects, such as the thin crescent moon to comets (Schaeffer 1990).

## The Genesis and Organization of This Book

The chapters of this book focus on the study of Native North American astronomical traditions—what have come to be called by the interdisciplinary name of "ethnoastronomy." Although a few anthropologists and folklorists have written about astronomical traditions in the course of their ethnographic research—most notably, Dorsey (1904), Gifford (1940), and Harrington (1916:37–69)—little organized research was done until recently. In the 1960s, astronomers and a few archaeologists began to probe prehistoric sites in the United Kingdom, Egypt, and Mesoamerica for information concerning the astronomical practices of prehistoric peoples. In the early 1970s, ethnoastronomical research supported archaeoastronomy, the study of the astronomical implications of archaeological sites. Scholars working in the New World quickly realized that the traditions of living peoples, or of their immediate ancestors, might shed light on what was being found, primarily by astronomers, in the archaeological record. Archaeoastronomers, as they had begun to call themselves, quickly teamed up with anthropologists and folklorists (Williamson 1981) to search through the wealth of ethnography available in the publications and archival collections of the Smithsonian Institution, the Field Museum, and similar institutions.

When anthropologists and folklorists began to look into the literature—whether published, in unpublished field notes, or their own data—they found much astronomy in myth and folklore. Its previous treatment had taken the form either of statistical compilations with notes (Gifford 1940), or of historic–geographic plotting of origin, migration, and variation of common stories in attempts to find the genesis, or urform (Thompson 1953). Using theoretical paradigms from anthropology and folklore of the 1970s and 1980s, and with encouragement from astronomical colleagues, anthropologists and folklorists became ethnoastronomers, looking not to dead cultures but to existing ones with viable astronomical systems (Hudson and Underhay 1978; Farrer and Second 1981; Urton 1981; Tedlock 1982; Young 1988).

Much remains to be done. In many ways, in fact, the work is just beginning. To address this lacuna, Williamson organized a symposium for the ninety-eighth meeting of the American Folklore Society, held in Baltimore in 1986; Farrer provided critical commentary. Our focus then was the entirety of the New World, a geographic and cultural area too vast to allow meaningful synthetic statements to be made with our present level of knowledge. The symposium papers and the ensuing discussion demonstrated that Native American stories provide a rich source of insight about cosmology and cosmogony as well as providing a deeper understanding of native astronomical practices. It seemed to us that a volume focused on the astronomical practices of Native North America would contribute both to the interdisciplinary study of ethnoastronomy and to a better understanding of the place of folklore scholarship in it. Hence, we asked several of our colleagues in the disciplines of anthropology, astronomy, English, folklore, and religion to examine their own field sites and data related to Native North American astronomy.

The book is organized geographically, beginning in the east, moving to the Southeast, and on around the sunrise circle. We begin and end in the same place, purposely imitating both the Sky realm and its interaction with Earth and the motions of the celestial sphere that repeat the vast cycles that suggest to people how they should live.

ACKNOWLEDGMENTS

A number of people, either knowingly or unknowingly, have contributed to this book. We especially thank the authors, who bore with our suggestions for revisions cheerfully and for the most part quickly. We are grateful to our reviewers for taking the time to read through the manuscript and make thoughtful suggestions. Special thanks are due to Beth Hadas, director of the University of New Mexico Press, who encouraged the creation of this volume, and editors Jeff Grathwohl and Barbara Guth, who successfully guided it through the publishing process.

Finally, we thank the many Native American collaborators who provided the stories and other ethnographic material without whom this book would have been impossible. Their insights into the nature of the cosmos have enriched our lives immeasurably.

## References

Allen, Richard H. 1963. *Star Names: Their Lore and Meaning*. New York: Dover. Originally published as *Star-Names and Their Meanings*. New York: Stechert (1899).

Aveni, Anthony, ed. 1977. *Native American Archaeoastronomy*. Austin: University of Texas Press.

———. 1980. *Skywatchers of Ancient Mexico*. Austin: University of Texas Press.

———, ed. 1989a. *World Archaeoastronomy*. Cambridge: Cambridge University Press.

———. 1989b. *Empires of Time: Clocks, Calendars, and Cultures*. New York: Basic Books.

Benson, Arlene, and Tom Hoskinson, eds. 1985. *Earth and Sky: Papers from the Northridge Conference on Archaeoastronomy*. Thousand Oaks, Calif.: Slo'w Press.

Blackburn, Thomas C. 1975. *December's Child*. Berkeley and Los Angeles: University of California Press.

Brewer, Sallie P. 1950. Notes on Navaho Astronomy. In *For the Dean: Essays in Anthropology in Honor of Byron Cummings*, Erik K. Reed and Dale S. King, eds. 133–36. Tucson: University of Arizona Press.

Carlson, John B. 1989. Romancing the Stone, or Moonshine on the Sun Dagger. In *World Archaeoastronomy*, ed. Anthony F. Aveni. Cambridge: Cambridge University Press.

Chamberlain, Von Del. 1982. *When Stars Came Down to Earth*. Los Altos, Calif.: Ballena Press.

Curtis, Natalie. 1968. *The Indians' Book: Songs and Legends of the American Indians*. New York: Dover. First published in 1907.

Cushing, Frank H. 1896. Outlines of Zuni Creation Myths. Washington: D.C. Bureau of American Ethnology Annual Report 13:321–447.

Dorsey, George. 1904. Traditions of the Skidi Pawnee. Memoirs of the American Folk-Lore Society 8.

———. 1906. The Pawnee: Mythology. Carnegie Institution of Washington Publications 59.

Drucker, Philip. 1937. The Tolowa and their Southwest Oregon Kin. *University of California Publications in American Archaeology and Ethnology* 26(4): 221–300.

Eddy, John A. 1974. Astronomical Alignment of the Big Horn Medicine Wheel. *Science* 184:1035–43.

Farrer, Claire R. 1991. Living Life's Circle: Mescalero Apache Cosmovision. Albuquerque: University of New Mexico Press.

———. 1986. Mescalero Apache Terminology for Venus. *Archaeoastronomy* 9: 59–61.

Farrer, Claire R., and Bernard Second. 1981. Living the Sky: Aspects of Mescalero Ethnoastronomy. In *Archaeoastronomy in the Americas,* ed. Ray A. Williamson, 137–50. Los Altos, Calif.: Ballena Press.

Gifford, Edward Winslow. 1940. Culture Element Distributions: XII-Apache-Pueblo. University of California Publications in Anthropological Records 4:1–208. Berkeley: University of California Press.

Haile, Fr. Berard. 1947. *Starlore among the Navaho.* Santa Fe: Museum of Navaho Ceremonial Art.

Harrington, John P. 1916. *The Ethnogeography of the Tewa Indians.* Bureau of American Ethnology Annual Report 29.

Hoskinson, Tom. In press. A Survey of California Ethnoastronomy. In *Ethnoastronomy of the Americas,* ed. Von Del Chamberlain and M. Jane Young. Thousand Oaks, Calif.: Slo'w Press.

Hudson, Travis. 1984. California's First Astronomers. *Archaeoastronomy and the Roots of Science,* ed. E. C. Krupp, 11–81. Washington, D.C.: American Association for the Advancement of Science.

———. 1985. Skywatchers of Ancient California. In *Earth and Sky: Papers from the Northridge Conference on Archaeoastronomy,* ed. Arlene Benson and Tom Hoskinson. Thousand Oaks, Calif.: Slo'w Press.

Hudson, Travis, and Earnest Underhay. 1978. *Crystals in the Sky: An Intellectual Odyssey involving Chumash Astronomy, Cosmology, and Rock Art.* Socorro, N.M.: Ballena Press.

Loeb, Edwin. 1926. Pomo Folkways. *University of California Publications in American Archaeology and Ethnology* 19(2):149–404.

McCluskey, Stephen C. 1977. The Astronomy of the Hopi Indians. *Journal of the History of Astronomy* 8:174–95.

Minnaert, Marcel. 1954. *The Nature of Light and Color in the Open Air.* New York: Dover.

Momaday, N. Scott. 1970. Man Made of Words. In *Indian Voices: The First Convocation of American Indian Scholars,* 49–62. San Francisco: Indian Historian Press.

Monroe, Jean, and Ray A. Williamson. 1987. *They Dance in the Sky: Native American Star Myths.* Boston: Houghton Mifflin.

Mooney, James. 1900. Myths of the Cherokee. Bureau of American Ethnology Annual Report 19.

O'Bryan, Aileen. 1956. The Dine: Origin Myths of the Navaho. Smithsonian Institution Bureau of American Ethnology Bulletin 163.

Patencio, Francisco. 1943. *Stories and Legends of the Palm Springs Indians.* Los Angeles: Times–Mirror Press.

Schaeffer, Bradley E. 1986. "Atmospheric Extinction Effects on Stellar Alignments." *Archaeoastronomy: Supplement to the Journal of the History of Astronomy* 10:S32–S42.

———. 1990. Basic Research in Astronomy and Its Applications to Archaeoastronomy. Paper presented at the Third International Conference on Archaeoastronomy, St. Andrews, Scotland, September 10–14.

Silko, Leslie Marmon. 1981. How to Write a Poem About the Sky. In *Storyteller,* 177. New York: Seaver.

Spier, Leslie. 1930. Klamath Ethnography. University of California Publications in American Archaeology and Ethnology 30.

Stephen, Alexander M. 1938. *Hopi Journal of Alexander M. Stephen,* ed. Elsie Clews Parsons. *Columbia University Contributions to Anthropology* 23.

Stevenson, Matilda Cox. 1903. The Zuni Indians. Bureau of American Ethnology Annual Report 23.

———. n.d. Unpublished notes in the Smithsonian National Anthropological Archives.

Strong, William Duncan. 1929. Aboriginal Society in Southern California. University of California Publications in American Archaeology 26.

Tedlock, Barbara. 1982. *Time and the Highland Maya.* Albuquerque: University of New Mexico Press.

Thompson, Stith. 1953. The Star Husband Tale. *Studia Sepentrionalia* 4:93–163. [Journal from Oslo, Norway—Universitetsforlaget, pb.]

Urton, Gary. 1981. *At the Crossroads of the Earth and the Sky.* Austin: University of Texas Press.

Williamson, Ray, ed. 1981. *Archaeoastronomy in the Americas.* Los Altos, Calif.: Ballena Press.

———. 1984. *Living the Sky: The Cosmos of the American Indian.* Boston: Houghton Mifflin.

Woolf, Virginia. 1953. *A Writer's Diary: Being Extracts from the Diary of Virginia Woolf.* London: Hogarth Press.

Young, Jane. 1988. *Signs from the Ancestors.* Albuquerque: University of New Mexico Press.

Zeilik, Michael. 1987. Anticipation in Ceremony: The Readiness Is All. In *Astron-omy and Ceremony in the Prehistoric Southwest,* ed. J. B. Carlson and W. J. Judge. 25–41. Albuquerque: Maxwell Museum Press, Papers of the Max-well Museum of Anthropology, no. 2.

———. 1989. Keeping the Sacred and Planting Calendar: Archaeoastronomy in the Pueblo Southwest. In *World Archaeoastronomy,* ed. Anthony F. Aveni. Cambridge: Cambridge University Press.

Zuidema, Tom. 1977. The Inca Calendar. In *Native American Astronomy,* ed. Anthony F. Aveni, 219–60. Austin: University of Texas Press.

# 2

■■■■■■■■■

## Cosmos and Poesis in the Seneca
## Thank-You Prayer

■■■■■■■■■

### PAUL ZOLBROD

*Paul Zolbrod is best known for his book on the Navajo creation story,* Diné
Bahane'. *Here, through the device of a seventeen-part poem, he elucidates the economy
with which Seneca people have a mnemonic for creation and the ordered world in
which they live. The poetry of the prayer reflects the inherent poetry of the sky and
earth.*

It may be all too easy to overlook the effect on everyday life of Seneca
astronomy or the cosmology of the other Iroquois tribes, to say nothing of
the sky-watching activities of eastern woodland peoples in general. Sub-
dued, displaced, and often acculturated before evidence could be systematically acquired, those groups have supplied less evidence for the kinds of
investigations in archaeoastronomy possible among tribes in other parts of
North America where data are easier to acquire. By the time researchers
began assembling information, star lore had declined among Iroquoian
peoples (Foster 1974:74). Furthermore, natural conditions have offered
archaeologists fewer opportunities to gather evidence of prehistoric life in
the moist East in the way investigators have been able to find and interpret
artifacts in the more arid Southwest. And dense forests combined with
frequent cloudiness in places like Pennsylvania and upstate New York make
for a narrower and less spectacular view of the sky. So Americanists who
have studied those peoples have not focused on astronomy. Thus we do not
consider the implications of sky watching among them, as we do among the
Plains tribes or desert peoples.

That does not mean that the Seneca or the other Iroquoians did not
watch the sky and create detailed models of the cosmos. Buttressed by what

we know about mythology, poetic evidence ranging from Old World texts like the East Indian *Mahabharata,* the Bible, and Hesiod's *Theogony,* to Native American texts like the Mayan *Popol Vuh* (Tedlock 1985) or the Navajo *Diné Bahane'* (Zolbrod: 1984) indicates that all peoples observed the heavens. To do so is to become civilized in the most fundamental sense; and one of the first tangible marks of any civilization is a poetic conception of the creation of Earth and Sky wherein activities we now call scientific or consider religious or poetic all converge. Thus, careful scrutiny of evidence not at first readily associated with sky watching might yield insights about people like the Seneca that otherwise would be missed.

For that reason, I would argue, we would do well to match the verbal artifacts of a people with whatever evidence of their astronomical practice we can recover to gain a better understanding of their conception of the heavens and of their way of integrating cosmic vision and everyday living here on Earth. In fact, if we work harder to integrate our understanding of poetic practice with what we are learning about tribal sky watching, we can learn more from cultures like that of the Seneca, who only appear to yield less information than ethnoastronomers customarily find. And in harvesting that information we discover that an earlier celestial awareness has left a powerful legacy even where the kind of sky watching still practiced, say, by the Pueblos' pekwins of the upper Rio Grande or San Juan watersheds of the Southwest no longer occurs.

A case in point is the Seneca Thank-You Prayer, which is among other things a considerable piece of poetry. As well as any native American lyric I know, it illustrates how a stylized ceremonial utterance articulates an ancient vision of the cosmos and perpetuates deep-seated tribal beliefs accrued from ancient celestial observation. Recited at the beginning and conclusion of virtually every ceremony except those honoring the dead, it is, in fact, more familiar to the Seneca people today than the creation cycle on which it is based (Tooker 1979:56) and which in the earliest recovered versions reflects considerable systematic celestial observation (see Hewitt 1903:227). In effect, it summarizes the making of the universe, which apparently must be verbalized at the major longhouse gatherings held each year at times determined by the position of the Pleiades (Wallace 1969:50; Foster 1974:110). More than that, however, it functions as a reminder that the cosmos is marked by certain patterned features that interface with such human affairs as planting, harvesting, fall hunting, and spring gathering. And it reminds ceremonial participants that the universe is a place wherein human beings are locked in an ongoing conflict between vast forces such as good and evil or life and death.

The lyric exists in several English translations, one of which is reproduced here. First published in Mexico in 1969, this version appeared in the United States in 1972, in Jerome Rothenberg's monumental anthology of Native American poetry, *Shaking the Pumpkin*. Although Rothenberg transcribed it in the summer of 1968 on the Allegany Seneca Reservation at Streamburg, New York, he credits the actual translation to Richard Johnny John, "a singer & songmaker in his own right, absolutely fluent in Seneca & with a poet's delight in getting the right combinations in whatever language" (1972:403). I chose this text because it is the most poetically appealing in my judgment and because several Seneca informants have assured me of its accuracy. To some extent, Rothenberg's printed rendering of the poem anticipates the work of Dennis Tedlock (1972b) and Dell Hymes (1981), who have explored ways in which print can be arranged to reflect many of the intrinsic poetic qualities of orally performed Native American utterances.

Tedlock warns that the prose employed in earlier translations of such material registers none of the special manipulations of the storyteller's voice and "rolls on for whole paragraphs at a time without taking a breath: there is no silence in it" (1972a:xix). Likewise, Hymes (1981:58) complains that older verse translations of Native American lyrics tended "to be valued as outcroppings of a pristine primitivity" and were not really "perceived as poems," often because those who translated them were insensitive to the "continuing tradition of philology in most of the languages in which the poems exist" (58). The distinction between poetry and more ordinary kinds of discourse that scholars like Tedlock and Hymes recognize is important to the study of archaeoastronomy, I believe, because it indicates how an awareness of the cosmos can summon a vision requiring a special sort of articulation stylized to match what is observed in the way a kiva, a hogan, or a tipi provides a model of what is seen by carefully monitoring the sky (Williamson 1984). Between them, Tedlock and Hymes have established a procedure for recasting oral performances in print more vividly than earlier translators could. As a result, it is now easier to demonstrate that cosmogony has traditionally been a common theme in Native American poetic performances, and to observe connections between sky watching and poetry making.

Thanks to the quality of Richard Johnny John's language and Rothenberg's typographical design, this rendering of the Thank-You Prayer matches the standards established by translators like Dell Hymes and Dennis Tedlock. What is missing, however, is an explanation of its place in the context of the Seneca creation myth. Briefly, that cycle tells of a quarrel between the great chief Tharonhiawagan, or Sky Holder, and his wife, Mature Flower, in a preternatural domain above the sky. Their conflict begins when he accuses her of becoming pregnant by another male and thrusts her headlong out of the sky. She lands on an island that expands out of a terrestrial sea, and there she bears a daughter who, in turn, is impregnated by the wind and gives birth to the culture hero Good Mind. There, he assembles rivers and mountains with his grandmother's help; oversees the creation of plants and animals and positions overhead the sun, the moon, and the stars; designates four primal messengers to preside over the entire expanse in the four cardinal directions; and finally engenders human life. Meanwhile, an evil twin, Warty One, contrives to offset Good Mind's efforts by unleashing "the rattlesnake and great bugs and loathing worms (Parker 1989:68). He also perverts the animals created by Good Mind by giving them an appetite for human flesh and pollutes the streams of pure water with mud and slime. Thus is created a world whose perceived harmony parallels that seen in the heavens—a world so fully balanced that good is offset by evil and humankind must struggle vigilantly to reconcile well-being with sickness, abundance with scarcity, and life with death (Hewitt 1903:221–54; Parker 1989:59–73; Tooker 1979:35–47).

Here is the complete text. Unless otherwise specified, the annotated comments and observations are my own.

## Thank You: A Poem in Seventeen Parts

*1. The Earth*

*Now so many people that are in this place.*
*In our meeting place.*
*It starts when two people see each other.*
*They greet each other.*
*Now we greet each other.*
*Now he thought.*
*I will make the Earth where some people can walk around.*
*I have created them, now this has happened.*
*We are walking on it.*
*Now this time of day.*
*This is the way it should be in our minds.*

---

In all probability, the speaker is the culture hero Good Mind, grandson of Tharonhiawagan, the Sky Holder, and his bride Mature Flower. He occupies the barren earth alone. He longs for human company, which he decides to create, but first he must make this a good world for those people. In at least one version of the original Seneca creation story, his grandmother participates in the accomplishments listed throughout the poem.

Foster (1974 : 127) indicates that a ceremony is "declared open with the speaker's announcement that the people's minds have been 'brought together,'" then it is terminated with the announcement that they will "*divide their minds*" (italics his).

*2. Grass and Weeds*

*Now he thought.*
*There should be grass & weeds should be all over the Earth.*
*Now this has happened.*
*Now he thought.*
*From this.*
*There should be some that will be used for medicine.*
*Now it blocks the way of it.*
*We aren't here forever.*
*Now this time of day.*
*We give thanks for grass & weeds.*
*This is the way it should be in our minds.*

---

A slightly wider circumference is "described" here.

Healing, much of which is associated with plant life, is a very important activity and is closely associated with spirituality, especially because of the evil brought by Warty One, Good Mind's mischief-making twin.

Again, notice the link between the *thought* of Sky Holder and the statement that "This is the way it should be in our minds."

*3. Springs, Rivers and Lakes (i.e., Fresh Water).*

*Now he thought.*
*I will make Springs.*
*Where water will be coming from.*
*On this Earth.*
*There will be Springs.*
*The River & the Lakes.*
*He thought.*
*There will be no trouble finding them.*
*Wherever you are on this Earth.*
*Now this time of day.*
*We give thanks for the things we named.*
*This is the way it should be in our minds.*

---

Water is dynamic. It can rise with the ebb and flow of seasonal change, rainfall, and so on. Watch the idea develop that this is a very dynamic world, full of motion and animation.

In some versions, water is mentioned prior to grasses. In effect, "stanzas" two and three are reversed. As expected of any text that comes out of a preliterate tribal source, there are variations from version to version.

*4. Bushes and Forest*

*Now he thought.*
*There should be bushes & also the Forest.*
*He thought.*
*The people can keep warm from it.*
*Now a certain tree is there.*
*He gave authority for it to be the Head One.*
*In the Forest.*
*People will call it Maple.*
*There is a certain time here.*
*When water will be coming from it.*
*He thought.*
*The people could make use of it.*
*Now this has happened.*
*The water was flowing when the warm weather came to Earth.*
*Now this time of day.*
*We give thanks for the bushes, Forest & Maple.*
*This is the way it should be in our minds.*

---

In some versions this section follows sections 5 and 6 below (Foster 1974:142).

The maple, with its rising sap, is a special tree. Reference is made to the late winter ceremony, which commemorates movement out of the earth. The sap rises and the maple sugar is running. The Maple Festival is the first in the the annual ceremonial cycle (Foster 1974:111). The implication is that the earth is dynamic and alive, even as winter draws to a close.

## 5. *Cultivated Food*

*Now he thought.*
*I will do this.*
*He left it for us.*
*Something that should be for the people's happiness.*
*They will be strong in body from it.*
*He left us all this food.*
*He scattered this all over the Earth.*
*Now we will give* one *thanks.*
*That he has left us all this food to live on.*
*On this Earth.*
*This is the way it should be in our minds.*

---

Here the implication is that seeds can be carried from place to place and planted. Also, they nourish human bodies which house the minds of people. Hence, "food" is elevated above the trees. The dynamic pattern progresses; that which nourishes the human body assumes the added motion of those bodies. In many versions, Culivated Food and Strawberries would exist as a single category of hanging fruit, or else there would be one section for Cultivated Food (or Seeds, or Sustenance), and then a separate section for hanging fruit, of which one variety is strawberries, a special kind of hanging fruit (Foster 1974 : 140−43).

### 6. *Strawberries*

*Now where the grass grows.*
*The first berry that ripens will be called the short strawberry.*
*He thought.*
*They should give thanks among themselves & also give thanks to him.*
*For all persons that are left on this Earth.*
*Now this time of day.*
*We give thanks for the Strawberries.*
*This is the way it should be in our minds.*

---

Here we see one of the poem's apparent discrepancies, since strawberries are not as tall as trees or bushes. But strawberries have a very special significance, and have had since ancient times. They are the first fruit of the year; they are said to have special medicinal value; and it is believed that they sprout along the road to the world above the sky (see Chafe 1961 : 2−8, 21, esp. n. 17; Foster 1974:62). Hence, they are associated with spring, rebirth, existence in the heavens, and so forth.

7. *Animals Running Around*

*Now on this Earth.*
*He found out.*
*The Earth was so barren.*
*He made the animals & for them to be running around.*
*This is for the people to enjoy.*
*Now this has happened.*
*We give thanks for the animals running around on this Earth.*
*This is the way it should be in our minds.*

---

Here, the poem begins to refer to things visibly animate. One appealing incident in the creation story describes how Good Mind fills a cavity in the ground with oil and then draws one animal at a time from it. He presents each one to his Grandmother and they give it a name, starting with the largest—the bear—and going to the very smallest, most earthbound, all the way down to the chipmunk and mole. Notice the contrast between that sequence and the small-to-larger sequence of the Thank-You Prayer.

### 8. Birds in the Air and Wind

*Now another thing       In the Air-&-Wind*
*He made the fluttering of the birds there.*
*& the different sounds of the birds.*
*This is for the people to hear.*
*This is for them to enjoy who I made for it.*
*Now this time of day.*
*Now we give thanks for the Birds that are fluttering in the air.*
*This is the way it should be in our minds.*

---

Now the poem's focus extends beyond the earth's surface. This verse is transitional. Watch how the movement continues not only outward, but also from the tangible to the less tangible, the visible to the less visible.

## 9. Air

*Now he thought.*
*At a certain place.*
*From which the air is moving around everywhere.*
*They will breathe easily by it.*
*While walking around on this earth.*
*Now this is happening.*
*Just the way he thought it to be happening.*
*Now this time of day.*
*We give thanks for the Air.*
*For the place with the net on it.*
*Which is making the Air move everywhere on Earth.*
*This is the way it should be in our minds.*

---

Air is related to breathing. Breath for Native Americans is the highest facility, since it is the meeting place for mind and speech. It is a common notion among tribes that as an articulated manifestation of breath, poetry in the form of prayers, chants, oratory, and so on is a special kind of activity.

## 10. *The Thunderers (Rainfall)*

*Now he thought.*
*I will give authority to them to carry the dampness & the Rain with them.*
*They will take care of rivers also to dampen the gardens.*
*Now this has happened he has these servants now.*
*He also made it*
*so that we are relatives.*
*The people should call them Our Grandparents.*
*The Thunderers.*
*Now this time of day.*
*We give thanks to the Thunderers.*
*For they come from the West.*
*This is the way it should be in our minds.*

---

   In the creation story, Thunder comes to Good Mind and volunteers to help make a good world. "What can you do?" Good Mind asks him. "I can wash the earth and make drink for the trees and grass," he replies. Thunder and its attendant rainfall implies a relationship between the sky and the earth. What rises must fall. Thus the pattern of dynamic relationships continues. According to Foster (1974 : 144), it is the duty of the Thunderers "to carry water to wash the earth, to replenish the bodies of water, and to help in the growth of plants. They also have the duty of keeping the monsters below the earth."

11. *Sky*

*Now he thought.*
*There should be a sky over their heads.*
*So they can look up at it.*
*Now this has happened.*
*We look up to see the sky over our heads.*
*Now this time of day.*
*We give thanks for the Sky.*
*This is the way it should be in our minds.*

Observe the movement toward cosmic dimensions. In its infinite expanse, the sky is even more abstract than air and thunder. Sky can also be associated with the mysterious zone separating this world and "the up-above world" where Good Mind's grandmother and grandfather once dwelled.

### 12. *The Sun—Source of Energy*

*Now in the sky.*
*He created two things.*
*That they should be in the sky.*
*They are the ones to give light.*
*So the people could see where they are going.*
*The people I created.*
*Now this has happened.*
*At this time of day.*
*There is plenty of light.*
*He has given authority.*
*To the one who gives light for the days to have light.*
*Now this time of day.*
*We give thanks to our Brother the Sun.*
*This is the way it should be in our minds.*

---

Traditionally, Sun is the ruler of the day in Native American mythology, always associated with power.

### *13. The Moon*

*Now when the Sun has rested.*
*Because there is a length of time that he passes over the Earth.*
*The shadow will pass over the earth.*
*Now he has authorized another.*
*She will be the one to give light*
*so that everything will go on all right if something should happen*
*to the families by night.*
*Now he had given her more things to do.*
*He has authorized her to take care of the months.*
*She just changes from one end of the month to the other.*
*Also there are little ones being born.*
*The people count it by these months.*
*Now this time of day.*
*We give thanks to our Grandmother the Moon.*
*This is the way it should be in our minds.*

---

Notice the implicit dynamic relationship between the sun and the moon, representing, among other things, a cyclical arrangement.

The moon is female and is associated with the passing months, that is, with time. We have here, then, an increasing level of abstraction, considering time, sexual relationships, and the movement from day to night and back again.

Note: As a lifelong resident of the Lower Great Lakes region, where cloudy days are commonplace, where morning-long mistiness is frequent, and where thick hardwood forests combine with narrow valleys to subdue the horizon, I surmise that the moon is the most reliable—or, better still, the least unreliable—celestial timekeeper. Thus, it becomes a more important calendrical marker than do the sun or the stars.

## *14. Stars*

*Now in the sky.*
*He thought.*
*I will create all around her.*
*The stars will be all over the sky.*
*In the past.*
*They all had names also directions so that nothing would go wrong*
    *wherever you were on this earth.*
*It is still the same way that he made it.*
*Now we will set our minds yes we will give thanks for all the Stars in the sky.*
*This is the way it should be in our minds.*

---

Stars and starlore are generally associated with mystery.

"The Stars are the only extra-terrestrial spirit force without clearly defined duties. This is probably because star lore is a thing of the past." (Foster 1974:74). Foster (75) also lists some of the things stars are now believed to do or to have done.

15. *Good and Evil: the Warty One and Handsome Lake*

*Now.*
*He found out.*
*On this Earth.*
*All kinds of evil had come to it.*
*From a small item even.*
*Even just thinking it you were creating this evilness.*
*Now he thought*
*I will come in through this person.*
*He will be the one to tell them what I think of it.*
*He picked out Handsome Lake.*
*Yes he is to tell these people.*
*What they should follow.*
*Now this has happened.*
*Now we hear the Word of our Creator.*
*Now this time of day.*
*We give thanks to our Big Man*
*Handsome Lake.*
*This is the way it should be in our minds.*

---

This verse replicates the ongoing dynamic relationship between good and evil. In the story the two brothers quarrel, fight, compete, etc. Warty One, for instance, slays their mother, makes poisonous plants and weeds, insects and poisonous snakes. In other words, he forces Good Mind to work for good. Implicitly, he is responsible for establishing the relationship between life and death.

Foster (1974:81) writes, "Seneca longhouse speakers begin with the theme that the Creator saw a dire situation on Earth. . . . He sent Handsome Lake to 'straighten out' the minds of the people." See the full context of Foster's statement (1974:80–83). Handsome Lake is not treated simply as another spirit force whose functions are to be described and given thanks for. The subject is treated biographically as a brief narrative of the prophet's life. For a fuller account of Handsome Lake and his place in Seneca lore, see Wallace (1969).

## 16. The Four Winds

*Now he thought yes I should have servants.*
*Yes four Beings should be enough.*
*To protect the ones I had created.*
*Now this is in their power.*
*They are doing the job that he handed them.*
*Now we give thanks to the Four Beings.*
*This is the way it should be in our minds.*

---

Reference is made here to the outer world, "Beyond the dome we call the sky," where, according to the Seneca Creation Story, "there is another world" (Parker 1989:59).

The four beings are the messengers of Sky Holder, identified as The Wind who dwells in the east; the Thunder, who probably dwells in the north; the defending force, probably associated with the south; and the Heavy Night associated with the west. One of them, the Wind, is the father of Good Mind. These four beings represent the infinity of space and the origin of all motion. They suggest the most far-reaching cosmic directions. They are, says Foster (1974:75–76), "the highest and most powerful of the Creator's helpers." Their origins are unknown; it is even questionable whether the four beings existed in the pantheon prior to the time of Handsome Lake.

17. *The Word: Back to the Earth and the Center*

*Now he thought.*
*At a certain place.*
*I will stay there.*
*All that I made will be finding its end in it.*
*Now this time of day.*
*We have given our word & our thanks for it.*
*For whatever he gave us.*
*Now this time of day.*
*We will give him our thanks for it.*
*At this time of day.*
*This is the way it should be in our minds.*

---

The creator, reports Foster (1974:83), "is said by several [of his informants] to dwell in a world 'on the other side of the sky.'" It would follow, then that "our word" mediates between the up-above and the earthbound. Hence, we can see it as a plunge back to earth.

If Good Mind finally occupies the sky-world or the up-above world, so to speak, we mortals still see the earth as his making under his care. By paying homage to him and his works, we establish our earthbound relationship to his skybound creative spirit.

The implicit earth–heaven relationship suggests the quarrel in the sky world, where the Great Chief and his wife are in conflict and where that conflict leads to a chain of events resulting in the creation of the earth and of man on the earth.

The prayer reiterates the story of creation in a strikingly schematic way that is characteristic of the stylized way in which the cosmos is represented by other Native American cosmogonic stories—or so I would postulate. The poem's focus radiates steadily outward from the centrally immediate, the stationary, the earthbound, and the concrete to the distant, the mobile, the celestial, and finally the abstract. This orderly way of observing from the nearest at hand to the most distant, or from the most immediately concrete to the most remotely abstract, is apparently fixed in the Iroquois world view. As an analogue, consider the great Iroquois condolence ritual, performed upon the death of a member of the Confederate council, and in which the bereaved moiety is represented allegorically as a brother totally disabled by his grief. He cannot breathe, feel, see, hear, or speak. And before he is able to function once more as an active member of the community of tribes, his senses must be revived so that he is again made aware, first, of the husk mat on which he sits inside the lodge, where his suffering has imprisoned him, then on its immediate surroundings out of doors, and progressively of the trees and shrubs surrounding the lodge and all that exists beyond. Thus cured, he can finally fix his attention at last on the sky, clear to its outermost limits where there are generated the ideal laws and customs that bind the six tribes in a harmonious polity of confederation (see Bierhorst 1974, especially 147–150). Only then can he respond with reason to the corpse of his lost brother by helping to install a new chief so that tribal life can be resumed in the social constellation of the larger confederacy of tribes.

Analogously, notice how, in stanza 1 of the text, the "earth" underfoot is first emplaced, "where some people can walk around." Then, in stanza 2, "grass and weeds" are distributed carpetlike "all over the earth." Springs are next made, in stanza 3, "where water will be coming from"; and in stanza 4, the "bushes" and "the forest" are then created, filling the space yet a little further above the ground. Following that, in stanza 5, Good Mind creates food, which I believe is a reference to cultivated crops whose seeds can be deliberately carried by people, as well as wild seeds moved passively by forces like the wind. Next, Good Mind creates the sacred strawberry in stanza 6, a most special kind of food because it is the "first fruit of the year" (Wallace 1969: 13). Animals are then created in stanza 7, who, unlike growing things, can move about actively on their own, followed by birds in stanza 8, whose capacity to fly "In the Air & Wind" lifts them above the earth. And in subsequent stanzas, celestial space is filled by the placement of "the air"; of thunder and its accompanying rain; of the sky overhead; of the rotating sun, the cyclical moon, and the constellations together with the endless array of individual stars; and finally of the "Four Beings," who appear to occupy the most conceivably remote extremities at each of the cardinal points (Parker 1989:59–73).

Hence the poem invokes earthly phenomena, celestial objects, and heavenly forces in a progressive arrangement of spheres enfolding spheres further and further out from an earthbound center. Seen that way, it suggests a design of concentric circles and reflects an awareness of the orderly dimensionality of space in a cosmos alive with spiritual forces moving cyclically in harmony with celestial objects and stellar configurations.[1] Recognized are three tiers of being—one on the surface of the earth; one in the sky; and one beyond the sky, where the contention between Sky Holder and Mature Flower first began (Foster 1974:103–7).

Similarly, each stanza in the poem can be broken down into three segments, each of which recapitulates a stage in the ritualized process of creation. One is a "determination segment," recited in a future tense which identifies the creator's intent; one is the "report segment," reflecting the physical appearance of some singularly visible item or items, recited either in the indicative tense designating either the present or an immediate past; and one is the "performative statement," which conveys in a durative grammatical mode a precept or set of enduring conditions (Foster 1974:136).

The emerging sense of design is static and, at the same time, dynamic because of the way attention is compelled to move further and further from an inner focal point fixed by a schematically appointed pattern of expression, seemingly across progressively distant zones of sensory perception, to the absolute extent of anyone's ability to conceive of them—until it is drawn back by the limits of the human imagination to the center once again. I am led to that conclusion by the ordered structure of the poem, made all the more evident by the evocative power of Richard Johnny John's language and Rothenberg's careful arrangement of the printed text.

I am struck, too, with the way the concluding stanza refers back to its very first line of the poem. First, the participants all gather in stanza one— "in this place . . . our meeting place," seeing and greeting each other in the ceremonial longhouse. Upon assembling, they listen to a recitation of the prayer, then dance in clockwise circles around a pair of singers, with their collective focus gradually widening to the very limitation of their capacity to perceive space. The whole procedure represents a systematic movement of focus from the most palpably immediate to the most abstractly remote and from the self to immediate members of the surrounding community and beyond, toward a grasp of what dwells in the sky as far as human conception allows. Step by step, the components of the universe from the nearest to the most remote are recognized in the prayer until speaker and audience must revert back upon themselves in a struggle to imagine Good Mind, whom I take to be the "he" of the poem's opening, envisioning the world he wishes to create in its appropriate cosmic surroundings.

The movement of the dancers at the ceremonial gathering functions as a counterpart to the language of the poem, so that it may be said that the ceremonial longhouse becomes a model of the cosmos at its most unified and cohesively dynamic. The ceremony is a festive occasion. People come from all points and greet each other as they assemble. They share some special dish of food according to the season, dance, eat again as they exchange gossip and parting farewells, and then depart in a renewed spirit of community. This, indeed, is "the way it should be" in everyone's mind on ceremonial occasions, where such a framework is invoked and reenacted in terms of the unified vision of the cosmos, which terminates as it begins, with the individual mind struggling to find its proper place in a vast, organic cosmic array.

While I have not given up the search, I have looked in vain for direct testimony to ongoing sky-watching activities among available Seneca sources and other Iroquois lore. Nor have I been able to learn from Seneca people I know whether any kind of naked-eye astronomy goes on today. The kind of evidence I am looking for, of course, would allow me to refine further my understanding and my appreciation of the Thank-You Prayer, which I suggest deserves the attention of ethnoastronomers and literary critics alike. But even if nothing more can be learned about how these people orchestrate their view of the heavens with their ceremonial year and their daily lives, the text makes one thing very clear. Like all peoples, the Seneca have an ancient history of sky watching that leads them to a systematic view of the universe that predicates their existence as members of a tribe and as individuals. Furthermore, that view is preserved in a remarkably poetic statement that helps us to understand the lasting importance of an early tradition of celestial observation, even in a society that no longer practices it. More broadly still, it suggests that where other kinds of direct observation are not possible, the careful examination of a lingering poetic record can help us to understand that by watching the heavens and articulating the results of their observation, ancient peoples attained a sophistication we do not readily recognize. And, as is so often the case, that sophistication manifests itself artistically.

## An Afterword

I conclude with the assertion that the examination of poetry and the study of naked-eye astronomy are not as inimical to one another as we might think. Rather, there is an old connection we would do well to rediscover. Philip Sidney (1951 : 195), the sixteenth-century British poet and premier spokesman of renaissance literary theory, has written that the essence of poetry "standeth in that *Idea,* or fore-coceite of the work, and not in the work it selfe [*sic*]." He then goes on to say "that the Poet hath that *Idea,* is manifest, by delivering them forth in such excellencie as he hath imagined them . . ." Maybe Sidney's assertion applies here, where a verbal artifact materializes on the basis of patient naked-eye observation, accompanied by curiosity and a need to verbalize what is perceived. The movement of the sun and the phases of the moon, the splash of stars overhead, the revolving seasons, the cycles of life and death—so much of what is seen begs for explanation, especially when it yields orderly patterns. And if it is the role of the scientist to recognize the patterned orderliness, it is the poet's task to promulgate understanding through the orchestrated use of language. I once heard it said that inside of every good scientist there is an artist looking for elegance in the universe. At one time, before specialization set in, systematic observation and poetic expression occurred together. That bond appears to have been strong among tribal peoples. Washington Matthews (1884), a pioneer anthropologist who deserves greater notice for such perceptions, has argued that tribal myths from the Southwest display a capacity for scientific observation. When we consider the poetry generated by preliterate attempts to account for the cosmos, maybe we can modify the above statement: Inside of every artist looking for elegance there is a good scientist struggling for a verifiable reality. Perhaps observation and poetic speculation go "hand in hand," combining the known world with an invented reality, especially in the creation of so-called mythical accounts (see Rodgers and Zolbrod 1989).

When traced to its oral roots, poetry's essence resides in a vision which combines the actual with the imagined, verbalized for all to understand. In composing that art which we call poetry, Sidney goes on to say, the poet "goeth hand in hand with nature," using "the vigor of his own invention" to grow, in effect, "another nature, which expresses that comprehension that all men seek" (Sidney 1951 : 195). The impulse Sidney describes is universal among people everywhere, I believe, and is especially well demonstrated in preliterate stories of creation and in the lyrics that derive from them as they are perforce replicated in rituals and abstracted into enduring designs. Those who wish to learn more about the way Native Americans watched the sky, envisioned the universe, and then expressed that vision in the way they lived their lives would do well to regard such stories carefully.

## Notes

1. While certainly implicit in the poem, such a notion of concentric circles or spheres is in keeping with conceptions of circles or spheres common to tribes all over North America. I write about this elsewhere (Zolbrod 1988). See also Aveni (1984).

## References

Aveni, Anthony F. 1984. Native American Astronomy. *Physics Today* (June): 24–32.

Bierhorst, John. 1974. *Four Masterworks of American Indian Literature*. New York, Farrar, Straus, and Giroux.

Chafe, Wallace I. 1961. *Seneca Thanksgiving Rituals*. Washington, D.C.: Bureau of American Ethnology Bulletin 183.

Foster, Michael Kirk. 1974. *From the Earth to Beyond the Sky: An Ethnographic Approach to Four Longhouses Iroquois Speech Events*. Ph.D. diss., University of Pennsylvania.

Hewitt, J. N. B. 1903. *Iroquoian Cosmology*. Washington, D.C.: Bureau of American Ethnology Annual Report 21.

Hymes, Dell. 1981. *"In vain I tried to tell you:" Essays in Native American Ethnopoetics*. Philadelphia: University of Pennsylvania Press.

Matthews, Washington. 1884. Natural Naturalists. Washington, D.C.: Philosophical Society of Washington *Bulletin* 7:73–79.

Parker, Arthur C. 1989. *Seneca Myths and Folktales*. Lincoln: University of Nebraska Press. Reprinted from the 1923 edition published by the Buffalo Historical Society.

Rodgers, Glen E., and Paul G. Zolbrod. 1989. The Scientist as Storyteller: Storytelling as Science. *North Dakota Quarterly* 57:121–36.

Rothenberg, Jerome. 1972. *Shaking the Pumpkin: Traditional Poetry of the Indian North Americas*. New York: Doubleday. Reprint. Albuquerque: University of New Mexico Press, 1991.

Sidney, Sir Philip. 1951. An Apologie for Poetrie. In *The Great Critics: An Anthology of Literary Criticism,* ed. James Harry Smith and Edd Winfield Parks, 190–232. New York: W. W. Norton. Originally published in 1595.

Tedlock, Dennis. 1972a. *Finding the Center: Narrative Poetry of the Zuni Indians.* New York: Dial Press. Reissued with new preface, Lincoln: University of Nebraska Press, 1978.

————. 1972b. Pueblo Literature: Style and Verisimilitude. In *New Perspectives on the Pueblos,* ed. Alfonso Ortiz, pp. 219–42. Albuquerque: University of New Mexico Press.

————. 1985. *Popol Vuh.* New York: Simon and Schuster.

Tooker, Elisabeth, ed. 1979. *Native North American Spirituality of the Eastern Woodlands.* New York: Paulist Press.

Wallace, Anthony F. 1969. *The Death and Rebirth of the Seneca.* New York: Alfred A. Knopf.

Williamson, Ray A. 1984. *Living the Sky: The Cosmos of the American Indian.* Boston: Houghton Mifflin.

Zolbrod, Paul G. 1984. *Diné bahane': The Navajo Creation Story.* Albuquerque: University of New Mexico Press.

————. 1988. When Artifacts Speak What Can They Tell Us? *In Recovering the Word: Essays on Native American Literature,* ed. Brian Swann and Arnold Krupat. Los Angeles: University of California Press.

# 3

■ ■ ■ ■ ■ ■ ■ ■

## The Celestial Skiff:
## An Alabama Myth of the Stars

■ ■ ■ ■ ■ ■ ■ ■

### RAY A. WILLIAMSON

*Being a project director at the United States Congress' Office of Technology Assessment keeps astronomer Ray Williamson's mind ranging between outer space and the sublunar world. The author of several books for adults and children, as well as numerous technical reports, Williamson here shows how the work of older ethnographers can be used to address questions of today, especially those concerned with the relationship between the earth and the sky. Through informed deduction, he identifies an important constellation of the Alabama and links its movement to a primary agricultural ceremony, the Busk.*

Compared to other Native American groups, such as the Chumash (Hudson and Underhay 1978), the Pawnee (Chamberlain 1982), or the Zuni (Young and Williamson 1981), we know relatively little of the calendars kept by Native American tribes of the Southeast such as the Cherokee, Creek, and related groups or their starlore. Yet the ethnologies and folklore of the southeastern tribes contain numerous tantalizing suggestions that they depended on regular observations of celestial phenomena to guide their yearly round of activities. By the time Western science developed an interest in the cultural practices of these groups, their lives had been severely disrupted and many of them had taken on Western traits. What information is left derives primarily from the work of Mooney and Swanton, ethnographers within the Bureau of American Ethnology, who worked with these tribes in the early part of this century. In addition to recording details of daily life, religious beliefs, games, and ceremonies, Mooney and Swanton also collected a number of myths and tales, some of which have celestial content.

One of these, "The Celestial Skiff," which was collected by Swanton (1929:138–39) about 1912 from Alabama Indians then living in Texas, is especially important because, in addition to revealing southeastern Indian attitudes toward the earth and the sky, it contains information about their knowledge of celestial patterns and their calendar. "The Celestial Skiff" tells the story of sky beings that descend to earth and humans that ascend to the sky. Although the recorded story neither mentions the stars nor identifies the stellar patterns of the celestial canoe by which the sky and earth people interact, it supplies enough contextual information about Alabama Indian beliefs and practices to suggest strongly that it is part of the constellation Ursa Major (or the Big Dipper).

The story is an allegory in which few of the important celestial or earthly events are mentioned by name. It embodies both sacred and secular activities shared by other southeastern tribes, such as an emphasis on agriculture, the ball game, the annual Fall Busk Ceremony, and related dances. The story also reveals important interrelationships among these aspects of Alabama Indian life and the nightly and seasonal movements of the stars.

The Alabama are culturally closely related to the Creek, the Chickasaw, the Choctaw, and other southeastern tribes, and share many of the same customs and religious practices. The elements of many of their stories are also similar. Today, some two to four hundred Alabama living in east Texas still speak their native language (Lupardus 1979:3).

Relatively little is known about the early history of the Alabama. They are mentioned infrequently in the early journals of European exploration but were encountered by DeSoto in 1541 in what has become northern Mississippi. Later records place them on the "Alabama River just below the junction of the Coosa and the Tallapoosa [north of the modern city of Montgomery, Alabama]" (Swanton 1946:87–88). Because of pressures from the French and the British, as well as from other Indian groups, the tribe ultimately split up after France relinquished control over the region to England. Some tribal members moved to Mississippi, while others settled among the Seminole. Those who stayed in Alabama and joined the Creeks were active in the Creek War of 1813–14 and were later forced to move with the Creeks to Oklahoma. Most Alabama moved to what is now east Texas in the early part of the nineteenth century. Descendants of those Alabama who settled in Texas now live in Polk County on a state reservation some ninety miles northeast of Houston.

John R. Swanton recorded this and some sixty other Alabama stories while visiting with them and with the Oklahoma Alabama at various times between 1906 and 1913. He published the stories, along with an additional 240 stories from the Creek, the Hitchiti, the Koasati, and the Natchez, in "Myths and Tales of the Southeastern Indians" (Swanton 1929).

Swanton published most of his other information about the Alabama in his general study of the Creek (Swanton 1928a) and in his overall summary of southeastern Indians (Swanton 1946). His notes, which are stored in the National Anthropological Archives at the Smithsonian Institution, contain considerable additional information, yet very little regarding the Alabama calendar, or any interest they may have evinced in observing the movements of the celestial sphere. In addition, the stories Swanton collected are often disjointed and sometimes fragmentary, as if the corpus of a much richer oral tradition had already begun to come apart when Swanton began to collect them. Kroeber once opined that the material available to Swanton was "enormously diluted" by European influences and tribal disruption. "It was like working over tailings instead of following a fresh vein" (Kroeber 1940:3). However, Swanton did assemble a card-file dictionary of Alabama words, which resides in the Smithsonian National Anthropological Archives (Acc. no. 2435). This dictionary has made possible considerable progress in interpreting the stories he collected. Finally, because the Alabama are closely related by language and culture to other southeastern Indian groups, it is possible to glean many interpretive clues from Swanton's descriptions of them.

## The Celestial Skiff

1 Some people descended from above in a canoe singing and laughing. When they reached the earth they got out and played ball on a little prairie. As soon as they were through they got into the canoe again, singing and laughing continually, ascended toward the sky, and disappeared. After an interval they descended to the same place, singing and laughing, got out, and played ball again. When they were through they went back, got into the canoe, ascended toward the sky, and disappeared.

2 After this had gone on for some time a man came near a little while before they descended, stood on a tree concealed behind some bushes and saw them come down, singing and laughing, to the ground and get out. While they were playing the ball was thrown so as to fall close to the man and one woman came running toward it. When she got near he seized her and the other people got into the canoe, ascended toward the sky, singing continually, and disappeared.

3    The woman, however, he married. One time, after they had had several children, the children said, "Father, we want some fresh meat. Go and hunt deer for us." He started off, but he had not gotten far when he stopped and returned home. The mother said to her children, "Say, 'Father, go farther off and kill and bring back deer. We need venison very much.'" And the children said, "Father, go farther off and kill and bring back some deer. We need venison very much." When he did so, the children and their mother got into the canoe and started up, singing, but he came running back, pulled the canoe down, and laid it on the ground again.

4    After that the woman made a small canoe and laid it on the ground. When their father went hunting she got into one canoe and put the children into the small canoe and they started upward, singing. As they were going up the man came running back, but pulled only his children down, while their mother, singing continually, disappeared above.

5    But the children which the father had kept back wanted to follow their mother. They and their father got into the canoe, started off, singing continually, and vanished. Presently they came to where an old woman lived. The man said to her, "We have come because the children want to see their mother," and the old woman answered, "Their mother is dancing over yonder all the time, having small round squashes for breasts."

6    Then the old woman gave them food. She cooked some small squashes and gave pieces to each. When she set these before them, they thought, "It is too little for us." But when they took one away another appeared in the same place. When they took that one away it was as before. They ate for a long time but the food was still left. Then the old woman broke a corncob in pieces and gave a piece to each of them.

7    They went on and came to another person's house. This person said to them, "She stays here dancing." While they were there she went dancing around. They threw a piece of corncob at her but did not hit her. She passed through them running. The next time they threw at her when she came, she said, "I smell something," and passed through on the run. But the last one they threw hit her and she said, "My children have come," and she came running up to them. Then they all got into the canoe and came back to this world.

8    One time after this when their father was away all got into the canoe, started up toward the sky, and disappeared. The children's father came back and after he had remained there for a while he got into the other canoe, sang, and started upward toward the sky. He went on for a

while, singing, but looked down to the ground. Then he fell back and was killed (Swanton 1929:138–39).

The story begins by telling us that visitors from the sky descend to the earth to play ball for a time. They arrive on Earth in a canoe, "singing and laughing continuously." Swanton translates the Alabama term *pi'ła* as canoe. *Pi'ła*, however, is a general term that could also be translated as boat or skiff, and might refer to any one of a number of conveyances for crossing water (Lupardes, personal communication, October 1986). The southeastern Indians used a wide variety of boats, from simple reed rafts to large dugout canoes (Hudson 1976:314–15). The ball game of the story was undoubtedly a version of the highly popular southeastern Indian sport that was played with two rackets and a deerskin-covered leather ball (Culin 1903:602–3). Except for the use of two rackets rather than one, the game vaguely resembles lacrosse. After playing for a time, the sky people ascend and disappear.

The second paragraph reveals that at least one woman is among the game's participants. She is captured by a man who had been watching the game from concealment. This paragraph repeats the reference to singing as the sky people descend or ascend, as if singing provides the motive force for the canoe.

In the third paragraph, we learn that the Earth man marries the Sky woman and they have children. She attempts to return to the Sky, taking their children with her. Here again, the story refers to singing as the canoe ascends. The husband, however, returns from hunting too soon and pulls them back.

Paragraph 4 relates how the mother finally achieves her goal of escaping the bonds of Earth by building a second, small canoe in which to put her children. This canoe may well have been one of the small boats the southeastern Indians often built from skins stretched over a frame made of saplings. They looked more like a coracle than a canoe, but were easy to construct and carry and could be taken apart for portage to a new stream (Swanton 1928a:744; Adney and Chapelle 1964:212–20). This strategm allows her to rise to the Sky in the larger canoe, even though her husband once again returns too soon and prevents their children from following in the smaller one.

Because the children wish to follow their mother, in the fifth paragraph the father agrees to take them to the Sky to find her. They meet an old woman who tells them their mother is dancing, "having small round squashes for breasts." This reference and the contents of the sixth paragraph, in which an old woman gives the children as much squash to eat as they desire, suggest that it is harvest time, perhaps the Green Corn Ceremony, or the Busk, at which the Alabama and other southeastern Indians would dance, play ball, and feast for four or more days. The corncob that the old woman divides and gives to the children supports this interpretation.

In the seventh paragraph, the children find her dancing and attract her attention by hitting her with a piece of corncob. She seems not to notice them before being hit, but says, "I smell something," seemingly a reference to the fact that Earth people have a smell, while Sky people do not.

When the woman returns to Earth, she is apparently still not happy there, and in the eighth and last paragraph, she and the children escape Earth in the larger canoe. Though the father follows them in the smaller canoe, singing, he falls to Earth when he looks down, as if he cannot decide whether he should remain on Earth or travel to the Sky.

The story implies that he falls because he stops singing. On the other hand, he may have fallen to Earth because he looked back. Although the story does not mention any particular injunction against looking backward, as Thompson noted (1966:338), taboos against looking back are a common feature of Native American tales in which humans travel to the sky or to the underworld. Violation of the taboo often ends in the death of the person who looks back, as in the Cherokee story of the origin of the Pleiades, when one of the seven children who has danced up into the Sky looks back (Mooney 1900:258–59). It can also result in the loss of a loved one, as in the Orpheuslike Gabrielino story of a man who has rescued the spirit of his dead wife from the spirit world only to lose her when he looks back at her too soon (Heizer 1968:65– 68).

Although nowhere does the story even refer to the stars, the first three lines suggest strongly that the canoe of this folktale is a bright stellar pattern. The following analysis is based on this hypothesis.

### THE CANOE

The opening paragraph provides three essential clues to the identity of the celestial canoe. First, in northern latitudes, only a few bright constellations fall into the category of constellations that appear to swing down to the Earth and then rise again to the Sky. These are the circumpolar constellations, with the most prominent being, in European terms, the Big Dipper (Ursa Major), the Little Dipper (Ursa Minor), and Cassiopeia. Second, the pattern must be one that could appear to come down to Earth for the length of a ball game, which could last several hours. Finally, it must do so in the summer, when the Alabama would have been most likely to play ball.

The interaction between celestial coordinates and the horizon determines the appearance and disappearance of circumpolar stars. As seen from a latitude of 30° north, any star with a declination (angular distance north or south of the celestial equator) less than 60° will fall below the horizon when it crosses the meridian. At the latitude of the Alabama, whether in their original home (32°) or in Texas (30°), both the Big Dipper and Cassiopeia fit the conditions of appearing to touch the Earth, to disappear below the horizon, and later to rise up from it (Fig. 3.1). Observers placed at a latitude of +30°, will see the star Alpha Ursa Major, which lies at a declination of +62°, appear to dim as it falls lower in the atmosphere and skim the horizon as the Big Dipper swings around to the east. In contrast, from a latitude of 40°, the last star in the handle of the Big Dipper appears to graze the horizon (assuming a 0° horizon), and the Big Dipper remains visible all night. As seen from 30° north latitude, the bowl of the Little Dipper is too far north to fall entirely below the horizon unless the northern horizon extends higher than 12° (for example, while standing at the base of a large hill). It is therefore an unlikely candidate for the celestial skiff. In addition, the Little Dipper is much fainter than the Big Dipper and is recognized as a pattern by only a few societies.

Of the two candidate constellations, Cassiopeia and the Big Dipper, only the Big Dipper appears to sink below the horizon in the summer (Fig. 3.1), when the southeastern tribes apparently played several variations of the ball game (Hudson 1976:411). Cassiopeia exhibits such behavior in the early and late spring when ball games were not played.

What makes this identification plausible is the fact that the Big Dipper, along with the Pleiades, is one of the most consistently recognized and important constellations throughout the world (Gibbon 1964), in part because of its usefulness as a celestial clock and direction finder. The Navajo, for example, use the angular position of the Big Dipper to indicate when to plant corn, or to set the time of certain ceremonies (Brewer 1950:134). Alpha and Beta Ursa Majoris, the two stars that point to Polaris, the north star, are much brighter than it and are likely to be visible more often.

After reading this conclusion from the story's internal evidence, I discovered that the Creek Indians, the close cultural relatives to the Alabama, call the Big Dipper *Pilohagi,* which means "the image of a canoe"

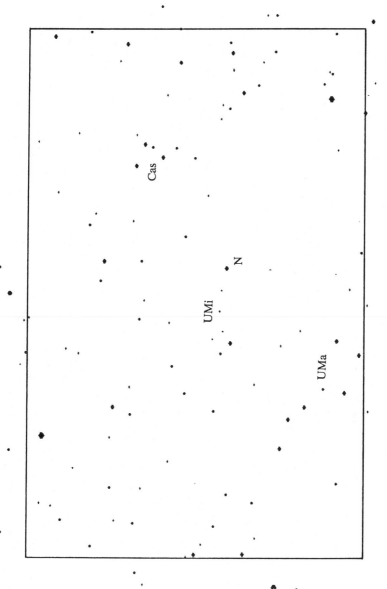

**Figure 3.1.** The night sky at 30° north latitude looking north (about 9 P.M. ST) in early summer.

(Swanton 1928a: 478). Finally, linguist Karen Lupardus (personal communication, October 1986) pointed out to me that Swanton (n.d. Acc. no. 2435, card 776) had recorded an Alabama constellation called *hotci'li pi'ła,* the Boat Stars, which he identified as the bowl of the Big Dipper.

Late July is the earliest time in the year when one can witness the entire sequence of appearing to come down to Earth and rise up again. This is also the time of year when the Busk was most often held. Then the Big Dipper would appear to set at about 1:00 A.M. and begin to rise soon after the first light of dawn appears in the East.

The best fit between the astronomical circumstances and the description in the story occurs around the autumnal equinox. On that date, assuming an average 3° local horizon, Beta and Gamma Ursa Major begin to set at about 9:00 P.M. EST, and Alpha and Beta Ursa Major start to rise at about 2:00 A.M. (Fig. 3.2). On the autumnal equinox the sun sets at shortly after 6:00 P.M. and rises a few minutes after 6:00 A.M.; twilight lasts about one hour and twenty minutes. Thus, the bowl of the Big Dipper begins to set approximately an hour and a half after dark. It starts to rise again two and a half hours before the first glimmer of dawn. When the "canoe" is well up into the sky, it disappears in the light of dawn. A month after the fall equinox, the Big Dipper would have already begun to set before dark.

## THE SMALL CANOE

One or more of the three stars in the handle of the Big Dipper, all fairly bright stars, are the best candidates for the small skiff because they appear to follow the bowl into the sky. Thus, they fit the conditions of the tale quite well. In addition, the Alabama word *tcinifa'se'kon,* in paragraph 4, which Swanton translates as small canoe, has the connotation in other contexts that it is carried along as a burden (Lupardes, personal communication 1986), which the stars in the handle might seem to be, as they follow after the bowl.

## THE BUSK CEREMONY

The Busk ceremony is not specifically mentioned in the story, yet the circumstances in the tale, including the plentiful supply of food and the dancing as well as the ball game, strongly imply than the tale takes place at the time of the Busk or afterward. The native listener would not need to have the point made explicitly, as he or she would know immediately from

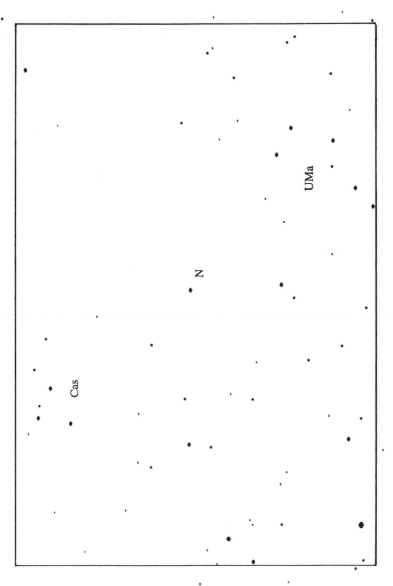

**Figure 3.2.** The night sky at 30° north latitude looking north (about 2 A.M. ST) in late September.

the various allusions just what time of year the actions of the story take place.

The Creek-related Indian groups, including the Seminole, held their Green Corn, or Busk, Ceremony when the earliest corn ripened. The exact date therefore depended on that year's weather patterns, the latitude, and the geographical setting of the village. However, it also apparently depended on observations of the stars and the moon. The ceremony was generally held in late July, though it could be held as early as June or as late as August. Observed for the sake of the tribe's well-being, the Busk was the major southeastern ceremony, and spring and early summer ceremonial activities were often devoted to preparing for it. The Creek held three "stomp dances" in preparation for the Busk; the first took place in April, although it might occur in May. The ceremony became known as the Busk as a corruption of the Creek term *poskita,* which means "a fast," in reference to the fasting and purging that took place before and during the Green Corn Ceremony. Before the ceremony, eating corn was taboo. The equivalent Alabama term is *poskitilga,* derived from the term *pos'ki,* to fast, to abstain from food (Swanton, n.d. Acc. no. 2435, card 1745). The Busk was apparently originally held at "the beginning of the first new moon in which their corn became full eared" (Adair, in Swanton 1928a:550n). Later, it was held at the time of harvest.

The Busk signaled the beginning of the year, and the Alabama kindled the year's new fire during the ceremony. Dancing and playing one or more types of ball game are significant parts of the Green Corn Ceremony. In some tribes, after the men and women danced all night, the men would play ball for several hours. In others, the women took part in a version of the ball game.

CORN WOMAN

This story also seems to be about Corn Woman, the being who brought corn and, according to some stories, beans and squash to the Indians. Although I could find no Alabama story specifically devoted to Corn Woman, the Creek, Koasati, and the Natchez told versions of it. Swanton (1929) collected six stories from these tribes relating to Corn Woman and the origin of corn and agriculture. Mooney (1900:242–49) collected a similar story from the Cherokee. The details of the stories vary, but they all agree that Corn Woman makes corn or corn meal by scraping it from her body. Other characters eat the corn she makes, but they wonder how she makes this wonderful food. When they discover that she scrapes it from her body, they become disgusted and refuse to eat the new food. She responds by telling them.

> You may not like to eat from me in this way, so build a corncrib, put me inside and fasten the door. Don't disturb me, but keep me there for four days, and at the end of the fourth day you can let me out. (Swanton 1929:9)

When they open the door on the fourth day (a sacred time span), the crib is full of corn. She later instructs the people about how to cultivate corn. Some stories specify that Corn Woman is an old crone; others leave the impression that she is much younger.

In "The Celestial Skiff," I believe we see her in two guises—as the old woman who feeds the children and the father upon their arrival in the Sky, and as the younger mother, the one who "is dancing over yonder all the time, having small round squashes for breasts." In this interpretation, the old woman symbolizes the fruits of harvest and the old year, while the young woman is the new corn. The old woman who feeds travelers small pieces of squash also appears in "The Men Who Went to the Sky" (Swanton 1929:139−41). In this related Alabama story, "The-Old-Sitting-Above" (God) gives the two men gifts of seeds from corn, watermelon, and beans, which they bring back to Earth.

In paragraph 7, the children throw pieces of corncob at their mother (the new corn) as she goes dancing by. This act cements their connection with her. During the first night of the Alabama Busk, each family brought roasted ears of corn to the Busk square, which was laid out in the cardinal directions. After everyone danced until midnight, some of the roasted ears were shelled and several men would throw kernels of roasted corn over the Busk house four times (Swanton 1928a:602). The following morning they kindled the new fire, which started the new year. For three more successive nights, the families would offer up roasted ears of corn, throwing a few kernels over the roof of the Busk house.

Three characteristics of Alabama cosmology can be understood by analyzing the actions of the mother. In one sense, she seems perfectly ordinary. She plays ball, has children, and dances—all things an Alabama woman would do. On another level, she is a Sky being who represents corn and the coming of agriculture. First, events of the Sky, such as the motion of the Big Dipper, are closely connected with earthly sacred occurrences such as the Busk. In addition, the beings who people the Sky are closely related to humans. Third, they are clearly quite different. Though commerce between the Sky and Earth is possible in specialized cases, through the celestial skiff, it is inappropriate for Sky beings to remain on the Earth and vice versa. The father stays on Earth; the mother remains in the Sky. The children belong to the Sky because, in this matrilineal society, they belong to the clan of the mother.

Other Alabama stories, such as "The Men Who Went to the Sky" (Swanton 1929:139–41), highlight the second two characteristics of Alabama thinking. In the several versions of this story recorded by Swanton, although the men are welcomed by "The-One-Sitting-Above" and presented with gifts of seeds, they are under strong injunctions to ignore the Sky beings through whose villages they pass during their journey. They must also return home soon.

Much of the story is also related to events and actions of the annual Busk ceremony. The connection in the story between the motion of the Big Dipper and the Busk suggests that at one time observations of the position of the Big Dipper may have played a part in the actual timing of the occurrence of the Busk, and perhaps in the timing of dances and other activities during the night. That astronomical observations undoubtedly had a role in determining the beginning of the Alabama Busk is suggested by the practices of the Creek, who set the time of their Busk and the three "stomp dances" that preceded it by the period of the new moon.

The Florida Seminole, who are closely related to the Creek and Alabamas, also arranged their Green Corn Ceremony, or Dance, by observing the regular motions of the celestial bodies. According to Capron, the Cow Creek Indians and the Big Cypress Indians date their Green Corn Dance by observing the new moon that occurs in the last of June or the first of July. Capron observes that the Cow Creek Indian who told him the day on which the feast would occur changed his estimate as the day approached, as a result of new information derived from lunar observations. The feast, or Picnic, took place two days after the first appearance of the crescent moon. The group called the Indians on the Trail hold their Green Corn Ceremony somewhat earlier, "when the 'Seven Stars,' the Pleiades, which have sunk below the horizon, make their reappearance [in the morning sky]" (Capron 1953:177). The latter appearance takes place shortly after the summer solstice, in late June. Although the Creek lunar observations are unlike the stellar observations I have posited for the Alabama, they demonstrate an interest among closely related southeastern tribes in celestial motions and appearances.

As noted earlier, the connection of the Busk Ceremony with the Sky was much stronger than simply setting a calendar by celestial events. Swanton (1928a: 546–47) tells us that according to "information obtained by one of the Tulsa Indians from an old Alabama . . . the busk medicines were sent down from God by two old gray-headed men. As soon as the old men had delivered them they disappeared, returning to the Sky." Corn and seeds for other crops also derived from the Sky (Swanton 1929: 139–43). In addition, the white smoke of the Busk fire was thought to reach the Sky. The smoke participated in unifying the Earth and Sky, just as the entire Busk ceremony was thought of as unifying the various discordant elements that had developed within the tribe throughout the year. It appears the Alabama used the constellation westerners call the Big Dipper to schedule the Busk.

## ACKNOWLEDGEMENTS

I am deeply indebted to Dr. Karen Lupardus for her guidance in understanding some of the pitfalls in interpreting Swanton's translation of the myth, and for her help in locating astronomical references in some of Swanton's published material. Dr. Lupardus allowed me to make use of her transcription of Swanton's field notes and literal translation of the story. She also shared with me her discovery in Swanton's unpublished material of the Alabama constellation called the Boat Stars. I appreciate the kind assistance of the staff of the Smithsonian National Anthropological Archives. Claude Bowen deserves special thanks for suggesting that the two women of the story represented Corn Woman.

# References

Adney, Edwin T., and Howard I. Chapelle. 1964. The Bark Canoes and Skin Boats of North America. *United States National Museum Bulletin* 230: 212–20.

Brewer, Sallie P. 1950. Notes on Navaho Astronomy. In *For the Dean: Essays in Anthropology in Honor of Byron Cummings*, Erik K. Reed and Dale S. King, eds. 133–36. Tucson: University of Arizona Press.

Chamberlain, Von Del. 1982. *When Stars Came Down to Earth*. Los Altos. Calif.: Ballena Press.

Capron, Lewis. 1953. The Medicine Bundles of the Florida Seminole and the Green Corn Dance. Smithsonian Institution Bureau of American Ethnology Bulletin 151.

Culin, Stewart. 1903. Games of the North American Indians. *Smithsonian Institution Bureau of American Ethnology Annual Report* 24.

Gibbon, William B. 1964. Asiatic Parallels in North American Star Lore: Ursa Major. *Journal of American Folklore* 77 : 236–50.

Heizer, Robert. 1968. The Indians of Los Angeles County: Hugo Reid's Letters of 1852. *Southwest Museum Papers* 21.

Hudson, Charles. 1976. *The Southeastern Indians.* Knoxville: University of Tennessee Press.

Hudson, Travis, and Earnest Underhay. 1978. *Crystals in the Sky: An Intellectual Odyssey involving Chumash Astronomony, Cosmology, and Rock Art.* Socorro, N.M.: Ballena Press.

Kroeber, A. L. 1940. The Work of John R. Swanton. *Smithsonian Miscellaneous Collections* 100 : 1–9.

Lupardus, Karen. 1979. *The Language of the Alabama Indians.* Ph.D. diss. University of Kansas.

Mooney, James. 1900. The Myths of the Cherokee. *Bureau of American Ethnology Annual Report* 19.

Swanton, John R. 1928a. Creek Religion and Medicine. *Smithsonian Institution Bureau of American Ethnology Annual Report* 42.

———. 1928b. Sun Worship in the Southeast, *American Anthropologist* 30 : 206–13.

———. 1929. Myths and Tales of the Southeastern Indians. *Smithsonian Institution Bureau of American Ethnology Bulletin* 88.

———. 1946. Indians of the Southeastern United States. *Smithsonian Institution Bureau of American Ethnology Bulletin* 137.

———. n.d. Unpublished notes, Acc. no. 2435, Smithsonian Anthropological Archives, Washington, D.C., 50,400 Alabama vocabulary cards.

Thompson, Stith. 1966. *Tales of the North American Indians.* Bloomington: Indiana University Press.

Young, M. Jane, and Ray A. Williamson. 1981. Ethnoastronomy: The Zuni Case. In *Archaeoastronomy in the Americas,* ed. Ray A. Williamson. Los Altos, Calif.: Ballena Press.

# 4

## ■■■■■■■■■

## "... by you they will know the directions to guide them": Stars and Mescalero Apaches

## ■■■■■■■■■

### CLAIRE R. FARRER

*Living on the desert floor next to the Mescalero Apache Indian Reservation for ten years serendipitously led to Claire Farrer's field focus; even when she is teaching anthropology at California State University-Chico, she longs for the New Mexican mountains. The author or editor of six books, and numerous articles, she has concentrated on ethnoastronomy for the past several years. In this chapter she takes a line from the Mescalero creation story to illustrate some of the ways in which earth and sky are linked and how what is written in the stars guides earthly action.*

Bernard Second, my primary Mescalero Apache consultant until his death in 1988, and I were outlining a book on ethnoastronomy. On June 15, 1988, the following conversation took place.[1]

CRF    I need a complete creation narrative for the beginning of this book. You know, each time we've talked about this, we keep getting interrupted or I ask a silly question that gets us off the track or you remind yourself of something you'd meant to tell me. I put a good story together, but it came from several different times. Tell me the story from the beginning.

BS    Wait. Let me think. ——— We do *not* forget. We remember.[2]

As I told you,
in the beginning of time
    when there was nothing except for the Eternal Power
He decided that He would create.[3]
So on the First Day
    He created the Sun and Mother Earth and the Moon and the Stars
    and the Wind,
    Rainbow.

On the Second Day
He created all the things that crawl and fly
   like birds, reptiles, worm, insects.
And on the Third Day
He created the four-legged of the world,
    the buffalo, deer, elk, antelope:
    all the ones that walk with hair on them.
And then,
    on the Fourth Day,
He created Man,
    the Apaches.

So
when He created Man,
([aside to CRF] and by that I mean mankind, women, too),
He told all of His creation,
He spoke to them and
He told them,
    "Because your relative is so weak and fragile, *all* of you are his
    relative and you will help him to live."

And then He,
the Power,
lined up all His creation.
And He told the Sun,
He said,
    "You I have created so that you will be My representative
    You
    will be that which Man sees."

And then the Moon,
He told the Moon,
    "You will be their eyesight at night."

And the Stars,
He said,
    "When they travel, by you they will know the directions to
    guide them."

And then the Wind,
He said,
    "You will carry Man's word."

([aside] So always be careful what you [head gesture to CRF] say on a windy day.)[4]

It is tempting to discuss all the facets of this rich narrative: its poetic content; how it sets up a base metaphor forming a template for living life; its structure divided into fours and balanced segments; its folkloristic content; the ontogeny recapitulated; its philosophical message; the informational content. In the past I have considered it quite literally; how the stars are used to time the girls' puberty ceremony (in press, 1987) and how the stars provide a guide to travel on the surface of the earth (1989). Now my focus is on relationships and the metaphoric, specifically the interplay between stars and people, between guiding lights and those for whom the lights shine. For, while surely the stars are guides to earth surface travel, the stars are also metaphoric guides to life as it should be lived. They serve as nightly visual reminders that there is a proper order to the created universe, to the celestial sphere, to the visible world, and to the behavioral–attitudinal world of *$^n$dé,* The People, the Mescalero Apache People.

Any message that is so important as to provide an order to, and harmony for, life is not one to be repeated only once and then set aside. Rather, it is a message that bears repeating many times in many contexts; it is a message that must be reinforced. Indeed, the message is repeated nightly as the stars rise in the east and set in the west; it is repeated yearly as different constellations appear in particular parts of the sky with a reassuring regularity. There is an ever-present and predictable order that in its very existence speaks eloquently of the harmonious universe of Creation.

Parts of the message are repeated in other narratives, such as how what Euroamericans call the Milky Way received its name or how and why particular groups of stars are connected and to what the connections refer.

The primary tenet of Mescalero Apache life is balanced harmony, *guzhuguja* [everything in order]. It is most often visually represented as a quartered circle that is referred to as *$^n$da$^?$i bijuuł siá$^?$* [life/creation—its circularity/completion—sits/is there]:

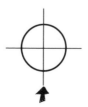

As Second and I demonstrated elsewhere (1981), this simple visual metaphor is transformed into a variety of designs that are said to be all "the same thing." For example, by connecting a few points, the quartered circle generates both a four-pointed star (symbolic of men)

and a crescent moon (symbolic of women).

Then, by cutting along the horizontal axis and following the points of the star, a mountain range appears:

In a similar fashion, behavior is generated from the messages encoded in the arrangements of stars in the sky. As an example, consider proper familial relationships. Mescalero Apaches believe that cooperation and generosity are essential within the group, the Tribe; without cooperation and generosity, some might perish. When some perish, the group is weakened; should the group be weakened sufficiently, the entire Tribe might be threatened.

On a microcosmic level, one is expected always to be generous to one's siblings and relatives of both ascending and descending generations. Thus, children are taught to share and to serve their elders while simultaneously being taught that all those in the matrilineally defined family, often with its matrilateral extensions, will provide food, shelter, and clothing whenever they have it themselves and, in any case, will provide support and love. It is not at all unusual for a child at Mescalero to decide to live for a period with a matrilineal relative, nor is it unusual for such a relative to welcome the child; for, if one in the family has, all have.

The importance of Tribal and family generosity is taught in a variety of ways, including by direct imperative to little children. Adults take their imperative from the night sky and what Euroamericans call the Milky Way.[5] Bernard Second related,

> When the world began.
>> our Twin Warrior Gods
>> they got in a fight;
>> they got in a fight.
> And one had a container of seeds.
> And so,
>> when they got in a fight,
> they hit it
> and
> it went all across the sky
>> like that. [Expansive hand gesture indicating the curving shape
>> of the Milky Way.]
>
> So
>> the Milky Way
>> is called "The Scattered Stars." [*syɣs naatsdił*]

To a Mescalero Apache person, this is not a just-so story. It speaks on a much deeper level. At the time of the beginning, when the universe was brought into being, Creator set in motion a perfect, balanced, harmonious, and beautiful world, a world not only *guzhuguja,* balanced, but also a world characterized by *ⁿzhúne,* exquisite in every sense of the word. While the Twin Warrior Gods behaved properly, the universe retained its inherent balanced order, with the stars in their appointed positions; but when they fought with one another—something those in the same matrilineage are not supposed to do—they literally and figuratively upset the order of the universe.

Creator, the Eternal Power, had originally stated that all in the universe were to cooperate with people, for people are the weakest link in the chain of creation; it is they who must lean on all other of Creator's efforts. It would have been tautological for Creator to have said that people, too, must cooperate with each other. Being in such a power-down position makes it incumbent upon people to tend very carefully indeed their relationships with all others in creation, whether animate or inanimate; they must be especially careful with their own interpersonal relationships, for there is nothing below them on which to lean. We people are the last in line, totally dependent upon the rest of creation that came into being before us. We are so weak that we could not exist without all that preceded us. Being so vulnerable, and so tenuously ensconced, makes it absolutely imperative that we get along with each other for we need each other so desperately. This is particularly true in one's own family; it is foolhardy to fight with a family member, especially one in the same generation, for the sibling links are lifelong.

So, rather than fix the rupture made by the fighting of two who should have known better, Creator left the residue of their improper behavior as a reminder to $^n dé$: one must be careful to maintain proper relationships, for to do otherwise is to tamper literally with the order of creation and its essential harmony and balance. The Scattered Stars (the Milky Way) serve as a nightly reminder to live in concert with one's fellow human beings, to live according to the template in the sky. The consequences of the failure to live properly are messy, nonordered, scattered, and imperfect. The lesson speaking of the threat to coherence and identity is one that is reinforced nightly. The messages are very clear to Mescalero Apaches: either live according to the Creator's plan or disrupt the balance and harmony of the universe; either cooperate with one another or lose your status as a separate Tribe. It is right up there in the sky to see; one cannot forget.

The consequences of a proper life are also encoded in the stars for all to see. To have lived a proper life is to have maintained balance and harmony throughout one's existence and, therefore, one may expect an orderly and proper existence in the next world, The Real World of Power and Potential rather than our Shadowed World of illusion and mirrored reflection (Farrer and Second 1986). The results of lives properly lived are beautifully displayed in a constellation that rises shortly before the sun in the summer. Mescalero Apaches identify a three-star constellation (Capella, iota Aurigae, and eta Aurigae) that Euroamericans group into Auriga, which itself is a part of the zodiacal constellation of Taurus. The Mescalero call the three-star constellation *taanashka?da,* or, in English, the Three Who Went Together, meaning the three who died at the same time.

Briefly, there were two sisters who both loved the same man.[6] Rather than fight over him and rather than have one sister be miserable all her life because of unrequited love, both the sisters agreed to marry him, to share him. This they did throughout their lives. Theirs was a harmonious household, they say. They became known not only for their caring for one another but also for their caring and compassion for all living things, and especially for their nurturance of others in the Tribe. When it was time for one of them to die, Creator, rather than separate them, took all three of them from the face of the earth simultaneously. But they were not lost, nor was their radiance from a properly balanced life diminished. Creator placed them in the sky together where they remain—sparkling, shining, and always linked— to remind The People of the positive consequences of a life well, and properly, lived.

While weak, The People are of special consequence to Creator. Yet it is their very weakness that has engendered both the chaos, as seen in the Scattered Stars, and the exquisite order, as seen in the Three Who Went Together. Creator knows that The People require the backside, the chaos, to remind them of the frontside, the order. Just look up any night, as the Mescalero Apache do. The stars are ever present, providing the directions to guide life.

## Notes

This chapter is dedicated to Bernard Second's memory and to the Mescalero Apache children he did not live long enough to instruct.

1. In addition to Second and me, David Carmichael, an archaeologist, was also present. Dave had been working at Mescalero for a few years on ethnobotany, ethnogeography, and hunting practices.

2. I have used a modified version of Dennis Tedlock's (1983) notational system to render Second's speaking style, using placement and spacing to simulate speech. Direct quotes from Second are indented rather than encased in quotation marks, which are reserved for quoted speech within the narrative. Further indentations from the left margin indicate slight pauses or changes in voice tone. Double spacing between segments indicates a longer pause; emphasized words are italicized. Parenthetical or explanatory statements are placed within parentheses, while my comments are in brackets. Upper case indicates the quintessential or specific, while lower case is used for the generic, as in "Buffalo" for the spirit animal and "buffalo" for the animal in general.

3. Mescalero Apache pronouns refer to first, second, dual second, third, and honorific fourth persons; there is no ascription of gender. However, since Second was here speaking in English, he utilized the English convention of referring to Creator as He. The Apache word for Creator [*Bik$^2$egudi$^n$dé*, According To Whom There Is Life] does not reference gender.

4. This is only a portion of the narrative related in June 1985. The complete narrative may be found in my book *Living Life's Circle: Mescalero Apache Cosmovision* (University of New Mexico Press, 1991).

5. This version of the Milky Way story was recorded on July 3, 1984, in the presence of Gene Ammarell, then Education Officer of the Fiske Planetarium at the University of Colorado, Boulder; Gene had accompanied me, with the assistance of an American Council

of Learned Societies grant I'd secured, to Mescalero in order to provide independent verification of my star identifications from a Euroamerican, scientific perspective as well as to help me gain additional information. He also produced several spectacular photographs of the night sky from the ceremonial mesa as well as photos of the stars used for timing the girls' puberty ceremony.

6. This narrative was never related to me as a coherent whole. Rather, I'd hear one part of it on one occasion and be told another part of it on another occasion. This is a composite of those several fragmentary tellings.

# References

Farrer, Claire R. 1987. Star Clocks: Mescalero Apache Ceremonial Timing. In *Amerindian Cosmology*, ed. Don McCaskill. Special issue of *The Canadian Journal of Native Studies* 7 : 223–36.

————. 1989. Star Walking: The Preliminary Report. *World Archaeoastronomy*, ed. Anthony F. Aveni, 483–89. Cambridge: Cambridge University Press.

————. In press. Mescalero Apache Ceremonial Timing to appear in *Ethnoastronomy: Indigenous Astronomical and Cosmological Traditions of the World*, ed. Von Del Chamberlain, M. Jane Young, and John B. Carlson. Los Altos and Thousand Oaks, Calif. Ballena Press and Slo'w Press.

Farrer, Claire R. and Bernard Second. 1981. Living the Sky: Aspects of Mescalero Apache Ethnoastronomy. *Archaeoastronomy in the Americas*, ed. Ray A. Williamson, 137–50. Los Altos, Calif. Ballena Press.

————. 1986. Looking through the Mirror of Life. *Parabola* 11(2):70–73.

Tedlock, Dennis. 1983. *The Spoken Word and the Work of Interpretation*. Philadelphia: University of Pennsylvania Press.

# 5

■■■■■■■■

# Morning Star, Evening Star: Zuni Traditional Stories

■■■■■■■■

## M. JANE YOUNG

*Jane Young's folklore Ph.D. from the University of Pennsylvania included advanced study in anthropology and linguistics as well. Currently associate professor of American Studies at the University of New Mexico, she recently published the definitive book on Zuni rock art. Here she intertwines stars, twins, narratives, and cultural symbolism to illuminate aspects of the Zuni understanding of the given and created world and some of the ways in which sky and earth are inseparable.*

The *Ahayu:da* or Twin War Gods play a central role in Zuni myths and folktales, especially those that focus on the time of the beginning. Basing my discussion on traditional Zuni narratives, I shall delineate the way in which these Twins, in their various aspects, contribute to an understanding of Zuni perceptions of the interaction between the earth and the sky.[1] Although these beings exemplify the importance of duality of Zuni cultural symbolism, they are neither identical twins, nor are they polar opposites. They seem, in fact, to be characteristic of a Zuni interest in dynamic asymmetry—an interest that is further reflected in the Zuni system of aesthetics in which artistic elements are rarely arranged according to a scheme of exact balance or mirror reflection (B. Tedlock 1984:259–61; Young 1988:105–7).[2] Despite their characterization as twins, the War Gods have distinctive names and attributes—they are Elder Brother and Younger Brother, *Ahayu:da* and *Matsailema*—and they have different personalities as well. Sometimes Zunis indicate that there are two sets of such twins: one pair, described as sons of the Sun who have existed since the time of the beginning, and another pair who are created by the union of the Sun and a waterfall during the Zunis' journey in search of the Center Place. In other instances, however, the two pairs seem to merge, both being referred to as "the Twins."[3] In any case, the roles of Elder and Younger Brother are similar, whether the discussion centers on one pair of twins or on two distinct pairs. For instance, in many Zuni narratives about these twins, the Younger Brother does most of the talking and impetuously initiates most of the action. Elder Brother is more deliberate and cautious than Younger Brother and often suggests, when they are in pursuit of a rather reckless adventure, that they should "Go home . . . and mind our own affairs" (Cushing 1901:176; see also Benedict 1935:1–6, 51–75; Quam 1972: 182–94). Nevertheless, Elder Brother is usually won over by Younger Brother and agrees to do what he wants. The elder brother's position as the senior, and generally wiser member of the pair, may be illustrated by the fact that the twins are usually referred to together as the *Ahayu:da,* using the elder's name to signify the pair.

In Zuni narratives that describe the time of the beginning, the Twin War Gods are culture heroes who bring the ancestors of the contemporary Zuni out of the fourth underworld to the surface of this earth; they contribute to making these people into "finished beings"; they shape the very features of the earth's surface (the Fifth World); they destroy or petrify the monsters that populate this world; and they create constellations, stars, and other astronomical objects by throwing the body parts of various monsters into the sky (Benedict 1935:1–5, 51; Bunzel 1932:584–602; Bunzel 1933:281–82; Cushing 1896:379–429; Cushing 1901:398–410, 423– 28; Cushing 1920:25–33; Parsons 1923:135–62; Quam 1972:129–33, 182–84; Stevenson 1904:24–46; D. Tedlock 1972:225–71). Thus, they play an important role that affects both the terrestrial and the celestial realms, and the beings who reside there.

In addition to depicting them as culture heroes or War Gods, some Zuni narratives also describe these twins as sons of the Sun Father—the Morning and Evening Stars, who serve as heralds for various ceremonial and agricultural activities (Cushing 1896:381; Cushing 1901:378–79; Quam 1972:129, 133; Risser 1941:215–26; Young and Williamson 1981:184). The Zuni name for the Evening Star translates as "the one that follows the sun" and the word for Morning Star translates as "big or great star" (Young and Williamson 1981:185–86). In certain Zuni narratives the Morning Star is referred to as "the one that goes before the sun:" (Cushing 1896:381; Cushing 1901:378–79). In the Zuni cosmological scheme, various planets—Venus, Mars, and Jupiter—play the role of Morning and Evening Star (Bunzel 1932:487; Dutton 1963:42; Stevenson 1904:26).[4]

According to some versions of this legend, these twins were born of the union of the Sun and Water—most often the water is in the form of a waterfall (Benedict 1935:1; Cushing 1896:381; Cushing 1920:24–26; Stevenson 1904:24; D. Tedlock 1972:226–27); hence, they are the result of the coupling of beings who inhabit the earth and sky, and their many subsequent adventures entail numerous interactions with such beings. The birth of the Twins is also linked with two of the most important aspects of Zuni ritual—prayers to the Sun Father asking that he allow the crops to thrive and prayers to the ancestors (kachinas) that they may send rain. The symbols of this pair, rainbow, lightning arrows, and a cloud shield, further emphasize the relationship to water or rain.

## The Twins in Zuni Worldview and Ritual Practice

Before turning to the role of the Twins in Zuni folklore and mythology, I will discuss their relationship to Zuni cultural symbolism and ceremonialism, thus providing a grounding for interpreting the actions of the Twins in these narratives. The Sun Father, the Twin War Gods, and the relationship between the earth and the sky all reveal a Zuni emphasis on duality that is integral to their worldview and the ritual activity based on that perspective. For example, in addition to paying keen attention to the sun's daily motion—its rise and set positions along the horizon—the Zunis carefully observe the yearly motion of the sun as well. They regard the extreme "swings" of the annual cycle—the winter and summer solstice rise and set positions—as the most critical times of the year, for it is then that the sun appears to stand still for four days during the journey along the horizon. To encourage "Our Father the Sun" to move again, particularly to assure that he turns around and continues his journey back along the horizon, the Zunis perform complex and vitally important rituals.

This apparent annual motion of the sun along the horizon serves to divide the Zuni year into two parts, each lasting for six months and each beginning when the sun reaches the solstice position and turns around. The winter and summer solstice ceremonies that occur at this time are both called *'itiwana* (the Center), although it is the winter solstice that marks the starting point of the new year cycle. In a kind of symbolic economy, the Zunis repeat the names of the months so that the first month of the winter season has the same name as the first month of the summer season, and so on, counting only six names in all. Winter and summer are thus more than complementary; they are reflections of one another. Nevertheless, distinctive ceremonies and activities characterize each half of the year. There are, for instance, a winter cycle and a summer cycle of ritual dances; certain narratives may be related in the winter but not in the summer, and so on. These examples illustrate that the idea of duality or balance is important in Zuni thought, a duality expressed in dichotomous terms such as morning/evening (sunrise/sunset), summer/winter, above/below. Furthermore, such duality is an important characteristic of Zuni verbal art; ritual poems and folktales are often organized according to pattern numbers of twos and fours, and sometimes these numerical patterns are directly related to the motion of the sun along the horizon or other astronomical phenomena (Bunzel 1929:23; Hymes 1980:7–51; Young 1988:98–99, 107–13). Although I have focused on the yearly motion of the sun, it is of further note that the Zunis consider the Sun Father to have two houses that he visits in the course of his daily journey: one in the eastern ocean and one in the western ocean. They associate this morning/evening duality with the Twin War Gods, in their aspect as the Morning and Evening Star.[5]

Just as the Zunis note the daily and yearly motion of the Sun, they also observe the stars throughout the night and year.[6] They regard some of these stars—such as the Morning Star, the Evening Star, and an enormous cluster of star groupings called Chief of the Night (Young and Williamson 1981:186–89)—as living beings. Others, especially those that form constellations, represent objects from nature—for example, the constellation called "pinyon seeds" (the Pleiades)—or depict elements central to Zuni ritual practice, like "the stick game ones" (not yet identified in terms of "Western" constellations). The Zuni names of a number of other constellations are based on their location or appearance—"those to the north," "seven ones," and "star zigzag" (Young and Williamson 1981:186). Finally, as I will discuss later, the Zunis believe that some constellations were formed when the Twins killed certain monsters and threw their body parts into the sky. Zuni narratives of the formation and/or actions of these various stars and constellations are prevalent, but it is important to note that the stellar beings who appear most often in the corpus of these narratives are the Morning Star and the Evening Star.

Although information on how the Pueblo Indians viewed and understood the stars is far from complete, searches through both the published and unpublished ethnographic data, as well as contemporary fieldwork, reveal that individual stars and star groupings were, and are, central elements in the ritual practice, legends, and graphic art forms of the Zuni Indians (Young and Williamson 1981:183–91). For example, Cushing

(1896:392), Parsons (1939:182), and Stevenson (1904:130, 131) have reported that stellar observation was very important for ceremonial and agricultural purposes at Zuni. Of primary importance for distinguishing divisions of the night were the positions of Orion, the Pleiades, the Great Dipper, and the Morning Star[7]—their rising or passage over the uncovered hatchway in the kiva roof often signaled the culmination of ceremonies or specific phrases of those ceremonies. For example, shortly after the rise of the Morning Star above the horizon, the women dancers at the August rain ceremony in 1891 donned headdresses decorated with the Morning and Evening Stars and began their dance (Stevenson 1904:194). Furthermore, the rising of the Morning Star during the winter solstice ceremony marked the time for the kindling of the New Year fire (Bunzel 1932:536; Stevenson 1904:130, 131); the rising of this star also marked the end of the all-night dancing and prayers during the famous Coming of the Gods, or *Shalako* ceremony (Parsons 1917:199; Stevenson 1904:249; B. Tedlock 1983:107; Wright 1985:31).[8] Stellar observation also played an important role in Zuni agricultural practice. Cushing explains that the Zunis first planted corn in the spring "by the light of the seven great stars [the Big Dipper] which were at that time rising bright above them . . . looking at the stars they saw how they were set, four of them as though around a gourd like their own, and three others as though along its handle!" (1896:392).[9]

In addition to their role in Zuni ritual and agricultural practice, stellar motifs are quite prevalent on Zuni altars, murals, and sand paintings, as well as on the masks, headdresses, and costumes of the kachinas (Stevenson 1904:194, plate XXXVIII, 245–46, plate LVIII, 250, plate LIX, 428, plate CII, 432, plate CIV, 454, plate CVIII, 459, plate CX, 491, plate CXVI, 529, plate CXXII, 543, plate CXXV, 550, plate CXXVI, 551, plate CXXVII). For the most part these visual depictions seem to represent single stars—predominantly the Morning Star and the Evening Star—rather than constellations. On Zuni altars, the Morning Star and Evening Star reflect their role as sons of the Sun as well as the importance of duality in Zuni ceremonialism. Zunis generally paint them on either side of, or on wooden slats in front of, the symbol for the Sun (Stevenson 1904:246, plate LVIII, 432, plate CIV, 491, plate CXVI, 543, plate CXXV, 551, plate CXXVII). Although in other parts of the Southwest scholars have suggested that certain rock-art images might represent the Morning and Evening Stars (Williamson and Young 1979:70–80), my documentation of the rock art surrounding Zuni Pueblo revealed very few images that Zunis discussed in terms of explicit astronomical symbolism. It is of note, however, that the wooden tablets placed next to the carved wooden images of the Zuni War Gods (to be discussed in more detail later in this chapter) contain depictions of the cumulus clouds, the crescent moon, the full moon, and a single star; other paraphernalia include a war club, a shield, a small bow and arrow, and a carved shaft that represents a lightning arrow (Stevenson 1904:113, plate XXI, plate XXII, plate CXXXVII, plate CXXXVIII, plate CXXXIX, 607)—perhaps a further reference to the cosmological role played by the Twins in their aspect as Morning and Evening Star, as well as their behavior as War Gods.

The central position of the Twins in Zuni ceremonialism and world-view as intertwined with their actions as culture heroes and creator gods (chiefly in their role as sons of the Sun) in Zuni origin myths and folktales. This role is related to, but somewhat distinct from, their behavior as Gods of War, a characterization of the Twins that sometimes involves the creation of a second pair of Twins who aid the Zunis in their battles against other peoples and destructive elements.

## Morning Star and Evening Star as Culture Heroes

In most versions of the narratives of the beginning, which the Zunis regard as their history, the people do not behave in a properly "human" manner; they do the reverse of what should be done (Benedict 1935:1–5; Bunzel 1932:584–91; Cushing 1896:383–84; Cushing 1901:401–10; Cushing 1920:26; Parsons 1923:136–39; Quam 1972:129–33; Stevenson 1904:28; D. Tedlock 1972:231–33, 263–64; D. Tedlock 1975:268–69.[10] They are dirty beings, somewhat similar in appearance to the salamander; they do not worship their father, the Sun, and in other ways do not behave correctly. They are not "finished," "ripe," or "human" beings, but rather "raw" or "non-human" beings (Cushing 1883:9–11; D. and B. Tedlock 1975:264–70; D. Tedlock 1979:499–508).[11] They live a life without order, lacking location in time and space; in the underworld there is neither linear time nor geographic location, for the people do not yet have a Center.

Taking pity on these poor creatures and also wanting their prayer offerings, the Sun Father sends his sons, the Twin War Gods, to lead the people to the surface of the earth. When the people reach this surface, after having traveled through the four underworlds, they are dazzled by the light of the Sun and are made human by the Twins. The Twins wash them, cut off their tails, separate their webbed digits, and remove the genitals from the tops of their heads. The Twins also harden or finish them in the same fire with which they harden the soft surface of the earth. Thus, the myth describes the existence of the Zuni people in the underworld as a period of inversion that ends when they reach the surface of the earth (Young 1988: 121–25). By taking the people from darkness into the light of the Sun Father and changing them from unfinished to finished beings, the Twins cause a reversal of what life had been like in the underworld, and this process further reveals the importance of duality in Zuni cultural symbolism.

Although I have described the actions of the Twin War Gods as "making people human," one can also look at this event in more symbolic terms, such as leading the people from the Darkness into the Light, from Ignorance into Knowledge.[12] The fact that some of the Rio Grande Puebloan groups ascribe this role to one group of the sacred clowns provides an interesting link with the Zuni example (Parsons 1932: 360; White 1962: 116). Certainly, for all the Puebloan groups, both the clowns and the Twin War Gods enact crucial and very serious roles in the time of the beginning. As I will discuss later, the Twin War Gods and clowns also share another important characteristic—the potential for humorous, mischievous behavior which is, at the same time, serious, powerful, and dangerous.

Once the Twins accomplish the "humanizing" of the people, they realize that they must undertake certain acts in order to protect them—such as reducing the number of predators (especially those that later become the Beast Gods) that roam the earth and killing dangerous monsters. First, they look around and decide that they should transform some of the predators, for the animals of prey are strong and "men are but poor, the finished beings of earth, therefore the weaker" (Cushing 1883: 14). When the Twins come across these animals, they strike them with the fire of lightning that they carry in their magic shield, changing these animals into stone, and making them into powerful fetishes who will bring good to the people instead of evil. As Cushing describes it, the Twins make the world safer for the people not only by hardening the surface of the earth, but by changing many of the early beings into stone:

> It happens that we find, here and there throughout the world, their forms, sometimes large like the beings themselves, sometimes shriveled and distorted. And we often see among the rocks the forms of many beings that live no longer, which shows us that all was different in the "days of the new." (Cushing 1883: 14–15)

But the Twin War Gods do more than "humanize" the people and protect them at the time of the beginning; they also offer them a very important choice that determines where they will go and what sort of lives they will lead. When the *Ahayu:da* bring the Zuni people out of the fourth underworld, other peoples, including witches, come out as well (but the Zunis are the first to come out). Although they journey together for a while, not all of these people want to go in the same direction, so the Twins devise a test that will divide the people (Bunzel 1932:595; Parsons 1923:141; B. Tedlock 1984:265; D. Tedlock 1972:265–66).[13] They create a beautiful raven's egg spotted with blue and a macaw's egg that is dull white. The Zunis, "the strongest and most hasty" (B. Tedlock 1984:265), choose the spotted egg and are thus told to go in the direction toward the Center Place. The other people choose (by default) the macaw egg and go away to the south. When the eggs hatch, those who chose the beautiful egg find that they have a black raven while the others have the beautiful multicolored macaws. Barbara Tedlock describes the Zuni choice delineated in this narrative as "comic–tragic" and integral to the Zuni system of aesthetics that incorporates both the "beautiful" and the "dangerous": "The beautiful eggs contained multicolored chicks that molted and matured into dangerous black ravens: for Zunis ever since, the beautiful has had the dangerous somewhere near or even bursting into the midst of it" (1984:265).

In their role as creator gods, the Twin War Gods also offer an important choice to the animal and bird people who, at the time of the beginning, resemble humans in both form and ability to speak. Deciding that "so much talking shortens [the birds' and animals'] lives," the *Ahayu:da* discuss the matter with Knife-Wing, the Beast God of the zenith (Risser 1941:223). Knife-Wing suggests that they summon the animal and bird people to see if they are willing to give up their humanlike qualities. They do this and the *Ahayu:da* say to them:

> We have decided that there is too much talking in the world. We think that you would be better off if you did not use so much of your energy in that way. We can change all that so that birds, animals, and man cannot understand each other. Then you would have more time for other matters. What do you think about it? (Risser 1941:223)

After much excited talk about this plan, the animals and birds finally agree that "if they should gain strength it would be better to give up the power of speech" (Risser 1941:223). The *Ahayu:da* then pierce the cheeks of each of these beings with a thorn and they assume the animal and bird forms that they possess today. The Twins also cause diversity in the language and dwelling places of these beings:

Each spoke his own language and went off in the direction assigned him. Their homes were no longer to be as the homes of men. The birds lived in the air and built their nests in the trees. The animals lived in caves or under the ground (Risser 1941:224).

In addition to these significant roles, the Twin War Gods also play a part in the creation of some of the constellations, stars, and the Milky Way. Some time after the people are made into finished beings and, following the instructions of the Sun Father, have found the Center Place, various monsters begin to threaten them. At this point the *Ahayu:da* live with their grandmother on the top of Corn Mountain, the sacred mesa southeast of the village. In an interesting inversion that is repeated throughout many of the tales that refer to these events, to "encourage" them to kill the various monsters that are troubling the people, Grandmother tells the Twins not to go where the monster is because it is too dangerous (Benedict 1935:51–53, 56, 58, 69, 71, 73, 291–92; Bunzel 1933:281; Quam 1972:182, 185–86, 188, 192, 203). In each instance, upon receiving this advice, they set out to do the very opposite—to find and kill the monsters. And there is every indication in such tales that this is just what their sly Grandmother wants them to do. The initial monster the Twins confront is a giant called Cloud Swallower who appears in the east: "he swallowed up each cloud as it came up and there was a great drought" (Benedict 1935:51).[14] On their journey to kill Cloud Swallower, the Twins meet with Gopher who offers to help them and takes them down into his hole "deep down in the ground." Gopher enables the Twins to reach Cloud Swallower by tunneling until his hole is "directly under Cloud Swallower's heart." The Twins draw their bow and shoot the monster; then they fling the body parts into the sky to create certain astronomical beings:

> They took his heart and threw it to the east and it became the morning star. They took his liver and threw it and it became the evening star. They took his lungs and threw them and they became the Seven Stars. They took his entrails and threw them and they became the Milky Way. They went home to Corn Mountain (Benedict 1935:51).

Significantly, this confrontation in the story provides the kind of earth/sky interaction that is characteristic of the Twins and of Zuni cultural symbolism in general. In order to kill this sky monster, the Twins must seek the help of one of the creatures who lives deep within the earth; this sort of dramatic opposition is prevalent in Zuni narratives. Furthermore, the *Ahayu:da* must seek the help of what one might assume to be a rather helpless creature. Yet, to the Zunis, all animals have power; for example, Spider Grandmother is often considered to be the embodiment of wisdom. It is also of importance that the Zuni Beast Gods (powerful animals of prey) include a being of the nadir or underground (mole) and a being of the zenith or sky (eagle or Knife-Wing) as well as four other animals that are associated with the semi-cardinal directions (Cushing 1883:16–19; Young 1988:99–103).[15]

All of these examples from Zuni traditional narratives illustrate that the original pair of Twin War Gods, the sons of the Sun Father, sometimes referred to as Morning Star and Evening Star, play vitally significant roles in the time of the beginning, protecting the people and starting them on their way to find the Center Place.

## The Twin War Gods

As is apparent from the previous discussion, the behavior of the Twins gradually changes. In the time of the beginning, they transform the Zunis and other beings, protect the people from monsters, and offer them a choice that determines the direction in which they will travel. As the people near the Center Place and once they are settled there, the primary role of the Twins becomes that of War Gods—powerful deities who have helped the Zunis to defeat their enemies throughout history and continue to do so in contemporary times. Although some scholars attribute this change to the creation of a second set of twins whose explicit charge is to protect the people by destroying their enemies, it is also possible that the change in the circumstances of the people yields a need for the Twins to focus more on the activities of war than on those of creation. For instance, as the Zuni people look for the Center Place, they sometimes encounter other groups who are hostile and battles ensue (Bunzel 1932:597, 599–600; Cushing 1896:417–25; Cushing 1920:34–35; Parsons 1923:142–46; Quam 1972:133–35; Risser 1941:224–26; Stevenson 1904:34–39). The Gods of War employ their great destructive powers to help the Zunis overcome their enemies and continue to do so after the Zunis establish their permanent village. Furthermore, the War Gods employ these powers today to protect not only the Zunis, but the entire world. The fact that the Gods of War affect Zunis and non-Zunis alike reveals an important concept in Zuni philosophy, for, although the Zunis occupy the Center Place, they do not regard that center as an isolated location. It is the center of the world, and the Zunis' residence there entails great concern and responsibility, not only for themselves and their own village, but for the entire world and its people. Indeed, I have heard a number of Zunis attribute the Vietnam War and other global conflicts to the fact that the images of the War Gods have been stolen from their mesatop shrines and put in museums or private collections. Zunis say that when all the War Gods are returned to their homes such destruction will cease.[16]

The *Ahayu:da* (Twin War Gods) are patrons of the principal war society at Zuni, the "Society of Bow Priests." In the past, it was necessary for any man who had killed an enemy to join this society so that his life would be protected from his enemy's vengeful ghost. The only exception to this rule occurred when the man was already a member of the Coyote Society or of one of the other war societies (Bunzel 1932:674; D. Tedlock 1979: 506). The members of the Coyote Society are expert in hunting and their patrons are the powerful Beast Gods of the six directions. The other two war societies have ceased to exist (D. Tedlock 1979:506). Interestingly, Cushing, an ethnologist who was adopted into the Zuni tribe in the late 1900s, found it necessary to obtain a scalp in order to be initiated into the Priesthood of the Bow (Green 1979:155). Although Cushing never recounted the details of this acquisition, which seemed to take place during a skirmish between a Zuni party that included Cushing and a group of Apaches, he did describe the ceremony of his initiation. This initiation included a ritual reenactment of surprising the enemy and then taking his scalp; significantly, this ceremony began "just as the morning star appeared" (Green 1979:155).

The function of the Society of Bow Priests has changed in recent times. For instance, although veterans of World War II were purified before entering the pueblo, this action was performed by the curing or medicine societies rather than by the Bow Priests (Adair 1948:109–10). Furthermore, the once-important Scalp Dance, held as recently as 1971, had become a "regular fall ceremony and was no longer a victory celebration over a new scalp" (D. Tedlock 1979:506). Nevertheless, Zunis still regard the War Gods, whose images reside in mesatop shrines, as particularly important beings.

Because the powers of the *Ahayu:da* are extensive and destructive, the Zunis must, through the vehicle of ritual action, draw these powers toward other ends in times of peace. Discussing the legal aspects of repatriation of the Zuni War Gods from museums, Elizabeth Childs underscores the necessity that the War Gods be constantly ritually propitiated in times of peace so that their potentially destructive powers will not be unleashed:

> The Zuni leaders have asserted repeatedly that War Gods embody an eternal spirit which protects the tribe and all the peoples of the earth if attended to by proper ritual. If a War God is out of its place, the religion holds that all of its mischievous and potentially malevolent powers are released on the world, creating disasters such as floods, wars, and earthquakes. In Zuni eyes, the harmony of the Universe and the future of Zuni in particular is endangered as long as a single War God is out of its shrine (Childs 1980 : 5).

Each year, certain Zuni religious leaders create new images of the Twin War Gods and take them to the shrines where the images from previous years are also clustered (Bunzel 1932 : 687 n.42). Although these images are constructed from wood, feathers, and paint, they become animate in the ritual process that surrounds their creation; in Zuni religion the War Gods are deities and present, animate objects of worship rather than symbols or art objects (Childs 1980 : 6). It is of note that these images remain exposed to the elements until they are finally eaten away by sun, wind, rain, and snow—perhaps an instance of potentially destructive powers returning to the forces that created them. Furthermore, the Zunis locate the shrines that contain the War God images on mesatops, the highest places surrounding the pueblo. Although the stone shrines sometimes surround the images, they are never covered over, but are always open to the sky. This is yet another example of the involvement of the Twins in the dynamic interaction between earth and sky that is integral to Zuni ritual life.

## The Second Set of Twins

As discussed earlier, although many Zuni traditional narratives portray only one set of Twin War Gods, who are usually associated with the Morning and Evening Star, other tales (along with contemporary commentary) detail the creation of a second set of twins (Bunzel 1932 : 597; Cushing 1896 : 417–24; Parsons 1923 : 41–43; Quam 1972 : 133; Stevenson 1904 : 34–35). According to such accounts, the Sun Father created these twins to act as war chiefs who would protect the Zunis from hostile peoples they began to encounter as they approached the Center Place. The Sun Father accomplished this creation by coupling with a waterfall at *Hanlhibinkya,* a place in Arizona near the present-day Zuni reservation.[17] Significantly, Zunis also describe this site as the place where the clans were given their names, stating that some of the petroglyphs that cover the boulders and other rock surfaces at this site are symbols of those clans (Young 1988: 146). This second set of Twins accompanied the people to the Center Place and took up residence on top of Corn Mountain. The Zunis believe that the War Gods still reside on the tops of some of the mesas surrounding the village. These deities are present at such places in the images that embody them (these images were made animate during the ritual process in which Zuni priests created them). Furthermore, because the Zunis regard the boundaries between past (myth time) and present (the "here and now") as permeable and part of a circular, temporal scheme, the beings of folklore and mythology are still an ongoing part of Zuni life (Young 1988: 116–19). They are ever present and continue to participate in the affairs of the pueblo.

Stevenson (1904: 34) refers to this second set of Twins as the "diminutive war gods," suggesting that they are derived from or closely related to the original pair, but somewhat reduced in stature; stature here may refer, of course, not to actual height but to symbolic importance. Certainly, these twins continue to perform many of the functions of the original pair—especially that of protecting the Zunis against various manifestations of danger—but they often do so in a mischievous, humorous manner. Tales collected by Ruth Benedict (1935: 51–53, 56–62, 69, 71, 73, 291–92), as well as versions collected by other ethnologists (Bunzel 1933: 281; Cushing 1901: 175–84, 401–10) and those compiled by the Zunis themselves (Quam 1972: 182, 185–86, 188, 192, 203), reveal that these Twins are frequently heedless of the consequences of their actions and disrespectful toward both their Grandmother and the sacred rain priests. For example, after killing many dangerous monsters, the Twins steal the thunder stone and lightning sticks from the rain priests and, against their Grandmother's advice, begin to play with them, causing it to rain very hard. Soon their own house begins to be filled with water and their Grandmother calls out to them to stop. The Twins respond as follows:

> The younger one said, "You had better put grandmother some place where she will keep quiet." The elder one went into the house and the water came up to his knees. In the corner was a big open cooking pot. He took his grandmother and threw her into the pot. Then he went out and played again. He laughed at the time (Benedict 1935: 62).

The *Ahayu:da* continue their play and their Grandmother drowns. They poke a hole in the house to let out the water, bury their Grandmother, and decide to split up, one going to Twin Buttes and the other remaining on Corn Mountain. They throw away the thunder and lightning, which the rain priests quickly retrieve.

Such tales reveal the Twins in a less "serious" aspect than one might expect of these creator gods. For example, a narrative collected and translated by Cushing that focuses on the Twins' decision to bring the people out of the fourth world begins thus:[18]

> Now, the Twain Little-ones, Áhaiyúta and Mátsailéma, were ever seeking scenes of contention, for what was deathly and dreadful to others was lively and delightful to them; so that ones of distress were ever their calls of invitation, as to a feast or dance is the call of a priest to us. (Cushing 1901: 401–2)

The tale goes on to describe the two as motivated by curiosity (the wishes of the Sun Father are not mentioned), laughing as they shoot arrows at the people, "cramming their mouths full" of huge morsels of food that they bolt down almost whole, punching one another and, in general, acting in a manner somewhat akin to that of Coyote the trickster in many Native American folktales (Toelken and Scott 1981:65–116). Nevertheless, this particular narrative concludes with the Zunis in a more beneficial state than they were before the Twins took an interest in them.

The "message" of such folktales is similar to that which is enacted by clown groups in Zuni and other Native American societies (Babcock 1984:102–28; Heib 1972:163–95; Ortiz 1972:135–61; B. Tedlock 1975:105–18). By dramatically depicting what should not happen, portraying how Zunis should *not* behave, they reinforce appropriate behavior (Young 1987a:144–45; Young 1988:113–15). For to be a good Zuni involves respect for one's elders (especially the older women of the tribe), behavior that is moderate, and the avoidance of contention whenever possible.[19] In the above-cited narrative segments, the Twins act in a manner that is the opposite of how Zunis ought to behave and the chaos that results from their actions is a subtle warning to those who do not behave as good Zunis about the unfortunate consequences they may experience.

One can offer a number of possible reasons for the appearance of this second set of Twin War Gods. Without Zuni commentary, of course, such "reasons" are quite subjective. Although in my ten years of fieldwork and acquaintance with Zuni friends we have sometimes discussed the creation of the second set of Twins and the consequent ambiguity in determining exactly which set was doing what and when in the narratives of the time of the beginning, I found time and again that my Zuni colleagues were not made uncomfortable by this ambiguity; nor were they interested in either pinning down whether in fact there actually was a second set (or just one set operating back and forth in time), or assigning totally discrete personalities or behaviors to the two pairs. This Zuni perspective suggests an interpretation of the second pair that I will discuss at the end of this section; but first, I think it useful to examine a few other possibilities—all of which may "merge" when one takes into account the importance of ambiguity, of multiple interpretations in Zuni cultural symbolism.

One might postulate that the reason for the creation of the second pair of Twin War Gods was that the first set really "belonged" in the sky in their role as Morning and Evening Star. According to this perspective, the first set would have returned to the sky after humanizing the people, hardening the surface of the earth, and fossilizing the monsters; hence the necessity for the creation of a second pair who would continue to protect the people once they settled in the Center Place. The following excerpt from a narrative in Quam's collection does, indeed, support this idea, but I have found no other such references.

> When the rains fell, as the rivers came rushing down where the water frothed about, the two Ahauda came into view. Thus far they had been seen as the stars that first brought the people upon their emerging. When that happened, the sun priests came forth and the Ahauda now stayed with their people while the stars went back up into the skies (Quam 1972 : 133).

My own knowledge of Zuni epistemology leads me to question this interpretation, for it implies an uncharacteristic spatial separation between the spheres of earth and sky. As I have discussed above and elsewhere (1988 : 116– 19), both spatial and temporal boundaries in Zuni belief are fluid. Therefore, various beings who are central actors in Zuni folklore and mythology are unrestricted by such boundaries. They have the ability to exist in past and present, earth and sky, simultaneously; they are continuously and intimately involved in the lives of the Zunis.

Another potential interpretation for the creation of the second set of Twins resides in the ethnocentric separation between religion and humor that non-Native American scholars often impose when attempting to understand Native American worldviews. According to this perspective, the first Twins were primarily awe-inspiring creator gods who acted with seriousness and propriety. Thus, the humorous, mischievous behavior of the second set would entail the necessity for a distinct separation from the first set—a distinct creation. This interpretation runs counter to Zuni world view, particularly as it is exemplified in Zuni ritual drama. For instance, one group of Zuni "clowns," the Mudheads (*Koyemshi*), frequently exemplify behavior in ritual drama that is oppositional to tribal norms.[20] They are buffoonlike in appearance and action, mocking accepted behavior, even mimicking the sacred, stately kachinas (deified ancestors personated by members of the religious societies), and making obscene gestures to the highly respected matrons of the tribe. This behavior is humorous precisely because it is a ritual reversal or inversion of appropriate behavior. The audience laughs openly at their antics, and this laughter seems to drive the Mudheads to new excesses; but the Mudheads play a serious and powerful role as well. Zunis talk of them with respect and fear, saying, "One must never refuse anything to the *Koyemshi* because they are dangerous"; they frequently attribute accidents they experience to improprieties toward these "clowns" (Bunzel 1932:947; Parsons 1939:105–6; Young 1987a:147 n.9). In addition, although the Mudheads perform hilarious clown routines during the summer rain dances when the kachina dancers have left the plaza to rest, they become quite sober when the kachinas return. As the kachinas dance and sing, the Mudheads act as directors of the performance, shouting out critical comments that are heeded by the performers; they also take on the role of interpreters, miming the words of the songs for the audience (B. Tedlock 1980:31). The "father" of the Mudheads stands next to the dance leader of the kachinas during the "serious" part of the rain dances and listens to him recite the sacred prayers (Parsons 1922:193; Young 1987a:147 n.13). The Mudheads also watch over the kachina personators as they dance and adjust parts of their costumes that come undone. Such a performance embodies not only humor, but antihumor; it permits a vision of the chaos that is ever ready to impinge on daily life should the necessary rituals and the attendant proper behavior be neglected; it is a vehicle through which the comic and the mysterious are intertwined. Similarly, the two types of behavior (serious and comic) enacted are not entirely separate; the boundaries between the two are not always clearly defined (Young 1987a:127–50; Young 1988:113–15).

These examples illustrate that religion and humor, laughter and danger, the serious and the comic are intertwined aspects of Zuni world view, and indeed, as I mentioned above, this is true for many Native American groups. One needs only to look at the figure of Coyote who appears throughout the traditional narratives of North American Indians as both a creator god and a trickster, often at one and the same time, to see this dynamic interaction.[21] Although such behavior might appear to be contradictory to those unfamiliar with Native American perspectives, it is quite consistent with an ethos that embraces ambiguity, multivocality, and a vision of "all possibilities" (Toelken and Scott 1981 : 80−90).

Having rejected these few suggestions concerning the reason for or meaning of the second set of Twin War Gods that I have put forth, I present the following hypothesis, which is based both on my fieldwork at Zuni and my prior attempts to understand the way in which ambiguity, multivocality, and permeable boundaries are integral to Zuni cultural symbolism (Young 1987a; Young 1988). I have previously emphasized that powerful images in the Zuni world—whether verbal or visual—are generally ambiguous and can be interpreted in a variety of ways. I regard these images as similar to those described by Turner (1967 : 295, 298) as nuclear or condensed symbols—those that have the ability or power to refer to many concepts simultaneously. But these meanings are not totally discrete; they are bound together in a complex system of interrelationships, so that the Zunis say of such meanings, "They're all the same thing" (Young 1988 : 104−7).[22] One can think of this ambiguity or multiplicity in another way, however. In addition to having the potential for multiple meanings, many of these powerful symbols have evocative power as well—evocative power that involves the transformation from one code to another such that verbal images can evoke visual symbols and vice versa. Finally, certain of these symbols also gain power from another sort of ambiguity—the type of ambiguity that enables such symbols to transcend conventional notions of time and space and become multitemporal and multispatial (Young 1988 : 113−19). I suggest that the Twin War Gods, although they are beings central to Zuni religion and cosmology rather than symbols per se, embody a similar kind of ambiguity, multivocality, and the ability to transcend conventional boundaries.

From this perspective, it is likely that both sets of Twin War Gods are "the same thing" in the sense discussed above. I would particularly emphasize here, however, the concept of ambiguity that is so strongly an element of Zuni world view. Thus, rather than resolving the issue by stating that there is clearly only one set of Twin War Gods who behave quite differently at different times, or that there are two sets who have distinct attributes, it is quite likely that both of these statements are true, and, depending on the particular verbal or visual context, one or the other may take precedence.

The principle of ambiguity also sheds light on the fact that the Twin War Gods sometimes take on the serious role of creator gods and sometimes are mischievous tricksters. (Being tricksters does not, of course, preclude their being creator gods.) Again, it is possible that one pair of twins embodies both of these behaviors. This idea fits well with the suggestion of a number of scholars of southwestern prehistory that the Zunis and their predecessors incorporated into their religion many elements of Mesoamerican religion in the kind of dynamic interaction and synthesis that occurs at Zuni in contemporary times as well (Anderson 1955:404–19; Ellis 1977; Ellis and Hammack 1968:25–44; Kelley 1966:95–110; Parsons 1933:611–31; Schaafsma 1975:2–14; Schaafsma and Schaafsma 1974:535–45).[23] Scholars of Mesoamerican religion have been perplexed by the multitude of gods in the pantheon and also by the differing aspects of the same god or goddess that are so diverse that the deity is given different names when taking on different aspects. Although the Twin War Gods take on different names and behaviors in various narratives, it is possible that these characteristics are similar to those of deities in the Mesoamerican pantheon, and there is only one set of twins. Furthermore, in his manifestation as Venus as well as his aspect as Sun, the Mesoamerican deity Quetzalcoatl is strikingly parallel to the Zuni and Hopi Twin War Gods, especially in their role as Morning Star and Evening Star (Caso 1958:15, 23–27; Young 1989:173).

Finally, we see the Twins (whether one pair or two) moving with ease between spatial levels such that one can envision them as residing in the sky as Morning Star and Evening Star, while operating on the earth as well. Thus, one can think of them as occupying two places at the same time. Certainly this involves the notion of the circularity or permeability of temporal boundaries, but it also involves a characteristic Zuni attitude toward place such that one place can have two (or more) very different aspects. For example, certain place names in the Zuni origin myth can refer both to an important site in the ancestors' quest for the center and to a known place in the contemporary physical world: Kachina Village, the home of the masked gods, not only has mythic existence in the past but physical existence in the present at the specific lake in Arizona to which the Zunis make a pilgrimage every four years. This example refers not only to place, however, but to time as well; in such instances, the boundaries between places and time periods fuse.

As for much of Zuni ethos and ceremonialism, past and present coexist: the time of the myth is one with everyday existence. In the case of the

Twin War Gods, one can say that not only do they exist in the celestial and terrestrial spheres at the same time, but they exist at all times (past, present, and future) simultaneously and, perhaps, like Coyote, "embody all possibilities." Just as Zunis perceive certain rock art images in the areas surrounding the pueblo as "signs from the ancestors"—messages that indicate their concern and involvement with contemporary Zuni life (Young 1988)—so are the Twin War Gods ever present. They are powerful forces that the Zunis must continually endeavor to keep in check, reminders of the balanced behavior that makes one a good Zuni.

Thus, the Twin War Gods are linked with other powerful images and beings that are central to Zuni life. They are frequently multireferential, standing for a number of things at the same time, contributing to an intensification of experience. Since Zuni audiences are quite familiar with traditional narratives that detail the exploits of the Twin War Gods, it is likely that a story (or stories) in which they are depicted in their mischievous aspect also calls to mind those narratives in which they play a more serious and dignified part. And either sort of verbal performance is also likely to bring to mind the images of the carved wooden War Gods in their mesatop shrines. Of special significance in the visual representation of the Twins is their appearance in the sky as Morning and Evening Star. Still keenly observed by Zunis today, they signify the time of the beginning when the Twins helped to bring the people out of the fourth underworld to the surface of the Earth Mother. Thus, they embody the intimate connection between those who dwell at the Center Place and those deities who live in the worlds above.[24]

# Notes

1. I have been conducting fieldwork at the Pueblo of Zuni—at uneven intervals—for the past ten years. My research interests have focused most strongly on the interaction between Zuni verbal and visual communicative systems. During this time, I became acquainted with orthography used by the Zuni Language Learning Program and I have tried to conform to that orthography for Zuni words used throughout this paper. I am grateful to Governor Robert E. Lewis, the Zuni Tribal Council, and the Zuni Archaeology Program for their continued support of my research. I especially thank the families of Margaret Sheyka, Arlen Sheyka, and Augustine Panteah for their hospitality and helpfulness during my various periods of fieldwork, but I am additionally grateful to all of those who have taken the time to talk with me about Zuni ways of looking at the world. I acknowledge a great debt to the editors of this volume—Ray A. Williamson and Claire R. Farrer—who have waited patiently for this article and given me valuable editorial suggestions.

2. I use the term *asymmetry* here to refer to the arrangement of elements (either those in verbal or visual art) in such a way that they are not exactly parallel or mirror reflections of one another. Although such arrangements can be unsettling to those who are accustomed to perfectly balanced compositions, it can unsettle in a purposive and dynamic way such that the resultant image impels one to consider new ways of thinking and visualizing. I contrast this with symmetrical arrangements that may grant one static repose, but do not necessarily challenge one to develop novel and exciting conceptual categories.

3. As I will discuss further in the final section of this article, the texts that center on the actions of the Zuni Twin War Gods collected by various ethnographers reveal a great deal of confusion concerning whether or not there is only one pair of twins, or two. They also differ considerably in the names they attribute to either pair of twins. Although, as much as possible throughout this chapter, I use Zuni orthography for Zuni terms, in the following discussion I use the orthography used by each individual ethnographer–scholar. According to Cushing (1901:378–79), *Áhaiyúta* and *Mátsailéma* are the names for the original pair. Stevenson (1904:24) states that this first pair of Twins—*Kow'wituma* and Wats'usi—were created when the sun impregnated "two bits of foam" with his rays. She refers to these Twins collectively as the Divine Ones. Stevenson discusses a second pair of Twins, which she refers to as "the diminutive war gods," that were created at *Hanlhibinkya* to help the Divine Ones who had grown weary of fighting the enemies the Zunis encountered in their search for the Center Place. Stevenson refers collectively to this later set of Twins as the *A'hayuta,* and individually calls them *U'yuyewi* and *Matsai'lema* (1904:34–45). Parsons (1923), Quam (1972:129), and D. Tedlock (1972:225–98) refer to both members of the pair as the *Ahayuuta* (Tedlock's orthography—*Ahauda* is Quam's rendering of the term), although Tedlock and Quam refer to the Twins who brought the people out of the fourth underworld, while Parsons uses *Aihayuta* to refer to the second pair of Twins who were generated at *Hanlhibinkya* while the people were searching for the Center Place. Benedict (1935:1) and Bunzel (1932:584, n.96) give the names *Watusti* (Bunzel uses the term *Watsutsi*) and *Yanaluha* to the "original" pairs of Twins, and Bunzel (1932:597) states that the second pair, the *Ahaiyute,* were generated by a waterfall at *Hanlhibinkya.* D. Tedlock (1979:501n.) gives the same names for the two pairs as do Benedict and Bunzel. However, in an earlier publication, D. Tedlock (1972:225–69) gives the names *Uyuyuwi* and *Ma'asewi* to the pair of Twins who were created while the people were searching for the Center Place, but refers to the pair together as the *Ahayuuta.* This is, by no means, a definitive list of all of the ethnographic references to the Zuni Twin War Gods, but should serve to illustrate the confusion surrounding the names and behavior of these beings.

The existence of various versions of tales is a typical occurrence in folklore scholarship and, frequently, no one version is regarded by its tellers or audience as more "correct" than another. Storytelling is a dynamic process and many factors contribute to change through time. D. Tedlock suggests that, in the act of performing, storytellers not only interpret a text, but frequently *improve* upon it (1983:236). Furthermore, Bunzel suggests that each of the religious societies at Zuni has its own version of the origin myth that sets out the charter for that particular organization so that "there is no single origin myth but a long series of separate myths" (1932:547). Similarly, there is no definitive text to point to as the one that tells the "true" story about the creation and activities of the Twin War Gods. The most conclusive statement one can make about these deities in Zuni narrative is that sometimes there are two different pairs of Twins, one primary, one secondary. In other texts, they are both assimilated into the same pair.

4. B. Tedlock (1983:100) also suggests Mars, Venus, or Jupiter for the Zuni Morning Star. There is much confusion, however, especially in the early ethnographic records, about which planet is serving as Morning or Evening Star at a given time.

5. For a much more detailed delineation of the Zuni cosmological system, see Young 1988 (especially chap. 3).

6. In addition to solar and stellar observation, the Zunis keenly watch the moon as well, but that practice does not relate directly to the Morning Star and Evening Star nor to a discussion of the Twin War Gods. For more information on Zuni lunar observation, see Young in press, and Zeilik 1986.

7. It is important to note that these are not the Zuni names for these star groupings. For more information on Zuni names, descriptions and observations of the constellations, see Young and Williamson 1981.

8. Of course, as B. Tedlock (1983: 107) observes, if there is no Morning Star on the particular morning that the all-night ceremony ends, then the first sign of dawn concludes this part of the *Shalako* ceremony. Bunzel (1932: 944) seems to concur with this observation.

9. Although I have framed this paragraph in the past tense, it is important to note that many of these practices are still continued by Zunis today.

10. I discuss the Zuni origin myth here in the present tense because Zuni "circular" attitudes toward the myth time and the "here and now" indicate that the time of the beginning is not over and done with, but constantly interacting with and informing what happens in the present. For more detail on the Zuni attitudes toward time and space, see Young 1988 (especially chap. 3).

11. The terminology I use here, although similar to that used by other scholars, is from my own translation of Zuni materials (see especially Young 1978), and from Zuni commentary about such terms that I recorded during my periods of fieldwork there.

12. I do not have any data to suggest that the Zunis make a direct connection between Darkness and Light and Ignorance and Knowledge; still, the transformation of the people from nonhuman to human, from behaving improperly to learning the appropriate ritual behavior (especially prayers to the Sun Father), may symbolize such a relationship.

13. Although Cushing (1896: 385−86) and Stevenson (1904: 40) mention this significant choice of eggs, they attribute the idea to one of the Zuni religious leaders rather than to the Twins.

14. Quam's version of this tale (1972: 182−84) is very similar to that recorded by Benedict, except that the monster in this tale is not called Cloud Swallower. In this rendition, a rodent helps the Twins and, when they kill the monster, "They let the heart go and then the heart flew into the sunset . . . they took the legs and threw them into the skies, and they became stars" (Quam 1972: 184). Bunzel (1933: 281−82) includes a narrative that is similar, in most respects, to that recorded by Quam. In Bunzel's version, the Twins throw the heart of Cloud Swallower to the East and it becomes the Morning Star. Cushing (1901: 423−28) has also recorded a Zuni narrative that describes the fight the Twins have with Cloud Swallower. In this version, however, the monster is turned into a tall pillar of stone, rather than stars or star groupings.

15. This description of the semicardinal directions as the ritual directions is a generalization. I am grateful to Barbara and Dennis Tedlock for pointing out to me that at Zuni the use of cardinal versus semicardinal directions depends on the particular ceremonial context. In his unpublished notes, J. P. Harrington gives "archaic Zuni words" used for the directions in Zuni ceremonies. He translates these directional words as the semicardinal directions, that is, "northeast, northwest, southwest, southeast," and states that they refer to the solstice extremes. See J. P. Harrington, n.d.

16. So disturbed have the Zunis been by the theft of War Gods from their mesatop shrines that they recently "consulted with Smithsonian staff for advice on installing a sound-sensitive alarm system that could be implemented at a mountain site without disturbing the physical integrity of the shrine" (Childs 1980: 6). During one of my visits to Zuni in the

early 1980s, one such burglar-proof structure that housed images of the War Gods was pointed out to me by a Zuni colleague (the brick structure could easily be viewed from the road on which we were traveling). My friend told me that the shrine did, indeed, have a burglar alarm system, and he added that it was open at the top so that the War Gods would not be protected from the elements, according to Zuni practice. This Zuni man did express concern, however, that someone might be able to get into the shrine from above—in a helicopter, for instance.

17. It is interesting to contrast this Zuni narrative of the birth of the Twins with one recorded by Stephen at Hopi (1929:13). According to this Hopi legend, a virgin was impregnated by the Sun when his rays penetrated a crack in the roof of the house and fell upon her. Later, the maiden exposes herself to falling rain, and, eventually, she gives birth to twins—one a child of the Sun and the other a child of the Water. Cushing (1901:429—74) details a somewhat similar Zuni narrative in which the Sun makes love to a religious leader's virgin daughter and she gives birth to two twin boys.

18. D. Tedlock has rightly questioned the reliability of Cushing's translations of Zuni narratives, especially in remarking that Cushing was given to exaggeration (1983:33—36). Still, Tedlock is referring more to a specific style of translation than to the accuracy of events reported. Furthermore, many of the narratives collected by other ethnographers that delineate the behavior of the Twin War Gods are similar enough to those recorded by Cushing (especially in terms of specific actions that take place) that I find it appropriate to include quotations from narratives collected by Cushing and other early ethnographers in this chapter. Still, the reader does well to keep Tedlock's cautions in mind; very few of the early ethnographers rendered Zuni narratives in a way that revealed their striking poetic quality.

19. See Young 1987b:436—45 for a discussion of the respect accorded to women in Zuni society. The behavior of a "really good Zuni" is further delineated in D. Tedlock 1979:507 and Young 1988:27—33.

20. According to Zuni mythology, the Mudheads are the result of the incestuous union of a brother and sister during the search to find "The Center." See Bunzel 1932:595—96; Cushing 1896:399—403; Parsons 1923:139—40; Quam 1972:131; Stevenson 1904:32—33; D. Tedlock 1972:267—68.

21. Although a plethora of collections deal specifically with Coyote, I will cite only a few. For a general introduction to the trickster figure in Native American mythology, see Radin 1956; for a more specific focus on Coyote as a comic—tragic figure, see Erdoes and Ortiz 1984:88—92, 140—42, 171—72, 223—24, 333—86, 470—71. Finally, Zuni narratives about Coyote's dual role include Benedict 1935:214—15; 219—21; Cushing 1901:203—68; Quam 1972:93—97, 117—25; D. Tedlock 1972:75—84.

22. For further discussion of such cultural "base metaphors," see Farrer 1980:125—59; Farrer and Second 1981:137—50; and Munn 1973:171—73.

23. I refer here to the fact that in the past and still today Zuni interactions with other groups frequently involve the exchange of ideas and material goods. Nevertheless, as I have argued elsewhere (Young 1982:42—48; Young 1988:37—39), the Zunis retain a stable cultural core that has changed little with respect to fundamental principles of worldview.

24. The Zunis view the Universe as consisting of a definite number of vertical layers: there are four underworlds, oriented toward the nadir, and each associated with a tree; then comes the surface of the earth (the center world—that is, the world currently occupied); finally, there are four upperworlds, oriented toward the zenith, peopled with various cosmological deities, and each associated with a different kind of bird. Although totaling nine levels, Zunis perceive them as four on either side of the central layer: the familiar world, the beginning point in the cycle of reincarnation. For further discussion of this Zuni perception of a multilayered Universe, see D. Tedlock 1979:499 and Young 1988:100.

# References

Adair, John J. 1948. A Study of Culture Resistance: The Veterans of World War II at Zuñi Pueblo. Ph.D. diss., University of New Mexico, Albuquerque.

Anderson, Frank G. 1955. The Pueblo Kachina Cult: A Historical Reconstruction. *Southwest Journal of Anthropology* 11 : 404 – 19.

Babcock, Barbara A. 1984. Arrange Me into Disorder: Fragments and Reflections on Ritual Clowning. In *Rite, Drama, Festival, Spectacle: Rehearsals toward a Theory of Cultural Performance*, ed. John J. MacAloon, 102 – 28. Philadelphia: Institute for the Study of Human Issues.

Benedict, Ruth. 1935. Zuni Mythology. 2 vols. Columbia University Contributions to Anthropology, 21. New York: Columbia University Press.

Bunzel, Ruth L. 1929. *The Pueblo Potter: A Study of Creative Imagination in Primitive Art*. New York: Dover Publications. 1972 reprint.

———. 1932. *Introduction of Zuñi Ceremonialism. Zuñi Origin Myths. Zuñi Ritual Poetry. Zuñi Katcinas: An Analytical Study.* Forty-Seventh Annual Report of the Bureau of American Ethnology for the Years 1929 – 1930, 467 – 1086. Washington, D.C.: Government Printing Office.

———. 1933. *Zuni Texts.* Publications of the American Ethnological Society, 15. New York: G. E. Stechert.

Caso, Alfonso. 1958. *The Aztecs: People of the Sun.* Norman: University of Oklahoma Press.

Childs, Elizabeth C. 1980. Museums and the American Indian: Legal Aspects of Repatriation. *Council on Museum Anthropology Newsletter* 4(4): 4 – 27.

Cushing, Frank H. 1883. *Zuñi Fetiches.* Second Annual Report of the Bureau of American Ethnology for the Years 1889 – 1881, 3 – 45. Washington, D.C.: Government Printing Office.

———. 1896. *Outlines of Zuñi Creation Myths.* Thirteenth Annual Report of the Bureau of American Ethnology for the Years 1891 – 1892, 321 – 447. Washington, D.C.: Government Printing Office.

———. 1901. *Zuni Folk Tales.* New York: G. P. Putnam's Sons.

———. 1920. *Zuñi Breadstuff.* Indian Notes and Monographs 8. New York: Museum of the American Indian. 1974 reprint.

Dutton, Bertha P. 1963. *Sun Father's Way: The Kiva Murals of Kuaua.* Albuquerque: University of New Mexico Press.

Ellis, Florence H. 1977. Distinctive Parallels between Mesoamerican and Pueblo Iconography and Deities. Unpublished paper delivered at Guanajuato, Mexico, August 1977.

Ellis, Florence H., and Laurens Hammack. 1968. The Inner Sanctum of Feather Cave, A Mogollon Sun and Earth Shrine Linking Mexico and the Southwest. *American Antiquity* 33 : 25 – 44.

Erdoes, Richard, and Alfonso Ortiz, eds. 1984. *American Indian Myths and Legends.* New York: Pantheon Books.

Farrer, Claire. 1980. Singing for Life: The Mescalero Apache Girls' Puberty Ceremony. In *Southwestern Indian Ritual Drama,* ed. Charlotte J. Frisbie, 125–59. Albuquerque and Santa Fe: University of New Mexico Press and The School of American Research.

Farrer, Claire R., and Bernard Second. 1981. Living the Sky: Aspects of Mescalero Apache Ethnoastronomy. In *Archaeoastronomy in the Americas,* ed. Ray A. Williamson, 137–150. Los Altos, Calif., and College Park, Md.: Ballena Press and Center for Archaeoastronomy.

Green, Jesse, ed. 1979. *Zuñi: Selected Writings of Frank Hamilton Cushing.* Lincoln and London: University of Nebraska Press.

Harrington, John P. n.d. Unpublished manuscripts and papers pertaining to fieldwork at Zuni. Smithsonian Institution, National Anthropological Archives.

Heib, Louis A. 1972. Meaning and Mismeaning: Toward an Understanding of the Ritual Clown. In *New Perspectives on the Pueblos,* ed. Alfonso Ortiz, 163–95. Albuquerque: University of New Mexico Press.

Hymes, Dell. 1980. Particle, Pause and Pattern in American Indian Verse. *American Indian Culture and Research Journal* 4(4):7–51.

Kelley, J. Charles. 1966. Mesoamerica and the Southwestern United States. In *Handbook of Middle American Indians,* vol. 4, ed. Robert Wauchope, 95–110. Austin: University of Texas Press.

Munn Nancy. 1973. *Walbiri Iconography: Graphic Representation and Cultural Symbolism in a Central Australian Society.* Ithaca and London: Cornell University Press.

Ortiz, Alfonso. 1972. Ritual Drama and the Pueblo World View. In *New Perspectives on the Pueblos,* ed. Alfonso Ortiz, 135–61. Albuquerque: University of New Mexico Press.

Parsons, Elsie C. 1917. Notes on Zuñi. *Memoirs of the American Anthropological Association* 4 (3–4):151–327.

———. 1922. Winter and Summer Dance Series in Zuñi in 1918. *University of California Publications in American Archaeology and Ethnology* 17 (3):171–216.

———. 1923. The Origin Myth of Zuñi. *Journal of American Folk-Lore* 36:135–62.

———. 1932. *Isleta, New Mexico.* Forty-Seventh Annual Report of the Bureau of American Ethnology for the Years 1929–1930, 193–466. Washington, D.C.: Government Printing Office.

———. 1933. Some Aztec and Pueblo Parallels, *American Anthropologist* 35:611–31.

———. 1939. *Pueblo Indian Religion.* 2 vols. Chicago: University of Chicago Press.

Quam, Alvina, trans. 1972. *The Zunis: Self-Portrayals by the Zuni People.* Albuquerque: University of New Mexico Press.

Radin, Paul. 1956. *The Trickster: A Study in American Indian Mythology.* New York: Schocken Books. 1972 reprint.

Risser, Anna. 1941. Seven Zuñi Folk Tales. *El Palacio* 48 (10): 315–26.

Schaafsma, Polly. 1975. Rock Art and Ideology of the Mimbres and Jornada Mogollon. *The Artifact* 13: 2–14.

Schaafsma, Polly, and Curtis Schaafsma. 1974. Evidence for the Origins of the Pueblo Katchina Cult as Suggested by Southwestern Rock Art. *American Antiquity* 39: 535–45.

Stephen, Alexander M. 1929. Hopi Tales. *Journal of American Folk-Lore* 42: 1–72.

Stevenson, Matilda C. 1904. *The Zuñi Indians: Their Mythology, Esoteric Fraternities, and Ceremonies.* Twenty-Third Annual Report of the Bureau of American Ethnology for the Years 1901–1902, 3–634. Washington, D.C.: Government Printing Office.

Tedlock, Barbara. 1975. The Clown's Way. In *Teachings from the American Earth,* ed. Dennis Tedlock and Barbara Tedlock, 105–118. New York: Liveright.

———. 1980. Songs of the Zuni Kachina Society: Composition, Rehearsal and Performance. In *Southwestern Indian Ritual Drama,* ed. Charlotte J. Frisbie, 7–35. Albuquerque: University of New Mexico Press.

———. 1983. Zuni Sacred Theater. *American Indian Quarterly* 7: 93–110.

———. 1984. The Beautiful and the Dangerous: Zuni Ritual and Cosmology as an Aesthetic System. *Conjunctions: Bi-annual Volumes of New Writing* 6: 246–65.

Tedlock, Dennis. 1972. *Finding the Center: Narrative Poetry of the Zuni Indians.* New York: Dial Press, 1972.

———. 1975. An American Indian View of Death. In *Teachings from the American Earth,* ed. Dennis Tedlock and Barbara Tedlock, pp. 248–71. New York: Liveright.

———. 1979. Zuni Religion and World View. In *Handbook of North American Indians, Southwest,* vol. 9, ed. Alfonso Ortiz, 499–508. Washington, D.C.: Government Printing Office.

———. 1983. *The Spoken Word and the Work of Interpretation.* Philadelphia: University of Pennsylvania Press.

Tedlock, Dennis and Barbara. 1975. *Teachings from the American Earth.* New York: Liveright.

Toelken, Barre, and Tacheeni Scott. 1981. Poetic Retranslation and the "Pretty Languages" of Yellowman. In *Traditional American Indian Literatures: Texts and Interpretations,* ed. Karl Kroeber, et al., 65–116. Lincoln and London: University of Nebraska Press.

Turner, Victor. 1967. *The Forest of Symbols.* Ithaca and London; Cornell University Press.

White, Leslie A. 1962. *The Pueblo of Sia, New Mexico.* Bureau of American Ethnology Bulletin 184. Washington, D.C.: Government Printing Office.

Williamson, Ray A., and M. Jane Young. 1979. An Equinox Sun Petroglyph Panel at Hovenweep National Monument. *American Indian Rock Art,* vol. 4, 70–80. El Toro, Calif. American Rock Art Research Association.

Wright, Barton. 1985. *Kachinas of the Zuni*. Flagstaff: Northland Press.

Young, M. Jane. 1978. *Translation and Analysis of Zuni Ritual Poetry*. Master's thesis, University of Pennsylvania.

———. 1982. We Were going to Have a Barbeque, But the Cow Ran Away: Production, Form, and Function of the Zuni Tribal Fair. *Southwest Folklore* 5 (4):42–48.

———. 1987a. Humor and Anti-Humor in Western Puebloan Puppetry Performances. In *Humor and Comedy in Puppetry: Celebration in Popular Culture*, ed. Dina Sherzer and Joel Sherzer, 127–50. Bowling Green. Ohio: Popular Press.

———. 1987b. Women, Reproduction, and Religion in Western Puebloan Society. *Journal of American Folklore* 100 (398):436–45.

———. 1988. *Signs from the Ancestors: Zuni cultural Symbolism and Perceptions of Rock Art*. Albuquerque: University of New Mexico Press.

———. 1989. The Southwest Connection: Similarities between Western Puebloan and Mesoamerican Cosmology. In *World Archaeoastronomy*, ed. Anthony F. Aveni. 167–79. Cambridge: Cambridge University Press.

———. In press. Astronomy in Pueblo and Navajo World Views. In *Ethnoastronomy: Indigenous Astronomical and Cosmological Traditions of the World*. ed. Von Del Chamberlain, M. Jane Young, and John B. Carlson. Los Altos, Calif., and Thousand Oaks, Calif.: Ballena Press and Slo'w Press.

Young, M. Jane, and Ray A. Williamson. 1981. Ethnoastronomy: The Zuni Case. In *Archaeoastronomy in the Americas*, ed. Ray A. Williamson, 183–91. Los Altos, Calif., and College Park, Md.: Ballena Press and Center for Archaeoastronomy.

Zeilik, Michael. 1986. The Ethnoastronomy of the Historic Pueblos, II: Moon Watching. *Archaeoastronomy*, suppl. to *Journal for the History of Astronomy* 10:1–22.

# 6

■■■■■■■■

# *Navajo Earth and Sky and the Celestial Life-Force*

■■■■■■■■

## RIK PINXTEN AND INGRID VAN DOOREN

*Both Rik Pinxten, whose Ph.D. is in philosophy, and Ingrid Van Dooren are associated with the Rijksuniversiteit Gent in Belgium where he is Director of the Seminarie voor Antropologie and she a research associate. They have collaborated on field research and book and article publication, most recently investigating Navajo space and geometry. Here they extend their recent work into the area of sacred space and place, considering aspects of the animating force sustaining life on earth and in the sky.*

The ethnography of the Navajo is so vast that few specialists in this field can keep an overview of everything published. Moreover, it seems to become ever more clear that generational and local differences are important. We will nevertheless disregard these differentiations here. In this chapter, we draw exclusively on our own field notes. Our contribution is small. However, against the background of the Navajo literature we know, we have the honest conviction that most of the data we relate either have never been published at all or have not been presented in the focus which is characteristic of the present volume.

Although the Navajo have been described at great length by a series of anthropologists, rather little is known about their astronomy. Haile, a lifelong ethnographer of the Navajo culture, mentioned this fact at the dawn of this century and repeats it in his published report about Navajo starlore (1947). According to Haile, those Navajo who are knowledgeable in these matters are rare. He suggests that starlore may actually be considered esoteric knowledge. We tend to have doubts about the differentiation between esoteric and exoteric knowledge, but it is nonetheless true that (a) some of the informants we worked with told us that knowledge about both the stars and their mythological aspects was "medicine man knowledge/talk" (*hataáli bisaad*), and that (b) only one (out of thirteen) of our informants actually did have considerable astronomical knowledge and was so recognized as such by all others. These particulars might be accidental, but on the other hand they might be taken to be indications which corroborate Haile's suggestion.

## Earth and Sky: Their Nature and Its Implications

A fundamental concept of Navajo cosmology is that of "placedness" of any particular phenomenon in the universe, in relationship with any series of other phenomena (Wyman 1983; Pinxten et al. 1983). Cosmological phenomena came into this universe through emergence, after which they were "placed" by the Holy Ones. Earth and Sky are the two major and englobing cosmological phenomena; they constitute the couple defining the ultimate boundaries of the Navajo universe. The creation story of Earth makes clear what the importance of Earth and Sky for human beings amounts to:

> What they (the gods) put on Mother Earth were the different plants. Mother Earth said, "From here on I will produce some different plants for human beings, for their use. All these different plants with different leaves and flowers will grow on my body." The Heavenly Father said, "In heaven I shall produce moisture to have all plants growing and blooming." (The same happens with animals to be hunted by the human beings.)
>     . . . So, after everything was all organized with Mother Earth, they [the gods] put the heaven in use too. So they lay the Earth underneath, and put Father Heaven on top. (C. M.)[1]

Earth and Sky are said to stretch out as anthropomorphic figures from the East (head) to the West (feet), the Sky lying on top of Earth like a man lying on top of a woman in the sexual act. They are stretched out in this position, however, without touching one another: there is some space between them, as there has been since the time of emergence. This space is filled up with layers of phenomena with each particular layer over and above the underlying one. In this way, everything that lives on top of the Earth (plants, animals, human beings) exists in a thick layer of air "which goes up only so far" (F. H.), above which are to be found the sun, then the moon and finally the stars. The stars are sometimes said to be attached to the Sky, as it were "hanging down from it" (F. H.) In the stories, Sun and Sky are often substitutable and both are referred to as "*Shitaa*" (my father).[2]

Both the Earth and the Sky/Sun give life force to everything in the universe between them, especially to everything living and growing. Some phenomena have a structuring force or wind inside them: a *níłch'i bii'histiia*. Others have a life force in them: a *níłch'i bii'sizįįnii*. Most phenomena have no such "winds" in them:

> We say *nahasdzáán bii'histiin* for the pillars that lift up the earth. And then from the Earth to the Sky you have *yádałhił bii'histiin*, the pillars of the sky. And all the Sacred Mountains, they have a *níłch'i bii'histiin*. But no animal has one. They only have *bijéí*, a heart. But that is not a *níłch'i*. But then people, they have a soul, a *níłch'i bii'sizįįnii*. That is what they live with, the breach. (F. H.)

The "living things" are inhabited by and are said to survive because of (a type of) the *níłch'i* (wind) in them. Precisely this *níłch'i* seems to stand for the aspect of life-force in them, that is, that type of power which keeps these living beings in existence. As the result of an agreement between the ancestors and the Earth and Sky at the dawn of this world, both Earth and Sun (Sky) keep giving force to living beings on a continuous and daily basis. However, they have to get something in return in order to be able to continue this transfer; each and every day Earth and Sun take lives: that is, the vital force of dying beings return to them. Because of this cosmological gift-recuperation system, the Earth and the Sun will continue the transfer of life forces to new generations of living beings. Eclipses of the Sun are said to indicate deregulation of this balance; the Sun is believed to have taken too many lives at once (for example, with a calamity leading to a great loss of lives), and the subsequent period is believed to be "free of death" for a while (F. H., T. B.).

> Inside of the Sun, Cornpollen represents the earth people, people who are now living . . . They say the eclipse of the Sun (*johana'ei dahats'ah*) is the death of the Sun. You do not eat, break up ceremonies, stay inside, etc. . . . Normally the Sun takes lives. With an eclipse the Sun is weakening, it can not take deaths that day. When it happens the Sun has to pay back to the people. (F. H.)

A full life, carried through to its optimal end, lasts 102 years. This number, which is used symbolically most of the time, refers to the conventional representations of the lifetime as 102 yucca leaves in the mocassin game. When one of our informants died at the age of 104, at least some informants (for example, T. B.) told us he went beyond the time allotted to a human being. When a person dies at "old age," the transition between life and death is believed to be safe; that is to say, the corpse is not dangerous for those living on. In a sense, an old person "has lived up his/her life force" (F. H.). However, most people die before they reach old age in this sense. Their death causes anxiety and often necessitates a ceremony to cure the survivors of evil effects caused by the illness and the death of the relative. In those cases, it is said that "the Sun and the Earth take a life" (T. B., F. N. C. M.) in return for the life-giving forces they invest in living creatures every day.

We could not reach totally satisfactory knowledge on this topic, we feel. This is most probably due to the supposedly dangerous nature of anything dead or dying, according to the Navajo. (Informants told us they underwent a ceremony whenever they had touched a corpse or a burial place.) It proved very difficult to engage in any kind of conversation about these questions. However, what we propose as a potential explanation of the difference in attitude vis-à-vis death of old age and death-as-danger with the dying of younger people goes as follows: when somebody dies of old age he has "used up his/her *nítch'i* to the limit" (F. H.), and consequently the *nítch'i* is reinvested in other beings in the course of such a life; however, when a young(er) person dies, the unused *nítch'i* is claimed again by Sun and Earth. The fear of a corpse of a young(er) person is caused by the unbalance or the lack of redistribution of *nítch'i*. In the case of a fulfilled life, this fear is out of place, since the cycle has been brought to its normal final stage. This interpretation, although based on some field data, is largely ours and we can only present it as a hypothesis. Some further data on the role of Sun and Earth seem to point in the direction indicated though (see below, next section).

Another aspect of the Sky has a definite role to play in the life of human beings, offering a second tension-laden relationship between humans and cosmological phenomena. According to Navajo belief, the North is the place from where all illness and misfortune comes. It is, of course, the direction where the Sun never comes, and it is explicitly identified as the place where the Big Dipper is located. In Navajo starlore, the Big Dipper constellation turns around its axis in the north; especially the North Star (represented by the male *Náhookǫs bikąą'di:* the north-star-on-top) and the second star to the south of it in the Big Dipper constellation (represented as the female *Náhookǫs bi'áádi:* the north [star]-remote-from-it) play an essential role here.* This couple is said to be revolving around the north at a

---

*Informants F. H. and T. B. pointed to individual stars here (*bikąą'di* and *bi'áádi*) within the Big Dipper constellation. On this point, they differ from Young and Morgan's interpretation (1980:542).

constant distance from one another, somewhat reminiscent of the structural relationship between Earth and Sky. Moreover, they "keep bad things away from people or call them back" (F. H.). That is to say, this couple in the Big Dipper constellation guards illnesses and calamities which can and do occasionally harass people. We return to this important couple in the following section.

So far, we are able to say that the give-and-take relationship between Earth/Sky and living beings focuses on the transfer of life force and its removal with death. A structurally similar couple of stars (male/female, at a constant distance from each other) situated in that part of the sky where the Sun can never come holds the key to the primary reservoir of disease and calamities for the Navajo. That is to say, this second couple is identified as a major agent in the causes of death or the continuation of a good life.

## The Stories and Their Social Correlates

The story of the Twins holds the key for an adequate interpretation of the importance attached to the Big Dipper constellation. After the emergence and the "placement" of things in this world, different calamities struck the world. The important mythical event, for the present paper, is the appearance of all sorts of monsters in the early times. Due to "unnatural sexual acts among other things" (Frisbie 1987: 19), the Earth was covered with monsters. According to our informants, the latter must be understood not only as diseases, but also as creatures that harassed and killed the ancestors. Changing Woman (a mythological figure linked with the seasons, life and growth, and fundamentally benevolent to all living things on Earth) bore the Twins, who are known as the Waterchild and the Monster Slayer (see, for example, Frisbie 1987). Two of our informants claimed that the Twins freed the Earth from the monsters in their search for their father, whom the informants identified as the Sun (C. M., F. H.). One version of this story goes as follows:

> There was a massive thing like a rock which fell over the Earth and killed people. The Twins chipped off pieces of it with their *kał* (club) until only the North was left. (F. H.)

That is to say, what covered the face of the earth was systematically demolished by the intervention of the Twins who managed to destroy it bit by bit, "slaying" it with their club. The only part they could not manage is that which lay in the upper northern region. Another version puts it like this:

> The Twin Monster Slayers were clubbing the big rock that covered Mother Earth and killed the people. Then the rock said, "I make this promise: I will go to the North and be good to earthpeople and not kill them anymore. Do not grind me to dust."
>
> It went to the North. From there it comes out now and then and sends bad things to remind people: colds, coughs, headaches, and so on. (F. H.)

This version was corroborated by C. M., who claimed that the "monsters" were "moved to the North to be guarded there by *Náhookǫs*." Both versions hold the same message, it seems: the monsters were basically overpowered by the offspring of Sun and Changing Woman, and the remainder was relocated in the north. The identification of the north as the place of origin for illnesses and calamities in the present-day Navajo world is mythologically indicated by the acts of the Twins. In daily attitudes and behavioral postures, this feature of the North is clearly recognized: in the *hooghan* (home) women should sit and sleep along the north side facing the South, while men should sit and sleep along the south side in order to face the North. Another important practice is witnessed during healing ceremonies, where the medicine man chases illness and "bad things" back to the North by blowing in that direction on a feather. Of course, the very fact that, according to myth, the Twins were unable to slay all the monsters and had to leave some in the North sets the stage for the appearance of illness and death in later time. It also announces the role of the medicine man and the range within which he should continue or repeat the struggle against illnesses for the people.

One more element of the story of the Twins should be mentioned. It is said that the Twins (and some other Holy People) in some instances showed human beings how to behave. The Twins are indicated in the language by *alkéé'naa'aashi'* (those following in each other's footsteps). To our knowledge, this term is used to refer to several of the "couples" found in Navajo stories: *sąah naagháí bik'eh hózhǫ́ǫ́n*, the male and female star of the Big Dipper; the *nílch'i bi'áadi* and *nílch'i bakáádi* in the Sacred Mountains; and possibly other couples can be mentioned (F. H., C. M.; see also Pinxten et al. 1983; Farella 1984). In most instances, the couple is seen as a male and a female figure. It is said that the *nílch'i* can enter the human spirit through the skull at the top of the head. This is why the newborn baby is put on the floor of the *hooghan* with its head directed toward the fire. Through the smoke of the fire, the ancestral social relationships of the baby and all preceding generations will be "communicated" to the newborn (F. H.). Smoking tobacco at a later age has the same meaning and impact. A good example of the way in which *nítch'i* has impact on human beings and, in fact, makes them able to cross generations is to be found in a quote from McNeley (1981 : 13), who quotes informant J. T.:

> Dark Wind, Blue Wind, Yellow Wind, White Wind, Glossy Wind, we will speak in accordance with their will—it happened [was said] like this. So, accordingly, one who speaks in our behalf has been present alongside us from back then. These same Winds speak for us and spoke for our later ancestors.

According to one informant, however, a particular impact stems from the Twins, whose *nítch'i* enter the human head by means of smoke in the form of *atkéé'naa'aashi':* the men have two openings in their skull, allowing for the two "followers of one another" to come in. The power of the Twins is thus invested in men, who, by this particular characteristic, are able to become responsible over women and children as head of the family (C. M., Farella 1984, and personal communication). This would imply that the Sky (by means of the Sun, father of the Twins) and the Earth (by means of Changing Woman mainly) organized, through the messenger– intervener role of the Twins, some of the social structure of the Navajo. We did not find these data explicitly corroborated by any other informant so far; on the other hand, such a view could be considered as an instantiation of the character of interrelatedness of everything with everything else in a closed world, which has repeatedly been recognized as a feature of the Navajo universe (Wyman 1983; Pinxten et al. 1983). An argument in favor of this view is the common statement that "between the Earth and the Sky there is air and the sun, and the moon and the stars; it is not empty. When it will be empty, it will be the end of the world" (F. H., as well as other informants).

A second argument in favor of serious consideration of C. M.'s view has to do with his particular status as a seer-thinker in the eyes of the Navajo. This implies that he overlooks and eventually reinterprets the Navajo universe as a whole. Since perceiving-thinking and talking (telling stories, for example) is, in fact, working with or on the universe, according to the Navajo view (see, for example, Witherspoon 1977), the thinker has a particular role and is liable to express views which may not be found explicitly with others. This leads us to the last point to which we wish to draw attention: the role of Coyote in the stories.

Coyote is a Holy Person, who seems to hold the "privileged" position of the one who disturbs order, mainly by taking risks other Holy People would shy away from. The best known story in ethnoastronomy is the one relating how Holy People gathered around Black God to "place the stars."

> The Holy People were placing the stars. *Ma'ii* (Coyote) came in and got annoyed by their slowness. He picked out a red star (*ma'ii sǫ*) from the bag with stars and placed it in the south. He said, "This is going to be my star." He took the bag of stars and threw it over his head. That is how *Yikaisdáhí* (Milky Way) was formed. The Holy People were making plans to place stars according to the season. Morning Star and Evening Star were going to be placed there. Because of Coyote only a few stars have been placed.
>
> Because Coyote picked his star in such a way, he said it would announce trouble, war or bad times. When you see that star you have to say a prayer, talking against the bad way (F. H.)

Because of this way of action, *ma'ii sǫ* appears only for "short periods during the year,"[3] and its connotation is "trouble" (F. H., T. B.). This feature corresponds with the general characterization of Coyote as a trouble-shooter or at least as the one who dares to take risks, to disturb a conventional order, and to push things in new or unforeseen directions. With his second action, Coyote ruined the plans of the Holy People to place and name all the stars: none of the stars of Milky Way were ever named and placed properly, since they were just scattered all over the sky in one big streak of anger.

Coyote is thus seen as a disturbing power, but also as a determining or renovating figure. It is in this sense that thinkers-seers among the Navajo are sometimes referred to as coyotes (for example, the seer C. M.); they seem to hold a similar position among human beings. That is to say, in contrast to their fellow Navajo, seers-thinkers are the ones who dare to take greater risks than common people by thinking through and speaking beyond the limits of tradition or convention and proposing alternatives, but also crea-tive, solutions for new problems. They are both feared and appealed to in cases of epidemics, calamities, politically insecure situations, and so on. The same ambivalence holds with regard to them vis-à-vis the holy figure of Coyote: they are disturbing order, but they are sometimes granted license to create new order (F. H.).

It will be clear that we could not offer any global view of Navajo ethnoastronomy. Some of the (sacred) material in this area has been pub-lished by others, but for the most part little information is available nor can it be obtained from Navajo informants. We focused on three cosmological elements, and their relationship with sociocultural patterns: the Sky–Earth couple and their relationship to life and death, the Big Dipper constellation and its relation with human illness, and Coyote (his star and the Milky Way) and his correlate among human beings. We hope this short paper may add some new information which may help to shed light on Navajo ethno-astronomy and how the celestial life force is lined to the Earth-surface people.

## Notes

1. The letters within brackets (C. M., F. H., T. B. and H. T.) refer to informants who provided us with some knowledge in this domain. Our debt to them is extremely great. We hope not to have misrepresented their views.

2. "Shitaa" is usually glossed "my father" in English; however, in this context a better gloss might be "my genitor" or "the one responsible for my life".

3. Unfortunately, we were unable to acquire more precise data on the length of appearance of *ma'ii sǫ*. This may result in part from the fact that very few people know about the stars and planets, and in part because of the secrecy attached to starlore. Consultants told us only that *ma'ii sǫ* appears for a short time—and that was it.

## References

Farella, John. 1984. *The Main Stalk*. Tucson: University of Arizona Press.

Frisbie, Charlotte. 1987. *Navajo Medicine Bundles or Jísh*. Albuquerque: University of New Mexico Press.

Haile, Berard. 1947. *Starlore Among the Navaho*. Santa Fe: The Museum of Ceremonial Art.

McNeley, James Kale. 1981. *Holy Wind in Navajo Philosophy*. Tucson: University of Arizona Press.

Pinxten, Rik, Ingrid van Dooren, and Frank Harvey. 1983. *The Anthropology of Space*. Philadelphia: University of Pennsylvania Press.

Young, Robert W., and William Morgan. 1980. *The Navajo Language: A Grammar and Colloquial Dictionary*. Albuquerque: University of New Mexico Press.

Witherspoon, Gary. 1977. *Language and Art in the Navajo Universe*. Ann Arbor: University of Michigan Press.

Wyman, Leland C. 1983. Navajo Ceremonial System. In: *Handbook of North American Indians*. Vol. 10, *Southwest*, ed. A. Ortiz, 536–37. Washington, D.C.: Smithsonian Institution.

# 7

■ ■ ■ ■ ■ ■ ■ ■ ■

## *The* Hooghan *and the Stars*

■ ■ ■ ■ ■ ■ ■ ■ ■

### TRUDY GRIFFIN-PIERCE

*An independent scholar as well as a practicing artist, Trudy Griffin-Pierce lives in Tucson where she makes frequent trips to continue her work with the Navajo star and crystal gazers she first engaged as part of her dissertation research at the University of Arizona. From having been adopted into a Navajo family and living with them occasionally through many years, she brings an immediacy to Navajo perceptions of the reality of celestial beings as she relates home to heavens.*

The Navajo homeland is located in the Four Corners area—the Colorado Plateau country where Arizona, New Mexico, Utah, and Colorado come together. The Navajo belong to the Athabascan language family, which they share with Apacheans in the Southwest as well as with Native Americans in Oregon, California, Canada, and Alaska. Although towns exist today on the Navajo Reservation, traditionally the Navajo lived in scattered, small family groups.

A concern for order in human life guides Navajo behavior. The Navajo word *hózhó*, which has no precise English equivalent, expresses concepts of beauty, harmony, blessedness, and satisfaction. The significance and pervasiveness of this idea is reflected in the statement that "abusing means disorderly treatment" (Pinxten 1983:29). All phenomena in the Navajo universe are interrelated and interdependent; all living beings serve one another to some extent. Consequently, everything has a place and a function in a mutually dependent chain that connects each feature of mind, body, earth, and celestial phenomena and ultimately includes the whole universe. When an individual abuses one element, he or she disrupts the whole system and is made ill by the forces thus unleashed.

This interrelatedness is reflected in the Navajo dwelling, which is called a *hooghan,* and in stories about the *hooghan.* As we will see, the *hooghan* embodies the concept of *hózhǫ.* The *hooghan* and the sky can also be conceptualized as reciprocals because the *hooghan* reflects cosmological order while the sky can be seen as a sort of *hooghan.*

These concepts are also exemplified in sandpaintings, which are created as a part of ceremonies that take place in the *hooghan.* Sandpaintings are an important part of Navajo healing rituals and play an essential role in the restoration of the patient to a state of health and harmony. These depictions, therefore, and the stories that accompany them reflect the Navajo emphasis on order and harmony, circularity and reciprocity. Sandpaintings synthesize the aesthetic, the sacred, and the medicinal by creating a visual model of the natural–supernatural worlds.[1]

This chapter focuses on the visual expression of one aspect of worldview—the transmission of normative standards of Navajo ethical behavior through stellar patterns. Specifically, it examines star patterns and moral teachings. I examine two constellations—the two *náhookǫs* (the Big Dipper and Cassiopeia)—which are conceptualized by some Navajo medicine men, or chanters, as a *hooghan.* As we explore the significance of the *hooghan* and its celestial counterpart, we will see how the two *náhookǫs* symbolize the concept of *hózhǫ.*

## Star Patterns and Moral Teachings

As Keith Basso (1983:45) has demonstrated with the Western Apache, geographical features of the physical landscape serve as "indispensable mnemonic pegs on which to hang moral teachings of their history." When a Western Apache sees a particular mountain, the name of the mountain evokes a particular historical tale that has moral significance. In this way, "the land makes people live right" (Mrs. Annie Peaches, in Basso 1983:2).

For the Navajo, celestial phenomena serve a similar function as visual reminders of key values. The stories associated with constellations provide moral guidance for the Earth Surface People, as the Navajo call themselves. Only by adhering to the right values can the Earth Surface People establish and maintain harmony in their lives and in the universe. The constellations serve as powerful symbols because they are universally visible. First Woman, in Newcomb's (1967:83) version of Creation, refers to this when she says,

When all the stars were ready to be placed in the sky First Woman said, "I will use these to write the laws that are to govern mankind for all time. These laws cannot be written on the water as that is always changing its form, nor can they be written in the sand as the wind would soon erase them, but if they are written in the stars they can be read and remembered forever."

To the Navajo, the constellations, sun, and moon are *diyin dine'é,* supernatural beings or Holy People. Even though the Holy People left the Earth Surface People (and are no longer visible to humans) at the time of Creation (Slim Curley, in Wyman 1970:324), these sacred beings remain nearby and are omnipresent. They are described as experiencing human emotions and are tied genealogically through the clan organization to the Earth Surface People (Reichard 1950:58–59). Thus, for the traditional Navajo, what Westerners call "celestial bodies" are really a class of living beings sharing emotional, genealogical, and physical proximity with humans.

## The *Hooghan*

Traditionally, the Navajo *hooghan* is the place in which the Navajo family lives its day-to-day life. Children are born in the *hooghan;* the family as well as motherless lambs sleep there; meals are cooked over the fire in the center of this dwelling; wool, which later will be woven into rugs, is dyed in pots on the *hooghan* floor; articles of clothing, as well as sacred paraphernalia, are stored within this structure. The *hooghan* is a place of instruction, where grandfathers tell stories during the long winter nights and daughters learn to cook and to spin during the day. As with all homes, it is a refuge of order and peace from the outside world.

The *hooghan* is also a place of healing; any Navajo home may be dedicated for sacred use when prayers identify it with the homes of powerful Navajo supernaturals. The ceremonial and the particular sandpainting for that ceremonial determine the sacred dwelling into which it is transformed. Through this transformation, the *hooghan* may become the first house built on earth in which the *diyin dine'é* planned the creation of the world; or it might be Changing Woman's home when she was still a girl at Huerfano Mesa in New Mexico; it could also become the Sun's magnificent celestial home with its many rooms full of jewels, livestock, signing birds, and beautiful fabrics; or the *hooghan* may be transformed into the luxurious home that the Sun built for Changing Woman in the Western Ocean where the Navajo clans of today were created (McAllester and McAllester 1980:13).

The primordial and cosmic houses celebrated in Navajo prayers and stories are unlike those in any other published literature; house beams listen and fall into place at the command of supernaturals as these beings create houses with cosmic ground plans (McAllester and McAllester 1980:13–15). And the houses created by these *diyin dine'é* are made of dawn, with rooms of turquoise and ladders of white shell with rainbows that extend into the interior.

In the beginning, when the first people emerged from the four underworlds to appear on the earth's surface, they had nothing. Before they could form the earth into a habitable place, they needed to gather together and plan. But in order to establish the order of the world, they needed to build the first *hooghan* where they could meet and discuss things for the future.

It was essential for the orderly unfolding of creation that the structure in which this planning occurred was constructed according to sacred specifications based on the four directions. The gods selected the four main support poles of the *hooghan* following the directional order that is proper in most ceremonies—the sunwise circuit—which begins with the East, moves to the South, then turns to the West, and finally, moves to the North.[2] In keeping with Navajo world view, the builder of the first *hooghan* thought about the suitable poles, discussed them with friends whose aid he would need, and then, with their assistance, brought the appropriate support poles to the site, where they were put in the proper cardinal positions, beginning with the East.

The following stanzas of the Chief Hooghan Songs demonstrate how fundamental the four directions and the *diyin dine'é* of each of these four directions are to the construction of the *hooghan*. By following these sacred specifications, *hózhǫ́,* expressed as a "long life" and "happiness," is built into the very foundation of the *hooghan*.

> Along below the east, Earth's pole I first lean into position. As I plan
> for it it drops, as I speak to it it drops, now it listens to me as it
> drops, it yields to my wish as it drops,
> Long life drops, happiness drops into position, *ni yo o.*

> Along below the south, Mountain Woman's pole I next lean in
> position.

As I plan for it it drops, as I speak to it it drops, now it listens to me
  as it drops, it yields to my wish as it drops,
Long life drops, happiness drops into position, *ni yo o.*

Along below the west Water Woman's pole I lean between in
  position
As I plan for it it drops, as I speak to it it drops, now it listens to me
  as it drops, it yields to my wish as it drops,
Long life drops, happiness drops into position, *ni yo o.*

Along below the north, Corn Woman's pole I lean my last in
  position
As I plan for it it drops, as I speak to it it drops, now it listens to me
  as it drops, it yields to my wish as it drops,
Long life drops, happiness drops into position, *ni yo o.*

(Wyman 1970:115)

Navajo chanter Frank Mitchell (Frisbie and McAllester 1978:245)
explains that after the gods built the first *hooghan* and established leadership
within this structure, "That [was] the start of the human race on earth."
Because the sacred specifications surrounding its construction were followed, the first *hooghan* became the proper site for the creation of life which
could then unfold *nizhónígo,* or "in an orderly and proper way." Today's
*hooghan* thus embodies the concept of *hózhǫ́,* both in its planning and in the
creative process of events which began within its walls. This is why Father
Berard Haile (n.d.) used the *hooghan* as a conceptual introduction to the
Navajo universe and why Farella (1984:87) refers to the *hooghan* as "one of
those master encodings . . . an economical starting point for understanding the whole of the Navajo world view."

## Sandpaintings

Navajo ritual both cures and prevents illness. According to Navajo
thought, illness is caused by natural phenomena (*diyin dine'é*), some species
of animals, the misuse of ceremonial paraphernalia or activities, and ghosts
(Wyman and Kluckhohn 1938:13–14). To cure the patient, the practi-
tioner must invoke the cause of illness and bring it under control. The
particular cause of the illness, rather than the physical symptoms, dictates
the particular ceremonial needed to cure the patient. The use of ceremonial

knowledge and the proper performance of orderly procedures in a ritually controlled context restores harmony, beauty, balance, and order. Thus, the actions and states of the individual are clearly linked with the rest of the universe.

Navajo ritual both restores and creates balance. Navajo ritual is organized around chants, which are ceremonials composed of a series of ritual procedures and conducted by a medicine man or chanter for a patient in order to cure illness. Each ceremonial has an associated origin myth that provides the sanction and rationale for the chant ritual by giving an account of how the chant's ritual procedures were acquired by some of the supernaturals and were given to the Earth Surface People. Thus, the chantway myth mediates between the natural and supernatural worlds.

The rites that compose a ceremonial can be combined into a two-night, five-night, or nine-night version. A sandpainting is but one of these component rites within a ceremonial; other rites include the consecration of the *hooghan,* the setting-out of prayer sticks, and the sweat bath. Only a few of the sandpaintings still being used today depict constellations.

The sandpainting assists healing in four ways: it attracts the supernaturals and their healing power; it identifies the patient with their healing power; it absorbs the sickness from, and imparts immunity to, the patient seated on it; and it creates a ritual reality in which the patient and supernatural interact dramatically. The supernatural beings are thought to be irresistibly attracted by seeing their portraits painted in sand; when they arrive, they become one with their images depicted on the *hooghan* floor. After the patient sits on the images of the supernaturals and the chanter has pressed sand from the various parts of the figures' bodies to the corresponding parts of the patient's body, the patient, through identification, becomes like the sandpainted supernaturals, powerful and immune to further harm. Gladys Reichard (1950 : 112) described the sandpainting rite as a "spiritual osmosis in which the evil in man and the good of deity penetrate the ceremonial membrane [the sandpainting] in both directions, the former being neutralized by the latter, but only if the exact conditions for interpenetration are fulfilled." It is the final purpose of the sandpainting that most concerns us in this chapter.

The cyclical nature of Native American time (rather than the linear, "progress"-oriented nature of modern Western time) makes it possible for events of the past to occur again in the present.[3] Because the past coexists with the present, the past is accessible to Native Americans in a way that it is not accessible to Westerners. The recitation of the chantway myth

through prayers, songs, and ritual procedures is understood as an actual—
not a symbolic—reenactment. (See Brown [1989] for a discussion of the
Native American cyclical perspective of time.) It is this concept of the
recreation of past events that makes a sandpainting so powerful and results
in the patient's transformation from observer to actor as he or she is taken
from the context of a family *hooghan* into a mythic world where miraculous
events are commonplace.

## Constellations in Sandpaintings

Figure 7.1 depicts the night-sky portion of a sandpainting of the sky and
the earth by a Navajo chanter to whom I will refer as Chanter A.[4] *Náhookǫs
biką'ii* (1) translates as "Male Revolver" and corresponds to the part of Ursa
Major that includes the Big Dipper (Griffin-Pierce 1986). (This particular
chanter reversed Ursa Major so that the two pointer stars point away from
Polaris.) *Náhookǫs ba'áadii* (2) is "Female Revolver" and is the same as
Cassiopeia. The Navajo names for these constellations describe their circular motion around Polaris which the Navajo refer to as their igniter, the
star that illuminates them and provides their fire and light.

Chanter A interprets these constellations (the Big Dipper and Cassiopeia) as a symbol of the Navajo home or *hooghan* as these two star
groupings revolve around Polaris, which represents the central fire in the
*hooghan* (Fig. 7.2). Together, these constellations represent "old people" or
"women folks," he said. "They tell us [by their positive example] to "stay at
home, to stay around your fire." Here, the implication is that these constellations set a moral example for the Earth Surface People to be at home
with their families to carry out their familial responsibilities.

Newcomb (1966: 156) also refers to polaris as the *hooghan* fire and to
Ursa Major and Cassiopeia as "the married couple who circled this fire but
never left it to find some other." She also says that two laws—the law
against two couples living in the same *hooghan* or doing their cooking over
the same fire and the law that forbids a young man to look at the face of his
mother-in-law—were "written in the stars" (Newcomb 1966: 156).

Chanter A offered a related but slightly different interpretation when
he referred to the two *náhookǫs* as leaders, as sources of wisdom and knowledge always available to the Earth Surface People. These constellations are
also visual reminders to leaders on earth that they must always be willing
and ready to help their people.

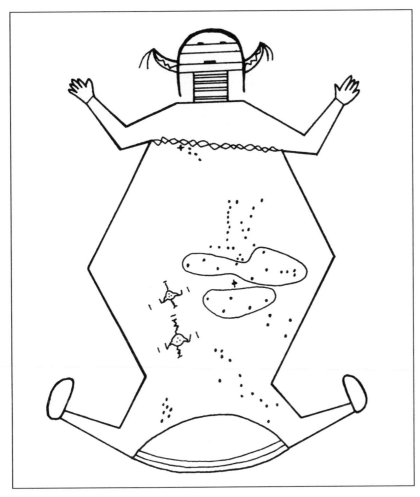

**Figure 7.1.** Chanter A's Father Sky with the Big Dipper and Cassiopeia circled.

## The *Hooghan* and the Two *Náhookǫos* (The Big Dipper and Cassiopeia)

*Náhookǫs biką'ii* (The Big Dipper) and *náhookǫs ba'áadii* (Cassiopeia) are thus a visual metaphor for the Navajo home or *hooghan,* a central focus for life, as these two beings revolve around Polaris—symbolic of the fire in the center of the *hooghan*—and the other stars revolve around the Big Dipper and

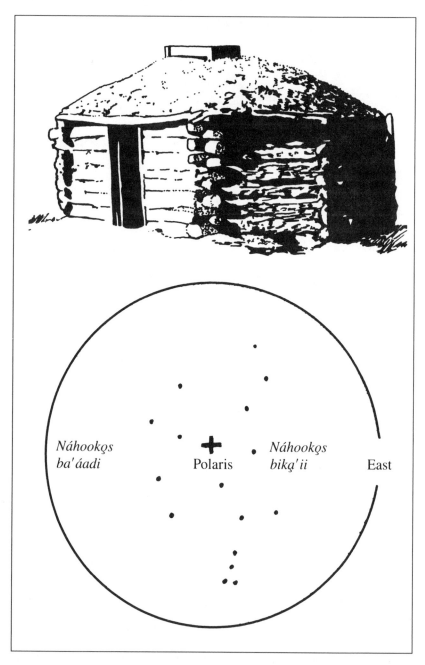

**Figure 7.2.** *Upper:* Navajo *hooghan. Lower:* the two *Náhookos* (from a sandpainting) revolving around Polaris, which represents the central fire in the *hooghan.* Navajo sandpaintings do not reflect the relative brightness of stars within constellations.

Cassiopeia (Chanter A). When I recounted this metaphor to Chanter B, he said, "That chanter gave you the *Hózhǫ́ǫ́jí* [Blessingway] version [of the two *náhookǫs*—the Big Dipper and Cassiopeia]," referring to the ceremonial which is considered to be the cornerstone and backbone of Navajo ritual.

*Hózhǫ́ǫ́jí* differs from the curing ceremonials not only in form (for example, Blessingway drypaintings differ in materials, designs, and use from the Holyway sandpaintings) but also in intent. The purpose of *Hózhǫ́ǫ́jí* is preventive in nature: Blessingway is held to ensure peace, harmony, success, and good fortune for the Navajo, their relatives, flocks, and other possessions, and, by extension, the whole tribe (Frisbie 1980 : 161).

What is of primary interest here is that the central concept of Blessingway is *sǫ́'a naghái bik'e hózhó*—related to the name of the rite. *Hózhǫ́ǫ́jí*—reflected on the intent of this ceremonial, which is "to secure a fine result in any phase of the life cycle, from birth to old age" (Haile, in Wyman 1970 : 7–8). *Sǫ́'a naghái bik'e hózhǫ́* has been discussed by many scholars of the Navajo, especially Farella (1984); this complex phrase can be translated as "according-to-the-ideal-may-restoration-be-achieved" (Reichard 1950 : 47). Although this interpretation is too brief to convey the full essence of such a complex concept, it remains the best gloss of this phrase.

Father Berard Haile (in Wyman 1970 : 10) explains the connection between Blessingway and the *hooghan*:

> Blessingway is vastly concerned with the hogan, a term which has been anglicized from the Navajo *hooghan*, the place home. This place home is the center of every blessing in life: happy births, the home of one's children, the center of weddings, the center where good health, property, increase in crops and livestock originate, where old age, the goal in life, will visit regularly. In a word, the hogan spells a long life of happiness.

A derived subceremony of the Blessingway focuses on the *hooghan* as a central focus for the maintenance of the order, harmony, balance, and peace necessary for the continuation and orderly functioning of the universe. This House Blessing Ceremony commemorates the building and blessing of the first mythological *hooghan* and implements instructions from the supernaturals for future generations to continue these orderly procedures, which are the basis for establishing *sǫ́'a naghái bik'e hózhǫ́* in the universe.

According to Frisbie (1980 : 165–66), the *hooghan* is a home and place of security and is equated with maturity and a willingness to settle down and to plan for the future.

Without a hogan you cannot plan. You can't just go out and plan other things for your future; you have to build a hogan first. Within that you sit down and begin to plan (Frisbie and McAllester 1978:244).

However, *hooghans* are much more than just dwelling places: they are important mythologically and are personified both as deities and as living entities. As we have seen, the *hooghan* is associated with Water Woman, Mountain Woman, Wood Woman, Changing Woman, and the Sun. The individual components of the *hooghan,* such as beams, earth, and fire, as well as its completeness is addressed in song and prayer (Frisbie 1980:166).

When Chanter A said that the two *Náhookǫs* (the Big Dipper and Cassiopeia) represented a *hooghan* that served as a reminder for "women folks . . . to stay at home," he was implicitly referring to the strength of the mother–child bond in Navajo society; this bond has been called perhaps the strongest (Aberle 1961:166; Lamphere 1977:70) and most important (Witherspoon 1970:59) tie in Navajo society. A child is born into the mother's clan and preferred residence is in the residence group of the wife's parents. The husband was often absent: in earlier times his absence was a result of hunting and raiding expeditions as well as kinship responsibilities to his sister's children, while today his absence results from wage work. Both in traditional and contemporary times, men's roles serve to reinforce the mother-child bond.

One of the chief *hooghan* songs of Blessingway, quoted below, directs the woman of the family to keep the *hooghan* neat and orderly both inside and outside. Wyman (1970:118) explains that

> In the song, "away from a woman" means that the hogan is assigned to the woman of the family and it is her duty to make it more attractive by the orderly arrangement of property inside and cleaning rubbish away from the outside premises.

The song to which Wyman refers contains these words:

*'e ne ya* . . . away from a woman . . . away from a woman.
It is my hogan where, from the back corners beauty radiates, it
    radiates from a woman.
It is my hogan where, from the rear center beauty radiates, it
    radiates from a woman.
It is my hogan where, from the fireside beauty radiates, it radiates
    from a woman.
It is my hogan where, from its side corners beauty radiates, it
    radiates from a woman.

It is my hogan where, from the doorway on and on beauty radiates,
it radiates from a woman, it increases the radius of beauty,
*golghane.*

(Wyman 1970:118)[5]

This song also mentions the hearth, or "fireside." The fire in the center
of the *hooghan,* represented by Polaris, is also of particular significance. As
Ruth Roessel, a Navajo writer and teacher (1981:72), puts it,

> Without the assistance of the fire and the poker there would be no Navajos
> today. During the beginning period [after the Emergence], the fire and the
> poker were capable of speech, and there was communication between the
> poker, the fire and the early Navajos.

The fire in the center of the *hooghan* is deeply intertwined with the
concept of the *hooghan* itself. This is reflected linguistically: "a no fireplace
home," or "a home where a fireplace is no more," designates a home in
which the fireplace has been abandoned—because the death of a younger
person has occurred in that home (Wyman 1970:10). In such a case, the
relative may burn the *hooghan,* or make an opening through the North side
to permit the passage of a corpse, or block the entrance and smokehole with
timbers to warn that a burial had been made in it (Wyman 1970:10). No
Navajo would approach such a site because of the association between
witchcraft and the dead.

The metaphor of the two *náhookǫs* (the Big Dipper and Cassiopeia) as
leaders also relates both to the concept of *są'a naghái bik'e hózhǫ́* and the
*hooghan* itself. The willingness and the maturity to take responsibility for
one's actions are qualities that ensure the maintenance of *są'a naghái bik'e
hózhǫ́* in the universe. The chief *hooghan* songs of Blessingway have this title
because they refer not only to their contents—a plan for the first *hooghan*—
but also to the person who will see that these plans are carried out.

Slim Curley, a Navajo chanter (in Wyman 1970:112), explains that
during the process of Creation, those involved said, "This much is clear,
that from the beginning of time this leading chief of ours had full knowledge of things, no doubt about it." This is a reference to the leading
headman, or *naat'áanii,* who knows

> which materials are suitable, where to obtain them, how to set them. His
> "full knowledge" also includes planning the hogan, asking friends for help,
> directing construction, talking matters over, etc., and is the keyword of one
> song (Wyman 1970:112).

The depth of the leader's knowledge is described in the following chief hooghan song:

Of origins I have full knowledge . . . *holaghai.*
Of Earth's origin I have full knowledge.
Of plant origins I have full knowledge.
Of various fabrics' origins I have full knowledge.
Now of long life's, now of happiness origin I have full knowledge,
   *holaghai.*
Of Mountain Woman's origin I have full knowledge.
Of various jewels' origins I have full knowledge . . .
                                                    (Wyman 1970:113)

The song goes on to describe a gradual progression of action that comes to a climax in the last song: first, the headman is credited with possession of full knowledge; then, he has the thought of putting this knowledge into practice; and, finally, he speaks of his purpose to others. This points to another quality of leadership: a strong leader possesses valuable knowledge that he draws upon as he carefully considers how he will put his plans into action before speaking of these plans to others.

The chief *hooghan* songs include a set of "planning songs." The words of the chorus reflect the emphasis on strong leadership:

*'e ne ya* . . . he gives orders and with it he gives orders as he passes
   by, *ni yo o.*
Now with Earth he gives orders as he passes by,
Now with vegetation he gives orders as he passes by,
With fabrics of all kinds he gives orders as he passes by,
With long life he gives orders as he passes by, with happi-
   ness he gives orders as he passes by, he gives orders as he passes
   by, *ni yo o* . . .
                                                    (Wyman 1970:121)

This song set is used at ceremonies for the induction of leaders because "headmen are supposed to be dependable and reliable planners in important public matters" (Wyman 1970:121). Wyman adds that the *hooghan* "is the logical place for planning of any kind" (Wyman 1970:121). This reiterates Frisbie's (1980:244) description of the *hooghan* as a symbol of maturity because it is there that one plans for his or her future.

In her analysis of Navajo chantway myths, Spencer (1957:40, 58–60) observes that the assumption of responsibility for the welfare of the family group and for the larger group are common themes in these myths, which are based on the conditions of Navajo life. The relatively isolated position of the family group imposes the necessity for familial cooperation, with the assumption of personal responsibility on the part of each family member. In chantway myths, indolence and irresponsibility lead to physical disaster, while industry and responsibility bring success.

Only through proper leadership can generational continuity be ensured. The two *náhookǫs* (the big Dipper and Cassiopeia) as leaders serve as a reminder to those on earth that we must provide strong leadership and accept responsibility for both present and future generations.

Finally, the enduring nature of the constellations as well as the image of the *hooghan* they represent is reflected in the songs of Talking God[6] from Blessingway:

> *'e ne ya* . . . the same [hogan] will continue, the same will continue,
>   on its surface it passes by.
> Exactly on Earth's surface it passes by,
> On its surface vegetation passes by, on its surface fabrics of all kinds
>   pass by,
> Chief long life, chief happiness, old age one says continues to pass by
>   on its surface, the same will continue, *ni yo o.*
>
>                                                    (Wyman 1970:120).

Talking God is saying that the inhabitants of the earth's surface pass on, and even the timbers of this particular *hooghan* may decay and collapse with age, but the concept of the *hooghan* continues on.

To symbolize that the *hooghan* type and its songs (in Blessingway) will continue on indefinitely, two stone slabs which are imbedded in the ground next to the eastern poles (which frame the East-facing doorway) are "set for" the *hooghan*. This means that wherever they are found, these stone slabs indicate that the mandate contained in Blessingway songs to continue the *hooghan* type of dwelling has been followed (Wyman 1970:14).

Just as the stone slabs symbolize the continuation of the *hooghan* and, thus, of the Navajo way of life, the daily occurrence of the dawn as the sun returns symbolizes the continuation of time and of life itself. Dawn (associated with the white and the east) is one of the four cardinal light phenomena, along with the blue of day–sky (associated with the South), the yellow of evening twilight (West), and the black of darkness (North). Each of these four light phenomena serves as a guide to people's movements and activities (Griffin-Pierce 1988). Dawn causes people to awaken: "he (or she) who has walked in it [the dawn] will enjoy every possession," says chanter Frank Mitchell (in Wyman 1970:370). Thus, by rising early, by "walking in the dawn," one is assured of abundance. Prayers and offerings at dawn outside the East-facing doorway of the *hooghan* ensure this prosperity.

The Milky Way (*yikáísdáhí*) symbolizes the white corn meal sprinkled by First Woman as she said her morning prayers (Chanter C). Ceremonials and with the dawn prayers as the sun rises; by visualizing the Milky Way as the corn meal used in these prayers, *yikáísdáhí* serves as a visual reminder to pray to the dawn as a life-giving source.

Prayers and offerings are of particular importance in showing respect and appreciation to the *diyin dine'é*. Harry Walters, director of the Ned Hatathli Museum at Navajo Community College, Tsaile, explains:

> If you see something out of the ordinary, it is a warning to remind you to restore the balance, to act like a Holy Person [*diyin dine'é*], to show respect to the mountains, animals, and people [including yourself]. Every chance we get we should acknowledge our gifts from the Holy People. If we forget the Holy People [including the Stars and Constellations] remind us. This is what it means when you see a Holy Person. You show respect and acknowledge their gifts to us by leaving offerings.

Chanter A explained that the purpose of the stars is to help the Earth Surface People to live the right way: "Before the Twins [the Sacred Twins who slew the Monsters which once inhabited the earth] and the Monsters were created, the *diyin dine'é* said, 'Someday there will be all kinds of misfortune in the world. We are creating the Stars to help the Earth Surface People to find their way, so that they can regain their faith and reestablish their balance and their direction.'"

Blessingway is designed to maintain and reinforce *hózhǫ́*. An important aspect of achieving and maintaining this ideal, valued state is to view life with the proper, reverent frame of mind. Reichard (1944, 1950) and Witherspoon (1977) have demonstrated how powerful thought is in Navajo culture. To think something is to cause it to be. Witherspoon (1977) explicates *sǫ'ah naaghái* as thought and *bik'eh hózhǫ́* as speech to show how intimately related these two processes are considered to be: speech is the outer form of thought, and thought is the inner form of speech. An unbreakable bond exists between thought and action, speech and event.

In Fig. 7.3 we see another example of the Navajo emphasis on concentration and clear thought processes. The reason Spider Woman taught the Navajo to make figures in string is to help the Navajo learn how to

**Figure 7.3.** Navajo woman making a string figure of *dilyéhé* (the Pleiades). (Line drawing after an original serigraph by the author.)

concentrate. "You learn to think when you make these," a Navajo girl told folklorist Barre Toelken (1979:95). The girl's father elaborated on the link between clear thought and living a good life, as well as on the link between the string figures and celestial constellations.

> It's too easy to become sick, because there are always things happening to confuse our minds. We need to have ways of thinking, of keeping things stable, healthy, beautiful. We try for a long life, but lots of things can happen to us. So we keep our thinking in order by these figures and we keep our lives in order with the stories. We have to relate our lives to the stars and the sun, the animals, and to all of nature or else we will go crazy, or get sick (Toelken 1979:96).

The depiction of the Pleiades (*dilyéhé*) in string represents the importance of clear, unclouded thought in order to receive the guidance necessary to "keep things stable and beautiful" so that one can live a long life. Only when one learns how to concentrate, how to use one's mind in proper ways, does one grow to understand and to respect the place and function of all living things in the universe. It is through this understanding of the interrelatedness of all things and through adherence to proper values that one contributes to the order of the universe.

As a cultural map, sandpaintings order and make sense of the natural–supernatural world around us. The patient, ill in spirit as well as in body, cannot help but respond to ceremonial efforts to reestablish order, efforts that occur at several levels of meaning.

First, there is the powerful image upon which the patient sits, the depiction of the *diyin dine'é,* drawn at the direction of a respected and trusted chanter. The chanter has guided the production of a ritually correct sandpainting. This sandpainting, which has previously healed many with similar illnesses, orders both the natural and supernatural worlds by correctly depicting particular images. The patient is aware that this sandpainting has been selected from the many sandpainting images known by the chanter because it is particularly suited for treating the patient's illness. The order reflected in the painting's visual representation of the world assists in reestablishing order in the patient's inner world of thought and feeling.

Just as all sandpaintings order the natural–supernatural world, sandpaintings of the heavens order a particular part of that world by emphasizing those constellations with particular significance for the Navajo. By filtering out constellations that are less culturally significant from the seemingly infinite number of stars strewn across the celestial sphere, the sandpainting depictions of constellations help the knowledgeable individual to focus on a select set of celestial entities.

These particular constellations evoke allegorical stories that help the Earth Surface People to live in the right way. Thus, depictions of constellations serve as mnemonic devices through which to remember moral stories. These visual and verbal images not only tell us what the Navajos find significant about the sky but also how the Navajos conceive of themselves and the right way to conduct their lives.

The visual depiction of constellations in sandpaintings transmits and reiterates the Navajo emphasis on order, balance, circularity, and reciprocity. Not only does the ceremonial itself work actively to restore this universal balance and order, but constellation depictions and the allegorical stories they evoke also remind the individual at a deeper level of how interrelated and interdependent his thoughts and feelings are with those of the rest of the universe.

The Navajo *hooghan* embodies the concept of *hózhǫ́* not only in its planning but also in the sequence of creation begun within its walls. The two *náhookǫs* (Cassiopeia and the Big Dipper), the constellations which symbolize the *hooghan*, are created in sandpaintings on the *hooghan* floor in a ceremonial context and demonstrate the interrelatedness of the universe as their depiction plays its role in the restoration of universal balance and order.

ACKNOWLEDGEMENTS

I appreciate the patient and kind assistance of Harry Walters, director of the Ned Hatathli Museum at Navajo Community College in Tsaile, Arizona, as well as other Navajo consultants who must remain anonymous. I also appreciate the assistance of Rain Parrish, Dr. Edson Way, and Steve Rogers, formerly at the Wheelwright Museum of the American Indian, Santa Fe, who made possible photography and documentation of five hundred sandpaintings at this museum. My thanks also go to Dorothy House, librarian at the Museum of Northern Arizona, and to Jan Bell, curator at the Arizona State Museum, who provided similar assistance at their institutions. I also appreciate the suggestions of Ray Williamson and Claire Farrer. I would also like to express my appreciation to Chanter A for allowing me to use his drawings as the basis for my drawings in Fig. 7.1 and 7.2. Figure 7.3 is my own original line drawing.

# Notes

1. Most Navajo ceremonials are used to treat the actual or anticipated illness of a patient or patients. Sandpaintings—which, more accurately, should be called "drypaintings" because they are made of sand *and* other materials —are also used when the ceremonial is not concerned specifically with curing. Even when the primary intent is not healing, there is usually a "patient," or "one-sung-over."

This chapter deals with sacred sandpaintings, which are created and destroyed in a ritual context. These are not to be confused with commercial sandpaintings—permanent paintings of pulverized dry materials which are glued onto a sand-covered wood backing— which are secular objects made by Navajo laymen for sale. For a discussion of commercial sandpaintings, see Parezo (1983).

Fieldwork for this chapter was conducted in the Tsaile and Pinon, Arizona, areas in spring 1984, spring and summer 1985, and winter 1985–86.

2. There are actually five poles because the two eastern poles which stand on either side of the entrance are known collectively as the East pole, so that one pole at each cardinal point may be mentioned in the songs. The intercardinal points are not significant to Navajo cosmology, in contrast to Pueblo belief and practice.

3. The concept of cyclical time is not exclusively Native American but is characteristic of many cultures which emphasize the spiritual over the technological. The annual celebration of Christmas and Easter, as well as the concept of the calendar itself, are inherited from a tradition with this kind of cyclical orientation. However, in modern Western culture, the pervasive concept of time tends to be linear and "progress" oriented. In the modern Western conceptualization of time, the past can be celebrated and commemorated but it cannot be reentered in any other than a purely symbolic manner. (See Eliade [1954] for a discussion of conceptions of time in the ancient cultures of Asia, Europe, and America.)

4. I have omitted the names of the Navajo individuals with whom I worked because Navajo opinions about sharing information about sandpaintings and astronomy vary considerably. Thus, I feel it is important to maintain the privacy of those with whom I worked. Although chanters agree on the identification of the major Navajo constellations, no two chanters depict the constellations in an identical manner.

5. This song reflects the extent to which the Navajo emphasize directional concepts related to the construction of the *hooghan* described earlier in this chapter. The "back corners," or rear base corner below the West pole of the *hooghan*, are first mentioned; then the "rear center," or the inner center between the fireplace and the West pole; then the "fireside," which is directly beneath the interlocked point of the *hooghan* poles; then the "side corners," which are on either side of the doorway (which always faces East): and, finally, the exit trail out the "doorway."

6. Talking God, generally addressed as "maternal grandfather" and known as the grandfather of the gods, is one of the great gods. He acts as a mentor, often supplying mythical characters with the solutions to questions put to them by other *diyin dine'é*. Reichard (1950:476) refers to Talking God as "the only god I have found with a sense of compassion."

# References

Aberle, David F. 1961. The Navajo. In *Matrilineal Kinship,* ed. David Schneider and Kathleen Gough, 96–201. Berkeley and Los Angeles: University of California Press.

Albert, Ethel M. 1956. The Classification of Values: A Method and Illustration. *American Anthropologist* 58:221–48.

Basso, Keith H. 1983. "Stalking with Stories": Names, Places, and Moral Narratives among the Western Apache. In *Text, Play, and Story: The Construction and Reconstruction of Self and Society,* ed. E. Bruner, 19–55. Washington, D.C.: American Ethnological Society.

Brown, Joseph E. 1989. *The Spiritual Legacy of the American Indian.* New York: Crossroad Publishing Company.

Eliade, Mircea. 1954. The Myth of the Eternal Return. New York: Pantheon Books.

Farella, John R. 1984. *The Main Stalk: A Synthesis of Navajo Philosophy*. Tucson: University of Arizona Press.

Frisbie, Charlotte J. 1980. Ritual Drama in the Navajo House Blessing Ceremony. In *Southwestern Indian Ritual Drama*, ed. Charlotte Frisbie, 161–98. Albuquerque: University of New Mexico Press.

Frisbie, Charlotte J., and David P. McAllester, eds. 1978. *Navajo Blessingway Singer, The Autobiography of Frank Mitchell, 1881–1967*. Tucson: University of Arizona Press.

Griffin-Pierce, Trudy. 1986. Ethnoastronomy in Navajo Sandpaintings of the Heavens. *Archaeoastronomy* 9:62–69.

————. 1988. Cosmological Order as a Model for Navajo Philosophy. Paper presented at the American Anthropological Meeting, Phoenix, Arizona, November 1988.

Haile, Father Berard. 1947. *Starlore among the Navaho*. Santa Fe: Museum of Navajo Ceremonial Art.

Lamphere, Louise. 1977. *To Run after Them*. Tucson: University of Arizona Press.

McAllester, David P., and Susan McAllester. 1980. *Hogans: Navajo Houses and House Songs*. Middletown, Conn.: Wesleyan University Press.

Newcomb, Franc Johnson. 1966. *Navaho Neighbors*. Norman: University of Oklahoma Press.

————. 1967. *Navaho Folk Tales*. Santa Fe: Museum of Navajo Ceremonial Art. Reprint. Albuquerque: University of new Mexico Press, 1990.

————. 1980. [1964] *Hosteen Klah: Navaho Medicine Man and Sand Painter*. Norman: University of Oklahoma Press.

Parezo, Nancy J. 1983. *Navajo Sandpaintings: From Religious Act to Commercial Art*. Tucson: University of Arizona Press.

Pinxten, Rik, Ingrid van Dooren, and Frank Harvey. 1983. *The Anthropology of Space: Explorations into the Natural Philosophy and Semantics of the Navajo*. Philadelphia: University of Pennsylvania Press.

Reichard, Gladys A. 1944. Prayer: The Compulsive Word. *Monographs of the American Ethnological Society*. no. 7. New York: J. J. Augustin.

————. 1950. *Navajo Religion: A Study of Symbolism*. Princeton, N.J.: Princeton University Press.

Roessel, Ruth. 1981. *Women in Navajo Society*. Rough Rock, Ariz.: Navajo Resource Center, Rough Rock Demonstration School.

Spencer, Katherine. 1957. Mythology and Values: An Analysis of Navaho Chantway Myths. *Memoirs of the American Folklore Society*, vol. 48. Philadelphia.

Toelken, Barre. 1979. *The Dynamics of Folklore*. Boston: Houghton Mifflin.

Witherspoon, Gary J. 1970. A New Look at Navajo Social Organization. *American Anthropologist* 72:55–65.

————. 1977. *Language and Art in the Navajo Universe*. Ann Arbor: University of Michigan Press.

Wyman, Leland C. 1952. The Sandpaintings of the Kayenta Navaho. *University of New Mexico Publications in Anthropology*. vol. 7. Albuquerque: University of New Mexico Press.

————. 1970. *Blessingway*. Tucson: University of Arizona Press.

————. 1983. *Southwest Indian Drypainting*. Albuquerque: University of New Mexico Press.

Wyman, Leland C., and Clyde Kluckhohn. 1938. Navaho Classification of Their Song Ceremonials, *Memoirs of the American Anthropological Association*, no. 50. Menasha, Wisc.

# 8

■■■■■■■■■

## Saguaro Wine, Ground Figures, and Power Mountains: Investigations at Sears Point, Arizona

■■■■■■■■■

### TOM HOSKINSON

*A mathematician with the Aerospace Corporation, Tom Hoskinson is the author of numerous papers about rock art and Native American astronomy, and co-editor of a major book on California ethno- and archaeoastronomy. This chapter illustrates the impossibility of separating ethnoastronomy from archaeoastronomy and provides part of our rationale for stating that ethnoastronomy is the blue portion of archaeoastronomy. Hoskinson utilizes the ethnographic record, the built environment, and knowledge of astronomy to unravel enigmatic designs on the desert floor.*

Sears Point (AZ:Y:3:1) is a prehistoric–historic archaeological site that occupies two small volcanic mesas and their associated drainages on the south bank of the Gila River in southwestern Arizona. The mesas are actually eroded portions of the Gila Plateau, which rises about twenty-one to twenty-five meters above the Gila floodplain. The mesas and their associated terraces are covered, in part, with desert pavement and with dense basaltic ejecta from nearby volcanic cinder cones. The desert pavement is a mosaic, a single stone thick, which lies on a clay stratum. The clay stratum is saline and sterile from accumulated evaporite deposits. Pavements of this type are very stable, and the stones which comprise them are covered with desert varnish, the usually glossy, dark brown to black surface deposit found on desert pavement or on other desert stones. Desert varnish only covers those portions of rock exposed to air. It is composed mostly of manganese and iron salts.

In the floodplain, which starts at the eastern base of the Sears Point Mesa, there is a large area that shows evidence of food gathering use over a long period of time. I believe that this area was a seasonal mesquite gathering and processing campsite.[1]

Historically, Indians from two different language families, Hokan and Uto-Aztecan, have been continuously present at this site. The Hokan language family members are the Yuman speakers. The Uto-Aztecans are the Piman speakers and the Ute speakers. A large historic–prehistoric village site is located on the north bank of the Gila River immediately across from AZ:Y:3:1. This village, called *Xakupi'nc* ("hot water") in the Kaveltkadom (Hokan/Yuman) language and Agua Caliente in Spanish, was occupied primarily by Yuman speakers who are believed to have belonged to the Kaveltkadom band of the Halchidhoma, (Spier 1978:1–47; Ezell 1963; Sedelmayr 1750), together with several Piman speaking families (Sedelmayr 1750). According to Garcés (in Spier 1978:33), in 1775 there were two hundred people living there. Agua Caliente was probably occupied for some time prior to the first recorded Hispanic contact on the Lower Colorado River in the sixteenth century; occupation continued into the early nineteenth century (Sedelmeyer 1750; Spier 1978; Ezell 1963). The Kaveltkadom are closely related to the Maricopa (Hokan/Yuman), and members of both tribal groups still live along the Gila River today. In addition, the Yuman-speaking Colorado River Indians are closely related to the Kaveltkadom and traditionally used the southwestern Gila River area (Cocopa, Quechan, Mohave, and so forth) as did the Yuman-speaking Kumeyaay (Diegueno) further to the west, and the Yavapai to the north. Several groups of Uto-Aztecan Piman speakers still live along the Gila River; the closest is the Gila Bend Tohono O'odham (Papago). In addition, the Uto-Aztecan–speaking Chemehuevi (Ute), who live along the Colorado River near Parker, traditionally used the southwestern Gila River area, according to tribal elders (Laird 1984).

Currently, Sears Point is visited by Tohono O'odham people from the Gila Bend and Sells areas, and by Quechan, Cocopa, Mohave, Chemehuevi, and other Colorado River people. Sears Point is regarded by these people as a sacred site.

The Sears Point site contains substantial lithic archaeological evidence that indicates that the site was used by Paleoindians (10,000–14,000 B.P.). In addition, a variety of prehistoric cultures, including the Desert Archaic (2000–9000 B.P., lithics, petroglyphs), Patayan (proto Yuman), and Hohokam (2000–600 B.P., lithics, ceramics, ornaments, petroglyphs), are believed to have utilized the site area. During the late prehistoric and post contact era, from about A.D. 1500 through the early 1800s, it appears that AZ:Y:3:1 was utilized primarily by Yuman and Piman Indians.

At the Sears Point site, there are about two thousand petroglyphs and perhaps fifty ground figures. Most of the ground figures in the Bureau of

Land Management's (BLM's) Sears Point Archaeological District (SPAD) are meanders and geometric designs created by rock alignments; several designs were formed by material removal, and others are lines formed of depressed stones that were apparently "walked" into the surface. Two of the ground figures form solstitial alignments involving a common far horizon terminal point, Granary Basket Mountain, which was recognized as a sacred mountain by the Yuman tribes of the Gila river and others (Spier 1978:23, 169–70, 252–54).

In this chapter, I explore the two solstitial ground figures mentioned above in the context of Piman and Yuman ethnographic traditions. My working hypothesis is that one, and probably both, of the figures was ceremonially and symbolically connected to the saguaro wine ceremonies held by both Yuman and Piman speakers at the June solstice. For the Pimans, the new year traditionally was celebrated during the saguaro harvest at the summer solstice (Saxton, Saxton and Enos 1983:120). For the Yumans, the saguaro harvest and the summer solstice had no connection with the new year; instead, it marked the time to celebrate war (Spier 1978:56–58, 146, 162–63, 269).

Saguaro fruit and seeds were a very important food resource to the desert dwellers of the Southwest (Curtin 1984; Nabhan 1982; Russell 1980; Spier 1978). The cactus fruit was gathered with a "saguaro hook" or "pitahaya pole" made from a saguaro cactus rib with a hook fixed to it (Russell 1980:103). Both the Yuman speakers and the Piman speakers along the Gila River celebrated the June solstice with a saguaro wine festival. Native American songs, speeches, and stories, as well as accounts of Spanish explorers, provide descriptions of the saguaro harvests and ceremonials.

Garcés (in Russell 1980:71), in the late eighteenth century, briefly described a saguaro wine festival held by the Pimas Gileños; and Venegas (also in Russell 1980:71), writing in 1759, provided a similar account for Indians of the California Peninsula.

Saguaro (and pitahaya) fruit gathering, wine making, and ceremonials appear to have been common to the entire region of northern Mexico, southern California, and southwestern Arizona. However, considerable cultural differences in ceremonial practices existed between the Yuman speakers and the Piman speakers. According to Spier's Halchidhoma consultants, the wine song *xatca'* was sung only in mid-June: "The Halchidhoma were the first to sing it, the Pima got it from them, and the Maricopa from the Pima" (Spier 1978:269). Curtin's Pima (Akimel 'O'odham) consultants stated that "the preparation and drinking of an intoxicating beverage (*ha-ashan navait*) made from saguaro is a religious ceremony of the Papago which, a Pima informant said, they would refuse to describe" (Curtin 1984:54). The Kaveltkadom saguaro harvest was heralded in mid-June by the early morning appearance of the Pleiades[2] (*xitca'*) on the eastern horizon (Spier 1978:146), when saguaro fruit was gathered and fermented into wine (*xatca'*). Then a ceremonial dance was held. Members of other tribes were invited to participate, but, by custom, they came in small groups, camping well away from the village. The song for this celebration was *xatca'*, sung at no other time. The song spoke about the saguaro wine, its bloodlike appearance and how it is made. It stated that their enemy had come to drink with them. They had fought, now they would drink together. The normal result of this ceremony was the decision to go on a raid, usually against the Yavapai. "When they were drunk they thought of war" (Spier 1978:58). In contrast to the Piman speakers, the Kaveltkadom saguaro wine ceremony did not mark the beginning of the new year (Spier 1978:56–58, 142–44, 146, 162–63, 269).

War was a fundamental component of the Yuman cultures, which, in general, held the belief that war was a source of spiritual power. The Kaveltkadom maintained that war was forced on them by the raids of the Quechuan and Yavapai. However, they took pleasure in planning war and brought up their sons to look forward to it. Spier relates that when war was contemplated, a shaman would invoke the spirits of the various tribal-power mountains to enlist their aid in the coming battle. When Yuman tribes faced each other in battle, it was common practice to draw a line on the ground. This line was thought of as a mountain, or line of mountains, magically raised to give protection (Spier 1978:160–70).

The Pima saguaro wine ceremonial heralds the beginning of the new year. As with the Kaveltkadom, the morning appearance of the Pleiades on the eastern horizon marked the beginning of the saguaro harvest. The Middle Run Song (Russell 1980:283–84) provides a beautiful metaphorical description of the sky at the time of the saguaro wine ceremonial.

Singing to the [*Makai* houses] in supplication;
Singing to the [*Makai* house] in supplication;
Thus my [shining] power is uplifted.
My [shining] power is uplifted as I sing.

Prostitutes hither running come;
Prostitutes hither running come,
[From the east direction.]

Holding blue flowers as they run.
Talking in whispers as they file along.

Along the crooked trail I'm going,
   Along the crooked trail going west.
To the land of rainbows I'm going,
   Swinging my arms as I journey on.

The bright dawn appears in the heavens;
   The bright dawn appears in the heavens,
And the paling Pleiades grow dim.
   The Moon is lost in the rising Sun.

With the women bluebird came running;
   With the women Bluebird came running;
All came carrying clouds on their heads,
   And these were seen shaking as they danced.

See there the Gray Spider Magician;
   See there the Gray Spider Magician
Who ties the Sun while the Moon rolls on.
   Turn back, the green staff rising higher.

In the preceding, I have substituted the material in brackets from José Lewis Brennan's (Russell's native Papago ethnologist) original translation of this song. Russell used "the gods" where I used "*Makai* houses" and Brennan used *Makai kik*(i), Magician houses. Russell used "magic" where I have used Brennan's "shining." I also added the phrase "From the east direction" from Brennan's translation.

The Makai houses are located at the four solstitial points and several other points along the Sun's path on the horizon. Earth Doctor and I'itoi are the most powerful supernaturals in Piman religious tradition, and both have houses at the eastern horizon. In addition, other Piman supernaturals such as Sinking *Makai,* Lightning, Thunder, Wind and Foam also have houses on the eastern horizon (Russell 1980:251). The songs sung at saguaro wine ceremonials prayerfully entreat Rain and his companions to return from the east and revitalize the Earth.

The song is dominated by celestial symbolism and metaphors. The prostitutes, or "running women," are a Pima metaphor for the Pleiades (Russell 1980:283–84; Saxon and Saxon 1978:9, 24; Saxton, Saxton and Enos 1983:97–98). I believe that the "crooked (*jujul*) trail going west" is a metaphor for the Milky Way in its aspect as the trail to the land of the dead. The Piman word *jujul* also means "zigzag"; in one of the Rain Songs it is used to describe the behavior of lightning: "lightning moving very zig-zag, roaring beautifully . . ." (Saxton and Saxton 1978: 335). Perhaps "crooked trail" is also a metaphor for lightning trail. The shaman's ladder to the sky is also known as the zigzag ladder (Russell 1980: 339).

I believe that the "land of rainbows" alludes to the land of the dead (Saxton and Saxton 1978: 9, 24), the Datura-induced trance state, and the mythic Rainhouse (*wa'aki*) at the far eastern horizon. Rainhouses are the source of fertility and renewal (Saxton and Saxton 1978: 335 – 40).

"The moon is lost in the rising sun" only at the time of the new moon. New moon occurs at the June solstice (plus or minus one day) only about one year out of eight (Fig. 8.1 – 8.4). For the Pimans, the lunar and solar cycles were primary components of the calendar system. Months are determined by lunar cycles (Mashath) which begin with the new moon. Years and cycles of years (Ahithag) are defined by the Sun. The new solar year begins at the June solstice (Underhill et al. 1979: 17 – 19; Saxton, Saxton and Enos 1983: 119 – 121).

"With the women, Bluebird came running." The women are the Pleiades, and Bluebird is, with high probability, the planet Venus in apparition as Morning Star (Russell 1980: 245 – 46, 284, 303, 334, 367; Ayer 1988: 5). The Pimans, the Paiutes, and others considered Bluebird to be a powerful supernatural who transformed his appearance, position, and sex by "bathing" for four days in the center of the sky. Thus, it is implied that in one of his aspects, Bluebird is a celestial object, probably a planet exhibiting retrograde motion. The Pima song indicates that Bluebird came running from the eastern horizon with the Pleiades. In June, in Papago country the mountain bluebird males are in their beautiful turquoise mating plumage and singing their mating songs. Mountain bluebirds, unlike their congeners, hover while feeding. During June, the bluebirds feed on saguaro cactus fruit (and sometimes become intoxicated). According to one of my papago consultants, "running" is a multiple entendre in the context of the June solstice and the Saguaro Wine Ceremonials. In this context, "running" means (a) running, coming along with; (b) defecating (due to the wine's purgative nature); (c) singing the puberty songs; (d) dancing to the puberty songs; and (e) whoring. Bluebird, in order to "run" with the Pleiades, must be a celestial object. The most prominent blue–white celestial object that appears cyclically near the Pleiades at the June solstice is Venus in apparition as Morning Star.

During the time period from A.D. 1950 through A.D. 2001, when Venus appears in the June solstice morning sky, it is within eleven degrees declination and two hours of right ascension from Alcyone (Eta Tau) in the Pleiades. Venus is not always present as Morning Star. However, it is in apparition as Morning Star either three or four years out of every eight (Figs. 8.1–8.4).[3] From my own naked-eye observations at the site between 1981 and 1990, Venus is visible when it rises thirty-five minutes or more in right ascension before the Sun.

Venus returns to approximately the same position in the sky every eight years. Five of Venus's 583.92137-day synodic periods = 2919.60685 days, which is 2.33075 days short of eight 365.24220-day tropical years. A better cycle length is 157 Venus synodic periods = 91675.65509 days, which is only three hours and seventeen minutes less than 251 tropical years. Other, perhaps less useful Venus cycles expressed in tropical years, that are not multiples of 8 or 251, are: 996, 1247, 1498, 1741, and 1749 (Hoskinson 1983).

At the June solstice, when Venus's declination is closest to Alcyone's, the two objects are farthest apart in right ascension. Conversely, when Venus and Alcyone are closest in right ascension, they are farthest apart in declination.

In A.D. 1197, 753 years (three 251-year cycles) earlier than the previous example, when Venus appeared in the June solstice morning sky (Fig. 8.3), it was within nine degrees of declination and two hours of right ascension from Alcyone[4] (Eta Tau) in the Pleiades.

It is important to remember that this song describes a specific set of events that occurred at a specific rather than generic June solstice. The presence of both Bluebird/Venus and the moon in the eastern sky at June solstice sunrise clearly indicates this.

The best short-term cycle for the moon and Venus is 8 tropical years, although some multiples of 251 tropical years also provide good cycles (Figs. 8.1–8.3). There are periods when the new moon and Venus cycles are out of phase (Fig. 8.4). For example, during the ninety-eight-year period between A.D. 893 and A.D. 991 the new moon does not occur at June solstice (plus or minus one day) in years when Venus is in apparition as Morning Star at the June solstice.

Gray Spider Magician "ties the Sun while the Moon rolls on" at solstice. Pima tradition regards the June solstice as a four day event. Sun rises at the same point for four days (at Pima latitudes) and then "turns back" to begin the journey toward his winter house after reaching his summer house at the June solstice.

The "green staff rising higher" refers to the ocotillo cactus (*Fouquiera splendens*) which begins to sprout brilliant green leaves in April and May.

# Day of the June New Moon

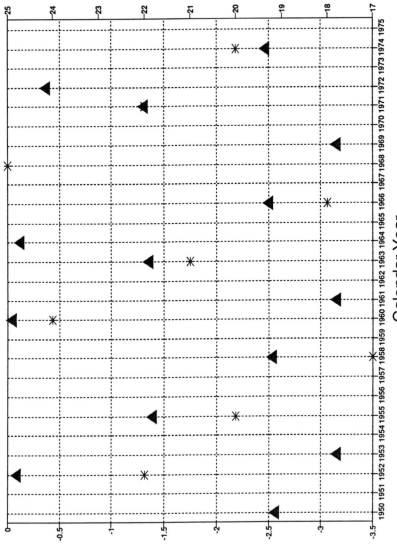

## Venus' Hrs. of Rt. Ascension from Sun

**Figure 8.1.** The June solstice. Venus and the new moon at sunrise (A.D. 1950–1975).

138

## Day of the June New Moon

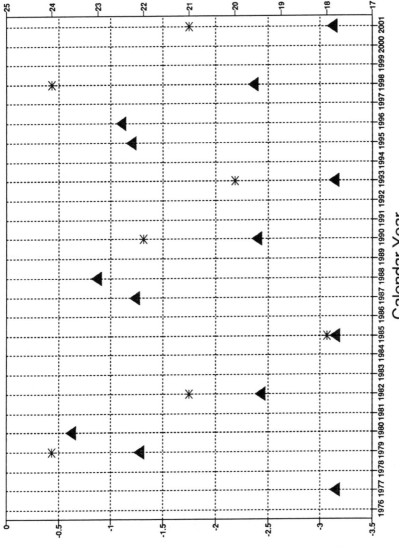

**Figure 8.2.** The June solstice. Venus and the new moon at sunrise (A.D. 1976–2001).

## Day of the June New Moon

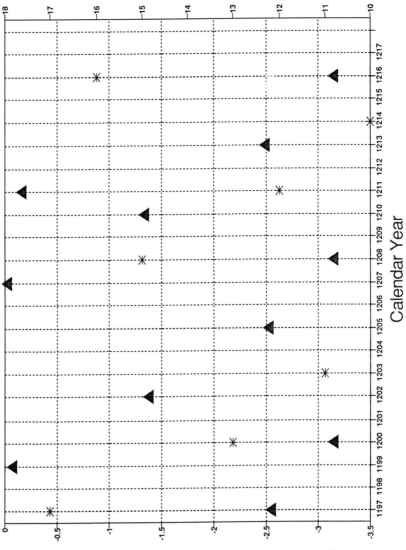

### Venus' Hrs. of Rt. Ascension from Sun

**Figure 8.3.** The June solstice. Venus and the new moon at sunrise (A.D. 1197–1217).

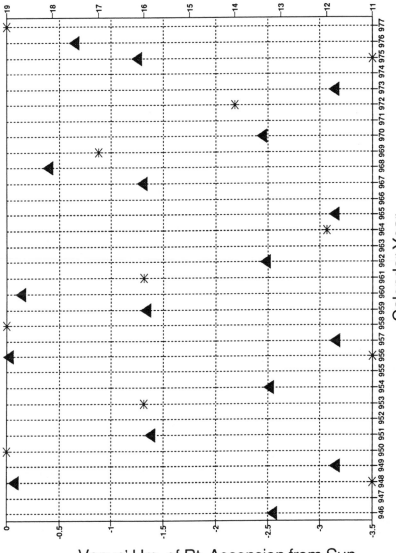

Day of the June New Moon

Venus' Hrs. of Rt. Ascension from Sun

Figure 8.4. The June solstice. Venus and the new moon at sunrise (A.D. 946–977).

141

The green ocotillo is cut by the Pimans and used ceremonially to renew shrines in April and May. Green ocotillo is also an anticipatory metaphor for the June rains and the corn, nourished by the rains which are the ceremonial consequence of a successful *nawait* festival (Underhill et al. 1979: 141−44).

As sunrise approaches during the current epoch on the June solstice, the Pleiades are clearly visible above the eastern horizon, and the Milky Way spans the sky from east to west with the bifurcated portions containing Cygnus and Aquila, respectively, clearly visible in the central western sky. At June solstice sunrise, precession will raise the Pleiades further above the eastern horizon as we look backward in time. All of this makes clear that the June solstice is the one the song refers to.

In the current epoch, at the December solstice sunrise the Pleiades have set and the Milky Way is distributed around the horizon, starting in the southeast, continuing up around the north polar sky, and disappearing in the northwest.

The Piman saguaro wine (*nawait*) ceremony lasts for four days and is performed to ensure rain and the renewal of fertility of the Earth, thus ushering in the new year. According to Papago oral tradition, the beginnings of the *nawait* ceremony are found in creation time, when the people petitioned *I'itoi* to make the mountain now called Baboquivari (rock drawn in the middle) smaller in order to create more room in the valley for fields. At this time, rain was plentiful. In order to shrink the mountain, *I'itoi* created saguaro wine and used it ritually. The shrinking of the mountain so angered Cloud, who lived there, that he left for the far eastern horizon with his sons, Wind and Rain. Now, under normal conditions, rain does not fall, unless Cloud heeds the prayers sent to him at the *nawait* ceremony (Nabhan 1982: 19−20, 26−27, 31−38; Saxton and Saxton 1978: 317−40). In June in Papago−Pima country the rain-bearing clouds always come from the southeast, moving along the imaginary line that connects the December solstice sunrise point with the June solstice sunset point.

The creation of ground figures (geoglyphs, rock alignments, sand paintings, and so forth) in creation time and in contemporary shamanic contexts is ethnographically well supported. DuBois (1901: 181−82) recorded a Diegueno creation story in which *Tuchaipai*, the creator, drew a line on the ground which established the sacred directions *Ynak*, East; *Auk*, West. Then the brother of *Tuchaipai*, *Yokomatis*, drew an intersecting line which established the sacred directions *Yawak*, South; *Katulk*, North.

A Piman basket design called *I'itoi Ki* (The House of *I'itoi*) incorporates the cardinal, intercardinal, and solstitial directions plus the center and the nadir into a mazelike motif (Fig. 8.5). Direction of movement is also

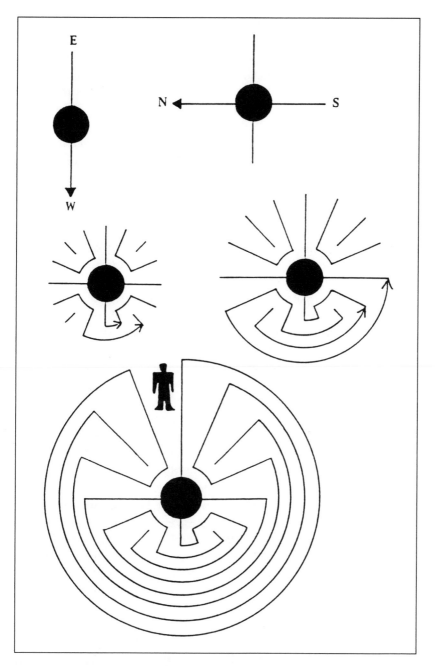

**Figure 8.5.** *I'itoi Ki,* the House of *I'itoi* (Elder Brother). (Tom Hoskinson, after Saxton and Saxton).

specified, counterclockwise, East to West and South to North. Baboquivari Peak is identified as the "center of the basket" (Saxton and Saxton 1978:371–73). This design motif is also incorporated into a ground figure that I am investigating, which is located on the Tohono O'odham Reservation in southern Arizona. The ground figure is contiguous with, and appears to be contemporaneous with, a Sells Phase (about A.D. 1220–1450) Hohokam occupation site.

Spier (1978:169–70) relates that Maricopa shamans would "raise" a power mountain (the long Sierra Estrella) by drawing a line on the ground. Such a shamanic usage of a power mountain by a powerful shaman would cause an insuperable mountain barrier to be raised along the line. In addition, a shaman might draw a circle on the ground with himself at the center and, in that manner, establish a magical circle of protective mountains. In their Papago and Pima vocabulary, Saxton, Saxton and Enos (1983:32) list the verb *kihchuth:* "building a house for, drawing a line around a patient to hold the healing power of a song."

Spier (1978:335) relates that Piman shamans would use magic to thwart Maricopa racers. "For instance, one of them would secretly sprinkle a reed full of water on the Maricopa racer before the race started 'in order to drown him' so that he could not run. Or they would run ahead of him and draw a line across his path, so that he would imagine it as a deep canyon which he could not cross. One of our men would clear it away by pulling a string across the line as though making a bridge. Both sides did this sort of thing to the other."

Russell (1980:254) describes the Piman sacred place *Haak Vaak,* (*Haak* Lying), which is a ground figure on a mesa situated about five miles north of Sacaton near the Gila River (Fig. 8.6). It was made by scraping aside the small stones with which the mesa is thickly strewn to form furrows about 50 cm. wide. As with most American Indian rock art, this ground figure is from an event that occurred during creation time. The shrine is active, and Piman people make offerings and prayers there today for power and long life. *Haak Vaak* provides a good example of Piman concepts of space and time, which are viewed by the Pimans as concentric, continuous, and simultaneous. If you have enough power and are in the proper place, then past, present, and future time and space are all simultaneously accessible to you. A person visiting the shrine has the potential to communicate directly with *Haak Vaak* and experience the events that led to the shrine's creation. This concept is obviously very different from the current and widely accepted view that space and time are discrete and sequential (Hoskinson 1984a).

**Figure 8.6.** *Ha-ak Va-ak* (*Ha-ak* lying). (Aerial photograph by Harry Casey.)

On the top, near the middle of the northern mesa that forms Sears Point, is a flat desert pavement area about 23 meters by 50 meters (see Figs. 8.7–8.12, beginning on page 150). Dividing the desert pavement area on the mesatop is a northeast/southwest line 23 meters long and about 10 cm. wide. Measurements made of the line with a transit show that it is oriented 61.5/241.5 degrees true azimuth.

The line was formed by removing rocks from the desert pavement, which leaves a light-colored line formed by the clay substrate. On the east, the line terminates at a large, heavily varnished basaltic rock firmly embedded in the clay matrix of the mesatop, anchored by caliche deposits. This rock is about .7 meters long, .5 meters high and .3 meters wide and has been sitting at its current location since the volcano threw it there. At the top of the rock, immediately above the point where the line terminates, is a smooth natural notch reminiscent of the rear sight of a gun (Fig. 8.7). A single petroglyph is pecked shallowly into the east face of the rock (Fig. 8.9). This glyph belongs to the Gila Petroglyph Style of Hohokam rock art (Schaafsma 1980:83–96). I speculate that this glyph may be a representation of a sun impersonator. James McCarthy, a Tohono O'Odham (Papago) man, describes the sun impersonator as "a round ball, red, and about seven feet high. His body was inside and he walked very slowly all around" (McCarthy 1985:17). In Papago, he was called *Ge Tascu Ewuadam,* meaning "Acting Like Sun." He appeared at sunrise with the sun (McCarthy 1985:18).

The west end of the line terminates in a small semicircular group of heavily varnished rocks of volcanic origin about 30 to 40 cm. in diameter, all firmly embedded in the clay and caliche matrix of the mesa. An observer who kneels or sits in the semicircle of rocks and looks down the line, through the "rear sight" toward the east (Figs. 8.7 and 8.10), will see a matching notch formed by the merger of Oatman Mountain (about 14 km. distant) and more distant mountains north of Painted Rock[5] (about 44 km. distant). The horizon elevation is about .15 degrees. In the current epoch, at sunrise on the June solstice a small sliver from the northern edge of the sun's disc appears, filling the notch spectacularly (Fig. 8.10). The sun slides up the notch, then the full disc begins to emerge on the top of the mountain. At solstice plus or minus four days the sun no longer appears in the notch, but rises on the top of the mountain. The horizon to the immediate south of the solstice rise point is "sawtoothed" and would lend itself to anticipatory observations.

The bearing of the line is 61.5 degrees true azimuth. The horizon elevation is about .15 degrees and the latitude of the line is 32.9 degrees north. Based on the bearing of the line and the Hohokam style of the associated petroglyph, I feel this alignment may be fifteen hundred years old and possibly older. The change in the sun's declination fifteen hundred years ago was calculated by the method of Bretagnon and Simon (1986) to be .188 degrees from the present value. Fifteen hundred years ago the June solstice sun rose .23 degrees north of where it rises today. Thus, fifteen hundred years ago, at first gleam of the June-solstice sunrise, the sun would rise with the center of the solar disc in the notch rather than the northern ⅛ of the disk that is observed now, in the current epoch (Fig. 8.10).

An observer kneeling behind the "rear sight" at the east end of the solstice line and looking down the line toward the southwest will see a matching notch in the next mesatop about two hundred meters away (Figs. 8.9 and 8.11). Investigation of this "notch" revealed no signs of human intervention or manipulation. Centered in this notch is the distinctive mountain peak (42 km. distant) called Granary Basket Mountain (see Figs. 8.9 and 8.11). This mountain was sacred to the Kaveltkadom and other Yuman people. As such, it was a important source of shamanistic dream power and knowledge.[6] It also marked the boundary between the territory of the Quechuan (often called Yumas) and the Kaveltkadom. It was believed that this mountain, if addressed with the proper shamanistic ceremonies, would ally itself with another power mountain and magically intervene during a war on behalf of the shaman's tribe (Spier 1978:23, 169–70, 247, 252–54).

Granary baskets (*cåkwi'n* in Kaveltkadom) were constructed by all tribal groups inhabiting the lower Colorado and the Gila river regions. These "granary baskets" or granaries were actually not baskets, but thick-walled, coiled, and woven cylinders that were either set into the ground or built upon a raised platform. A roof was then constructed over the top. They were three to five feet in diameter and three to four feet high. They lasted for years. Structures practically identical in shape, construction, and name were built for a girl's puberty rite, for menstrual and childbirth lodges, and for warriors undergoing ritual purification. The openings (doorways) to these ritual structures always faced toward the east (Spier 1978:90, 91).

At sunset on the December solstice, to an observer looking down the solstice line, the sun appears to touch down on the peak of Granary Basket Mountain (Figs. 8.9 and 8.11). It then slides down the north slope of the mountain and disappears into the northern part of the notch. The horizon elevation at the sun's set point is about .15 degrees. At solstice plus or minus five days, the sun sets north of the "notch." The horizon immediately north of the solstice set point is "sawtoothed" and would lend itself to anticipatory observations.

Figure 8.12 shows an aerial view of the site. The dash-dot line which starts in the upper center of the figure is a trail about 40 cm. wide formed of compressed desert pavement. One branch of the trail starts at the extreme western edge of the Sears Point Mesa. The other branch starts at the extreme northwestern corner of Sears Point. This trail proceeds south, joins the branch coming from the west, continues toward the solstice line (solid line in Fig. 8.12), stops just a few centimeters short of the line, and loops back to the north again for about fifteen meters, at which point it abruptly terminates in a small, randomly scattered group of basaltic rocks. These rocks are of volcanic origin and are heavily varnished, about 20 to 40 cm. in diameter and firmly embedded in the matrix of the mesatop. The two dotted lines that fan out from the terminus point of the solstice alignment are shallow depressions in the desert pavement that are about 6–7 cm. wide and form December solstice sunrise and cardinal east-west alignments (Hoskinson 1984a, 1985, 1986).

Near the middle of a mesa to the west of Sears Point is a flat desert pavement terrace about forty meters by sixty meters. To the east, the terrace extends to the near vertical rocky slope that forms the mesa edge. The mesa top is about seven meters higher than the terrace. To the west, the terrace extends about sixty meters where it drops off into a drainage below. Figure 8.13 shows an aerial view of the alignment and two associated ground figures. All three figures are made of dense basaltic rocks that are heavily covered with desert varnish. All of the rocks are firmly embedded in caliche from the matrix of the desert pavement. Thus, it appears that this complex of alignments is of considerable antiquity—dating at least from the early Desert Archaic period and possibly from the Paleolithic. Geological dating research is in process.

The largest ground figure is "J" or hook shaped with a "barb" just behind and on the outside of the hooked portion. The longest portion is a bit over seven meters long and is made up of twenty-four rocks that vary in diameter from 10 cm. to 20 cm. Nine rocks from 20 cm. to 40 cm. make up the curved portion. The "barb" (three rocks, about 30 cm. in diameter) is a little less than a meter long.

The long part of the ground figure is oriented 240 degrees true azimuth, measured with a Suunto KB14 optical sighting compass. It is aligned with a point on the south slope near the summit of Granary Basket Mountain. The horizon elevation is about .5 degrees. My photographs at sunset on the December solstice show the sun as it touched down on the peak of Granary Basket Mountain, about two solar diameters north of the point indicated by the alignment.

The "barb" of the ground figure is oriented three hundred degrees true azimuth, measured with a Suunto KB14 optical sighting compass. It is aligned with a "notch" on the eastern ridge of the Palomas mountains. The horizon elevation is about 0.1 degrees. I observed and photographed the 1989 June solstice sunset while sighting over the "barb." My photographs show the sun touching down about two solar diameters south of the "notch" indicated by the alignment.

I calculated the number of years (method of Bretagnon and Simon 1986) required to produce the change in obliquity of the ecliptic needed to bring the apparent position of the sun "into line" with these alignments. The sun starts lining up about 6000 years B.P. Six thousand years B.P. is right at the limit that Bretagnon and Simon have established for their period.[7]

To me, and to a Papago tribal elder I have consulted, the alignment shown in Fig. 8.13a strongly suggests a saguaro gathering hook. Circles (Fig. 8.13 b,c), as previously discussed, are traditionally used by Piman and Yuman speakers to either keep power in or out. These circles are about large enough to hold a single person. The proximity of the stone circles to the alignment suggests that they may have played a protective role against the power of wind, thunder, and lightning. Such protection is always an integral part of Pima saguaro wine ceremonials. The apparent antiquity of these ground figures, their alignment to the solstices, and the saguaro hook shape of the alignment, all suggest ceremonial saguaro wine and solstice connections extending at least into the early archaic period.

The ground figure described in Figs. 8.7 through 8.12 is a good fit to Yuman cultural traditions. It is a line drawn on the ground that "connects" three mountains. It halts and turns back the progress of a trail that comes from the direction of the Kaveltkadom west enemy (Quechuan) and the north enemies (Yavapai and Mojave). It may be that it is "renewed" as a protective barrier by the shadows cast down its length at the moment of June-solstice sunrise—the culmination of the Yuman saguaro wine (*xatca'*) ceremonial. As counterpoint, shadows trace the line in the opposite direction at the December solstice sunset—and winter was the preferred time for war.

**Figure 8.7a.** Solstitial linear ground figure, Sears Point, looking east. Arrow indicates horizon "notch" where the June solstice sun rises. (Photograph by Tom Hoskinson.)

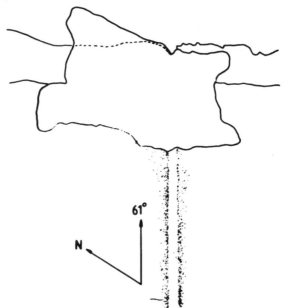

**Figure 8.7b.** Line drawing of solstitial linear ground figure, Sears Point, looking east.

**Figure 8.8.**   Solstitial linear ground figure near sunset, 21 December 1985, Sears Point, looking southeast. The ground figure is most visible in low-angle light and almost disappears when the light is directly overhead. (Photograph by Tom Hoskinson.)

**Figure 8.9a.** Solstitial linear ground figure, Sears Point, looking west. Arrow indicates Granary Basket Mountain, framed in a near-horizon notch. The sun "balances" on this peak at the December solstice sunset. (Photograph by Tom Hoskinson.)

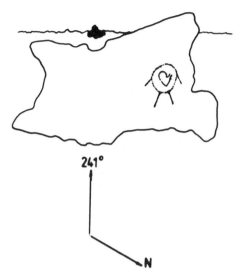

**Figure 8.9b.** Line drawing of solstitial linear ground figure, Sears Point, looking west.

**Figure 8.10.** June solstice sun rising in notch (arrow) at east end of solstitial linear ground figure. Refer to figs. 8.7a, b. (Photograph by Tom Hoskinson.)

**Figure 8.11a.** Near sunset on the December solstice. Looking west down the solstitial linear ground figure at Granary Basket Mountain framed in the near-horizon notch (arrow). (Photograph by Tom Hoskinson.)

**Figure 8.11b.** Approach sunset on the December solstice. The sun is just above the peak of Granary Basket Mountain (arrow). (Photograph by Tom Hoskinson.)

**Figure 8.11c.** Sunset on the December solstice. The sun appears to balance on the peak of Granary Basket Mountain (arrow). (Photograph by Tom Hoskinson.)

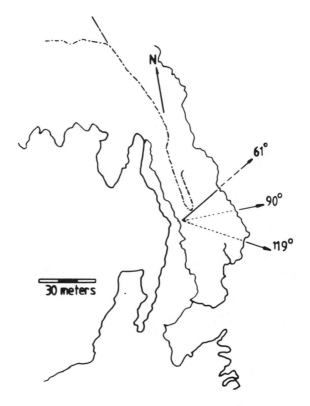

**Figure 8.12a.**  Line drawing of solstitial linear ground figure, Sears Point, aerial view.

**Figure 8.12b.** Aerial infrared photograph of Sears Point Mesa, flying from the east. Photograph shows many of the trails, solstitial linear ground figure (small arrows), and other ground figures. (Photograph by Tom Hoskinson.)

158 / *Tom Hoskinson*

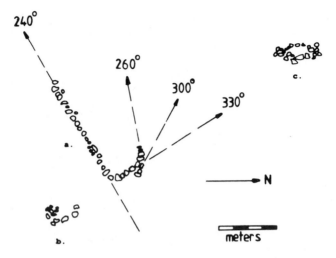

**Figure 8.13.** Line drawing of ground figures, mesa west of Sears Point, aerial view.

## Notes

1. On the rocky slopes of the site are found creosote bush, brittlebush (*Encelia Farinosa*), ocotillo (*Fouquieria Splendens*), saguaro (*Cereus giganteus*), and barrel cactus (*Echinocactus Lecontei*).

The Gila River flood plain which extends to the north and east of AZ:Y:3:1 is covered by a dense velvet mesquite (*Prosopis Velutina*) bosque. Occasional ironwood (*Olneya Tesota*), paloverde (*Cercidium Microphyllum*), willow (*Salix Goodingii Ball*), and the intrusive tamarisk (*Tamerix Pentandra*) are also found in the floodplain. Gourd (*Lagenaria Vulgaris*) vines are present, as are datura (*Datura Meteloides*), squawbush (*Lycium Fremontii*), and mallow (*Sphaeralcea Emoryi Var. Variabilis*). In the marshy places near the river are cattails (*Typha Angustifolla L.*).

The drainages of the SPAD contain velvet mesquite, ironwood, paloverde, jojoba (*Simmondsia Californica*), catclaw (*Acacia Greggii*), and cresote bush (*Larrea Tridentata*).

2. Spier is in error here. Probably quoting a consultant he writes: "They went for cactus fruit in the summer [mid-June] when the Pleiades (*xitca'*) appear on the eastern horizon [in the evening]." The material enclosed in square brackets was presumably added by Spier for clarification. However, in the current epoch, the Pleiades first appear on the eastern horizon in mid-June around 3:30 to 4:00 A.M.

3. The data for Venus and the Sun presented in Figs. 8.1–4 were calculated with a computer program written by the author that uses the methods of Brentagnon and Simon (1986). Right ascension and declination of Venus and the Sun were calculated for the site longitude (113 degrees West) at the sunrise closest to the June solstice. Day of the June new moon was calculated with the tables and algorithms developed by Jan Meeus (1983:4–1 through 4–36).

4. The effects of precession and nutation on declination and right ascension of Alcyone were calculated using algorithms developed by Jan Meeus (1982:63–75).

5. Painted Rock Mountains: This north/south mountain range lies about twenty miles west of Gila Bend, Arizona. It is also called the Sibupue Sierra (Sedelmayr 1750).

6. The Yuman speakers of the Hokan language family of the lower Colorado and Gila rivers attained shamanic states by individual dreams. It was common for dreaming to be induced and/or enhanced through the use of Datura Meteloides (in Spanish, *toloache*). Du Bois (1905:624) reported:

> Old [Diegueno] Indians have told me that after they had drunk the toloache the earth shone with dazzling colors; the commonest objects were transformed into beauty and colored with rainbow hues. They felt for a time possessed with power, wealth, and importance. Not everyone saw an animal in a vision. Those who had this experience were distinguished above the rest. They might become hechiceros or possess powers denied to the ordinary man.

During a shamanic dream, the dreamer invariably first was transported to the summit of his or her tribal power mountain. The tribal power mountain was always the first stop in a shamanic dream; while there, the individual contacted sources of power, which usually took the form of quartz crystals, stars, animals, and other power mountains. Powerful shamans frequently would solicit the aid (or noninterference) of power mountains belonging to other tribal groups. With regard to contests of shamanic power, Kelly (1977:74–76) describes Cocopa and Piman shamanic practices of "putting Monte Mayor" (*wi spa*, a Cocopa power mountain) into an opposing shaman's rattle, thus nullifying his power.

The Piman speakers of the Uto-Aztecan language family also viewed mountains as an important source of shamanic power. However, a Piman dreamer or seeker of shamanic power did not, as a rule, first dream of the tribal power mountain. Mountains were a source of power to the Pima, as were quartz crystals, stars, animals, and the Houses of the Makai. The Houses of the Makai (Magicians) had many aspects. In one instance, they were the solstitial points on Earth's horizon. They were also seen as mountains, stars, and adobe ruins.

7. At 6000 years B.P., Bretagnon and Simon claim that their method is accurate for the position of the sun to within 3.24 arc seconds of geocentric longitude. With naked-eye astronomy, it is very difficult to obtain measurements more accurate than one arc minute (sixty arc seconds). Thus, it appears that the ethnoastronomy investigator can expect to obtain excellent accuracy through use of the Bretagnon/Simon method. The method uses analytical theory to describe the orbital motion of the sun. Polynomials of high degree are used to approximate the orbital motion of the earth from the fixed ecliptic, to approximate precession in longitude and precession in obliquity. These polynomials are apparently the result of curve fitting data obtained from a theoretical model attributed to J. Laskar (Bretagnon, Simon, and Laskar 1986:39–50).

There is no body of empirical observation data available to verify the results obtained from the Bretagnon and Simon model for early dates. Bretagnon and Simon claim that their model yields accurate results out to 6000 B.P., based on comparisons between their model and results obtained from numerical integration.

# References

Ayer, Eleanor H. 1988. *Birds of Arizona, A Guide to Unique Varieties*. Frederick, Colo.: Renaissance House.

Brentagnon, Pierre, J. L. Simon, and J. Laskar. 1986. Presentation of New Solar and Planetary Tables of Interest for Historical Calculations. *Journal for the History of Astronomy* 17. Cambridge, England: University Printing Services.

Brentagnon, Pierre, and Jean-Louis Simon. 1986. Planetary Programs and Tables from −4000 to +2800. Richmond, Va.: Willman-Bell.

Curtin, L. S. M. 1984. By the Prophet of the Earth: Ethnobotany of the Pima. Tucson: University of Arizona Press.

DuBois, Constance Goddard. 1901. The Mythology of the Dieguenos. *Journal of American Folk Lore* 14, no. 54, 13:181–85.

———. 1905. Religious Ceremonies and Myths of the Mission Indians. *American Anthropologist* 7:620–29.

Ezell, Paul. 1963. The Maricopas: An Identification from Documentary Sources. *Anthropological Papers of the University of Arizona*, no. 6.

Hoskinson, Tom. 1983. A Survey of California Indian Astronomy. Paper read at the 1983 Smithsonian Conference. To be published in *Ethnoastronomy Traditions of the World*, vol. I, in press.

———. 1984a. Investigation of a Solstitially Aligned Linear Ground Figure. Paper read at the 1984 ARARA Conference.

———. 1984b. Celestial Traditions and Myths in the Rock Art of Sears Point, Arizona. Paper presented at the Little Rock Conference on Ethnoastronomy.

———. 1985. Transformation Themes in the Rock Art of Sears Point. Paper presented at the Santa Barbara Conference of the American Rock Art Research Association, in press.

———. 1986. Coyotes, Rainbows and Power Mountains. *Rock Art Papers*, vol. 3, ed. Ken Hedges, 91–102. San Diego Museum Papers no. 20, San Diego, Calif.

Kelly, William H. 1977. Cocopa Ethnography. *Anthropological papers of the University of Arizona*, no. 29.

Laird, Carobeth. 1984. *Mirror and Pattern, George Laird's World of Chemehuevi Mythology*. Banning, Calif.: Malki Museum Press.

McCarthy, James. 1985. *A Papago Traveler. The Memories of James McCarthy*. Tucson: University of Arizona Press.

Meeus, Jan. 1982. *Astronomical Formulae for Calculators*, 2d ed. Richmond, Va.: Willmann-Bell.

———. 1983. *Astronomical Tables of the Sun, Moon and Planets*. Richmond, Va.: Willmann-Bell.

Nabhan, Gary Paul. 1982. *The Desert Smells Like Rain, A Naturalist in Papago Indian Country*. San Francisco, Calif.: North Point Press.

Russell, Frank. 1980. *The Pima Indians*. Reprint of the 1908 publication with Introduction, Citation Sources, and Bibliography by Bernard L. Fontana. Tucson, Ariz.: University of Arizona Press.

Saxton, Dean, and Lucille Saxton. 1978. O'othham Hoho'ok A'agitha, Legends and Lore of the Papago and Pima Indians. Tucson: University of Arizona Press.

Saxton, Dean, Lucille Saxton, and Suzie Enos. 1983. *Dictionary: Papago/Pima—*

*English; English—Papago/Pima*, ed. R. L. Cherry. Tucson: University of Arizona Press.

Schaafsma, Polly. 1980. *Indian Rock Art of the Southwest*. School of American Research. Albuquerque: University of New Mexico Press.

Sedelmayr, Jacob. 1750. Entrada a la nación de los yumas gentiles . . . Tubutama [Sonora, Mexico], January 15, 1750. Manuscript in Arizona Pioneers Historical Society, Tucson.

Spier, Leslie. 1978. *Yuman Tribes of the Gila River*. Unabridged reprint. New York: Dover. Originally published in 1933, by University of Chicago Press.

Underhill, Ruth M., Donald M. Bahr, Baptisto López, José Pancho, and David López. 1979. Rainhouse and Ocean, Speeches for the Papago Year. *American Tribal Religions*. vol. 4, ed. Karl W. Luckert. Flagstaff: Museum of Northern Arizona Press.

# 9

■■■■■■■■■

# *Menil (Moon):*
# *Symbolic Representation of Cahuilla Woman*

■■■■■■■■■

## LOWELL JOHN BEAN

*Lowell Bean is a professor of anthropology at California State University, Hayward, and the author or editor of several books about California Native Americans. He is also one of the founders of Bellena Press. Here, Bean uses his substantial knowledge of Cahuilla folklore and ritual to examine the role of Moon in Cahuilla culture. It illustrates the importance of seeking out and relating astronomical knowledge to ritual behavior.*

Cahuilla cosmology is not completely understood, nor can it ever be, since no one studied it at a time when Cahuilla experts were available for consultation. Much knowledge was lost a century ago when the need for astronomical prediction and the value of and ways of transmitting esoteric knowledge disappeared as the result of forced acculturation in the nineteenth century. Fortunately, some knowledge is retained in the minds of Cahuilla elders today, which, combined with other knowledge recorded by anthropologists working with the Cahuilla in earlier years, provides us with some of the basic outlines of Cahuilla astronomy.

A review of Cahuilla ethnoastronomical data, existing in published and archival sources and acquired from ethnographic interviews in recent years, reveals a level of astronomical knowledge once thought to have been associated with what are agricultural peoples. Actually, the Cahuilla and many of their California Indian neighbors are better described as a proto-agricultural society (Bean and Lawton 1973: v–xlvii).

We are indebted to several authors for our understanding of Cahuilla culture. These include Lucile Hooper, who collected data among the Cahuilla of Palm Springs and the Coachella Valley in 1920; W. D. Strong, whose extraordinary collection of data among Southern California Indians, from 1926 to 1928, remains our finest ethnographic legacy of that area; John P. Harrington (n.d.), who acquired some fragments of data from the Cahuilla in the 1930s; Philip Drucker (1937), whose "Culture Element Lists" adds still more bits and pieces; and Francisco Patencio, a Cahuilla political and religious leader who dictated his remarkable *Stories and Legends of the Palm Springs Indians* in 1943.

I have, over the years, acquired data which are now being placed together with that of former scholars. Several Cahuilla elders have been consulted over the thirty-two years. These include Alice López, Salvador López, Cinciona Lubo, Jane Penn, David Quatte, Katherine Siva Saubel, Alvino Siva, Juan Siva, Saturnino Torres, and Victoria Wierick.

I am especially grateful to the editors of this volume for encouraging me to proceed because it caused me to ask questions which would not have been asked otherwise, and to review data I would otherwise not question in itself. This has led to an article on a sky person, *Tahquitz*, now in press in another report. A better understanding of the role of women and men in traditional Cahuilla society has emerged as well.

I began working with the Cahuilla in 1958, and I was told of Moon and her travail with *Mukat* very shortly after I became acquainted with and consulted with elderly Cahuilla women, who were especially important in religious affairs at that time. Moon was then, and is now, for many a culture heroine of enormous strength. Much of what is described herein is not practiced today, but remembered vividly and with great excitement by older Cahuillas: for example, the race of the new moon, and the awesomeness of the eclipse.

Celestial knowledge is still revered and fondly remembered despite the fact that most of it is gone or is alive only in ethnographic literature, the field notes of ethnographers, or the memories of a few Cahuilla. That which remains is a reminder of a rich ethnographic past. It serves as an identity marker of Cahuillaness in a contemporary world where Cahuillaness is only remotely significant, if at all, to their Euroamerican neighbors, but remains crucial to the Cahuilla themselves. The Cahuilla today are concerned about the sacred past despite enormous changes and the loss of many of their traditional ways. The ways of the Sun, Moon, stars, and various other sky phenomena and beings were pervasive and essential in Cahuilla philosophy. This knowledge is essential to understanding the traditional, as well as some of the contemporary, ways of the Cahuilla.

In this essay, I will comment on the place of Moon (*Menil*) in Cahuilla life and the continued presence of Moon as a significant symbolic representation of Cahuilla history and identity. It is no accident that some of the beings remained in Cahuilla memory and action longer than others. Moon was among those sky beings most loved by all Cahuillas and especially by women, who are today the great nurturers and reservoirs of traditional culture.

As the economic conditions of the Cahuilla changed, astronomical knowledge, which had been intimately associated with the economic need to know where and when plants and animals were available and when ceremonies were to be held, was less critical to survival. Specialized knowledge of the sky was the province of priests, shamans, and other male specialists. Since celestial beings were integrated with the management of the physical world, and were no longer a necessary part of the Cahuilla male's world, they became less important as Cahuilla men became increasingly involved in cash economies. The need subsided to pass on to future generations knowledge about Cahuilla rituals. The timing of ceremonies became less directly associated with the natural order of traditional Cahuilla cosmology. Nevertheless, a part of the knowledge and practice of most Cahuilla institutions and domains of knowledge was retained. That which remained was that which was still useful, applicable, and known to the majority of Cahuillas.

Those aspects of Cahuilla culture which were the domain of women's culture were retained longer than men's, since women's economic contributions and traditional ways remained longer: for example, the gathering of indigenous foods and the manufacture of subsistence technology. In contrast, since many areas were closed off to hunting and trade and men were introduced to more risk-free activities—wage labor, farming, and cattle raising—knowledge of the male's world decreased more rapidly than that of women. Even more than Moon, *Menil,* had prescribed in the beginning, women became the nurturers of the culture. They kept these beliefs and others known to most Cahuilla communities; that astronomical knowledge which was a part of the culture of men (or of elites and priests) was lost as those persons who engaged in it died and did not pass it on.

A further reason for the lacunae in these data is that esoteric scientific knowledge of the sort held by Cahuilla priests and shamans was powerful and was kept secret. Especially powerful was its possession by the elites who were in political control. It was not, therefore, casually revealed to anyone, especially to an outsider. Only special Cahuillas themselves were allowed access to it. As these specialists passed away, so did their knowledge.

Thus, in today's Cahuilla cosmology the dramatic personages of *Tahquitz* (Bean, forthcoming), who was and is known to all as a stealer of souls and a dangerous person, but the guardian spirit of many shamans, and *Menil,* the symbolic representation of all that is womanly in Cahuilla culture, are those sky people most remembered and useful to the Cahuilla today.

All Cahuilla peoples had a considerable knowledge about the sky. From the time children could first learn, they were taught about celestial phenomena, usually though the vehicle of stories and legends and the creation myth itself, which every Cahuilla knew in detail. Many of these tales contained dramatic and sometimes entertaining adventures about persons and phenomena of the early times who became the sun, the moon, various stars, and the Milky Way. Consequently, there was an awareness among all Cahuilla about the general functions and purposes of cosmology. One would expect an ordinary Cahuilla to know the major stars and constellations (Orion and the Pleiades), the morning star, and the phases of the moon, even though they did not have access to esoteric knowledge.

## The Universe

A number of philosophical assumptions about the Cahuilla universe and man's place within it have been discussed elsewhere (Bean 1972 : 160 – 82). The essential assumption concerns the existence of power, namely that the use of that power by various beings was/is the principal causative agent for the control and change of all things and events.

Power was created from a void in which two forces, male and female, came together in a cataclysmic event that took an egglike form. From this emerged the twin creator gods *Mukat* and *Temayawet.* Their creative and competitive energies began to form the world. Various acts were accomplished through the use of power.

The universe was created along with various anthropomophic beings, and all things. Of these, Moon was one of the earliest of beings, the only *nukatem* (those created in the beginning) who is identified as female and who resided with the Cahuillas in the beginning. Among the results of this creation is the mandate to have a hierarchically structured social universe. The cosmological model defines power and provides rules (existential and normative postulates) for interacting with power sources (Bean 1972 : 160–82).

The Cahuilla universe consisted of three parts including the middle world—flat, circular in shape, and surrounded by water but sometimes supported by various beings—and a world pillar. Placed one above the other, each part contained considerable sources of power, which was scattered subsequently and has been entropic since creation. The lowest world was especially dangerous, filled with powerful, often malevolent beings associated with the failed creator twin *Temayawet*. The middle world became the home of humans and various powerful nonmortals, the *nukatem*—for example, *Tahquitz*—and contained many places of residual power (Bean 1972:161–62).

The most important, most revered, world for the Cahuilla was the upper one, for it was the home of the most powerful celestials who were responsible for many significant events taking place below. They were *nukatem*, transformed beings who ascended to the skies from the middle world to escape death or maltreatment. They were like humans, sentient, with the strengths and foibles of men, but with greater power.

## *Menil*

Who is moon maiden? Why is she so important a figure to the Cahuilla? What does she mean to the Cahuilla? How does her presence affect everyday life? These are important questions for the understanding of a female deity in a vigorously patrilineal, patrilocal culture—a culture in which "power," economic matters, ritual, and social contacts were so conspicuously in the hands of men.

However, *Menil*'s place in Cahuilla cosmology is consistent with the extraordinary strength of character one sees in Cahuilla women. These are women of strong personality, who can and have taken charge when necessary—ritually, economically, and socially—as their peoples were damaged by diseases from Europeans; their children were despoiled by foreign educational systems; and there were losses of land and subsistence with consequent travails of poverty, political powerlessness, and a dependency status which has only barely improved in recent years. All of these factors and more have impacted their culture over the past two hundred years.

Moon is the mother of all Cahuilla people. She was the first woman and remains a great culture heroine, a reference point for Cahuillaness. Femaleness is one of the principal aspects of the original power–energy that resulted in the creation of the world when it combined with a male aspect, resulting in the creation of male twin creator gods—*Mukat* and *Temayawet*—who created the world and Moon herself.

## Creation of *Menil*

While the specifics of Moon's emergence in the beginning of time vary a bit from one Cahuilla clan tradition to another, the explanation of her origin is essentially similar among all Cahuillas. She was originally created so that *Mukat* and *Temayawet* could have enough light to see the creatures – beings that they had created in darkness. The Sun had been created earlier, but he was so bright and speedy that he slipped away and was not available for light. Alejo Patencio, a Cahuilla leader, referred to Moon "as a lamp still up there."

When some light came about because of the creation of Moon, enough so that they could see their creations, *Mukat* was displeased by the creatures that had been made by *Temayawet*. He didn't like their peculiar appearance—their webbed hands and two faces (front and back so they could walk either way and see behind themselves). Their toes were also pointing in both directions and their breasts were in the front and back, as were their eyes. The creators argued about the appropriateness of this and many other matters: for example, when things should grow and ripen, and how many moons there should be. At first they had fifty moons, but later wisely decided it would be as it is now. Eventually, *Temayawet* became angry and dissatisfied with *Mukat*'s decisions and left the world of *Mukat* and their creations, never to return. Then began a new phase of creation—that time when *Mukat* and his creations (*nukatem*) lived together.

## Moon's Teachings

While Moon was on Earth as a *nukatem,* she taught the others many things—to enjoy themselves and their world, to be socially organized and ritually responsible. Social order was first established by her; for example, she created moieties, clans, lineages, hierarchical social organization, and ritual. It was Moon who put one group of people on one side and said, "You are Coyote people," and put another group of people on another side and said, "You are Wildcat people," thus creating the exogamous moieties that guided much of Cahuilla social and ritual life (Bean 1972 : 85). According to Strong:

> After the creation all people including birds, animals, . . . who were
> then human, were talking. The lady moon used to take them far away and
> tell them how to sing and dance when they came back to the dance house.

She named one to be *net* and made a round house with a fence around it . . . for him to stay in. Then she made the other party go back and come singing and dancing to the house. She told the *net* to sing his song also. Those who were coming answered with the same song. She told them always to do this. Then she divided all the people and said these are *istam* and those are *tuktum*, and they must sing their own songs. For in the very beginning *temaiyauit* was *istam* and *mukat* was *tuktum* and all the things each created belonged to its creator's side . . . (Strong 1929: 109).

She told the coyote people to sing against the wildcat people as though they were singing enemy songs. Then the wildcat people would begin to dance; then they would do it the other way around. This was a game. She told them to build a little brush house and put one creature in the house to be chief. Then she told another group to come from far away singing and dancing to the house. This was the way they should do later through all the generations to come. She also taught them to run, jump, wrestle, throw balls of mud at one another, and to flip pebbles at another from their finger tips. Certain ones she picked out and said, "You are women. You must grind, and feed these others, who are men, that come dancing to the house" (Strong 1929: 136).

She colored various creatures in different ways, especially the snakes. It is said that they were her paintings. Later snakes were a popular design element in Cahuilla baskets.

According to Patencio, one song that Moon taught them was

all about the funny faces of the animals: the coyote, who was the youngest of them all, was the most teased of them all, so they sang the song about his long nose and his long tail, and the color of his eyes and his hide; and about the wild-cat the same way: all about his short nose and his short tail, and his bright eyes (Patencio 1943 : 8).

She told the people about moieties and moiety exogamy and explained what this meant. She told them they would have children, that they would have songs for them, and that they should be instructed in the right way to live and that old people were the best instructors, thus reinforcing such Cahuilla values as tradition, age, maleness, and hierarchical order as referents for proper conduct (Bean 1972 : 173). Many of the teachings of *Menil* are still used by Cahuillas.

She taught them a game in which a piece of cane was split into six parts at the joint. These were struck on a rock and the parts that fell underneath were counted. In another game, pebbles were thrown up while placing another, like "jacks" (Patencio 1943 : 30).

Moon also taught them about flat sticks marked on one side by XXXXs, which were thrown up on the flat of the hand and the marks then counted. It was that game that was named *con wel ah* (Patencio 1943 : 30). These and many other games were taught by Moon for women and girls to play.

Other games were invented for the men and boys. One was the hiding game, a favorite of the Cahuilla. A mark was made on the ground and a short bone was thrust into one of the points of the mark. Accompanying this game was a song about a star that was to hide the bone and slip it into the ground (Patencio 1943 : 31). Wagers often were made upon the result of the game.

Moon also taught the people to play what we call Cat's Cradle—a string figure game and a predictive technique necessary to know in order for the soul, it was said, to get into *Telmekish,* the land of the dead (Hooper 1920 : 360). They had to know many figures because as the soul traveled to the land of the dead they had to tell *Montakwet,* the shaman-person who guarded the entrance to *Telmekish,* what they meant. If they couldn't tell him, they would not be admitted. This same game, a favorite recreation for Cahuilla women, could predict the sex of a child.

While Moon was on Earth, life was especially pleasant. It was a paradisiacal time. The people "played" all day long, and they loved *Menil* very much.

An important aspect of Moon's teachings are utilized today when the bird songs—a cycle of songs taught to the early people in the times of creation by Moon—are sung. In these songs, which are usually sung at night, Moon's sacred time, many of the circumstances of ordinary things of life are described: places, journeys, hard times of tribulation of beings, birds, stars, places of snow, animals, weather conditions. A song was sung for each as it was approached by the travelers. The texts of these songs provided many object lessons, explanations, and a taxonomy about the natural world. The personages, whether in human form or their earlier forms, are personified and humanlike, as are all Cahuilla *nukatem.*

The songs tell of their experiences, successes, failures, foibles, and the lessons learned from their experiences. This cycle of songs, an important recreational and educational activity that lasts many hours, was sung at night as the Moon came up, usually from sundown to sunup, and provided a time when great happiness was expressed. Interestingly enough, these songs, so intimately associated with Moon, were associated with a behavioral license for women, who were otherwise restricted in Cahuilla culture.

At these occasions a woman could, and can now, be so forward as to ask a man to dance and flirt with her. It was a time when sex roles were somewhat relaxed.

Today, the songs are danced on most southern California Indian reservations, while more sacred song cycles are no longer or seldom performed. So they are now, even more than in the past, associated with the traditional past of the Cahuilla as well as with Luiseno, Kumayaay, and Serrano identities. Although many of the songs are sad in the stories they tell, they are times of great pleasure. This may be the most significant legacy of Moon (*Menil*), although many of her other teachings are still utilized and appreciated.

## The Beginning

Unfortunately, as time went on, *Menil* became the innocent participant in introducing the idea of death to the Cahuilla people. She followed *Mukat's* orders when he logically but duplicitously introduced the fact and need of death to the people. It was Moon whom he asked to instruct the people on how to make bows of wood and arrows of reeds with no points on them and to use them recreationally, harmlessly shooting at one another. Then, *Mukat* told the people to sharpen them to points and make stone points, and shoot at each other, guaranteeing them that there was no danger to themselves, even after they expressed concern about that possibility. People were killed, and the fact of death was revealed as was the place of afterlife, *Telmekish*. He had "tricked and joked" with his people (Strong 1929:138). In other versions, it is *Tahquitz,* a malevolent *nukatem,* who encourages the people to shoot at each other (Patencio 1943:12; Hooper 1920:323).

Those people still alive were sad at the loss of their relations, but they were still pleased that their teacher *Menil* was with them, but only, as it turned out, for a short time. Alejo Patencio, *net* (ceremonial leader) of the Kauisiktum Cahuilla, said in 1929:

> The moon was a naked, white, and beautifully formed woman. She slept apart from all the other creatures. One night *Mukat,* who had often watched her, leaned above her and touched her as he passed. Next morning the moon was weak, sleepy, and sore; she felt very sad. She planned to go away somewhere, but before going she spoke to all *Mukat's* creatures, saying, "I am going away, but you must go to the place where you used to play. Go there and play as before. In the evening you will see me in the west, then you may say ha! ha! ha! ha! and run to the water to bathe. Remember this

always." Then she disappeared and no one saw or knew what became of her. In a short while they saw the new moon rise in the west, and they cried, "ha! ha! ha! ha!" as she had told them and ran to bathe (Strong 1929:138).

Thereafter, women celebrated their menses with these special rituals and served their people as curers. Thus was born the new moon ceremony so important to the Cahuilla thereafter. In another version of this story, it is said that *Mukat* desired *Menil* as his wife. This made her very sad because he was her father.

> He did not tell her, but she knew it, and it made her feel very sad, for he was her father. She decided to leave, and told her people. She told them that there were a great many games she had not yet taught them, but that it was now too late. She said she would never die or have diseases as other people had, for *Tamaioit* had helped to create her (Hooper 1920:322).

Before she left:

> She told the women how to care for themselves during menstruation and pregnancy; they must not eat salt, meat, or fat, or drink cold water. She showed them certain herbs to use if they became ill.
> That night she left and got beetles and ants to crawl over her tracks so that no one would follow her (Hooper 1920:322).

Later, the tracks of all who died were wiped away by feathers, even later by cloth that was dragged around the ceremonial house (*kishumnawut*) at which the funeral rites were held so that the souls of the dead who traveled to *Telmekish* (the land of the dead) would not return to their living relatives. The theme of leaving gifts to those you leave behind and noting that there was much known that was still not given to you by departing culture heroes was carried out again when *Mukat* himself died, leaving many valuable (agricultural) plants and places of power where his blood (hematite) dropped.

> Everyone felt very badly and tried to find her. Coyote went to the water where they had always bathed to look for her. He saw her reflection in the water and thought it was she. He jumped in after her but couldn't find her (Hooper 1920:322–23).

(Later, in time he would pursue the dying *Mukat* and retrieve his heart to acquire power.)

> When he climbed out and looked in again, he was sure he saw her and again he jumped in, with the same result. As he came out this time, Moon, who had gone to the sky, spat on him. He looked up to see where the spit had come from, and he saw her. He begged her to reurn but she would not talk,

only smiled. He then returned to the others to tell them where their beloved playmate and teacher had gone. He felt very sad so he hung his head as he said, "Here she is, here she is." The people looked down where he was looking, but of course could not see. Finally someone happened to look up and there saw Moon in the sky. She seemed very far away and they all wept. Each night, for a long time, she went higher up, until she was where we now see her (Hooper 1920:323).

Similarly, when *Mukat* died it was Coyote who sought out the culture hero in order to recapture the sacred being.

Because Moon left, her people were angry with *Mukat*. This and the other events caused by *Mukat,* which they did not understand and with which they disagreed (for example, the need for death so that the world would not be overpopulated), led to their poisoning of him. Eventually he died, but while he was dying he requested assistance from his creations. Many came to cure him, but they only pretended to cure him, continuing to poison *Mukat,* their father.

The significance of death, the most significant theme in Cahuilla cosmology, is highlighted in Cahuilla's religious poetry when just prior to *Mukat's* death, while falsely and deceitfully being cured by his creations, he began to predict his own death. Francisco Patencio (1943) recalls that while being falsely cured by Crow, who gave him a medicine to eat,

> *Mo-Cot* ate them and they did him so much good that he sent the crow back again for more. Then *Mo-Cot* began explaining to his people, "Maybe I die in the month of *Sowl,*" which means before you can see the new moon. "Or the moon *Seva* (the crescent of the new moon). Perhaps I shall die in the new moon, *chan a,* or the half moon (*Ky vo*), or the moon *tan cha* (three-quarters), or the full moon (*te ve*).
>
> Maybe I shall die in the moon (*tes sa*) going back to three-quarters, maybe I shall die in the *Le we* moon. Maybe I shall die in the *ca ve* moon, maybe I shall die in the *he qua* moon. Maybe I shall die in *Too* moon."
>
> He told his people, "When I die, you better watch my creation coyote. When I die you must tell him to go for my creation Rockfire and Sunfire." He told this to his people (Patencio 1943:18−19).

In another version given to W. D. Strong by Alejo Patencio, the brother of Francisco Patencio, who preceded Francisco as *net* of the Kauisiktum people, he said:

> All my creatures have tried to cure me but I am no better. I know now that I am about to die. Perhaps I shall die in the dark of the moon, or in the faint light of the new moon, or during the young crescent moon, or during the older crescent moon, or in the first week of the new moon, or when the

moon has a cloudy ring around it, or during the clear half-moon, or when the half-moon has its rim parallel to the earth, or during the full moon when its spots show clearly, or when the full moon comes from the east and is red, or when it begins to wane and one side is flattened, or when it has half disappeared, or during the last dying moon (Strong 1929 : 140).

Thus the moon, at the death of the creator himself, is an important measure of time, a continuing and everlasting reminder of life, death, and regeneration.

## Menstruation and Women's Rituals

Moon is directly associated with menstruation, which is referred to in Cahuilla as *"menily pechi gaawish"* (to be menstruating) (Hill and Nolasquez 1973 : 162). During menstruation, Cahuilla women were isolated from others. It was especially important that things which were sacred or associated with male activities not be touched, walked over, or in any way closely associated with them. They were placed on a salt-free meat diet for several days and "bathed" in a pit filled with warm sand and herbs. Because of this, they were said to be free of painful menstruation or any irregularities associated with menstruation or childbirth.

Since Moon was so associated with women's things, special songs were sung at the girls' adolescent ceremonies about her. A ritual lasting several days was given for a girl when she first menstruated. It was continued thereafter, in part, by all Cahuilla women at every menstruation until menopause. Curtis records that

> On the occasion of her first menses a Cahuilla girl was laid recumbent on a bed of brush and herbs in a heated trench. Covered with a blanket she remained there throughout three nights, while men and women danced and sang songs alluding to the institution of this custom by Moon and to the proper conduct of menstruating girls. During the day her grandmother or aunt placed her on the floor of the house, where neither sun nor wind could strike her. When she was thirsty they gave her warmed water, since cold water would cause cramps; and for her two daily meals she received a small quantity of thin mush. No salt nor dried food was given, and a bone or wooden scratcher was provided, since scratching with the fingers was prohibited. She remained thus in seclusion and on a limited diet for one moon. The first menstruation generally occurred at the new moon, it is said, and the girl remained under care until that moon disappeared, when she received a warm shower-bath. At the rise of the next new moon the flow, it is said, did

not usually recur. If it did, the parents knew that the previous one was not her first period, that she had deceived them; and therefore a shaman was summoned to administer large quantities of bitter herb decoctions. At her second menstruation, and indeed, it is said, at every recurrence, the girl was kept in seclusion for six days, and ate no salt nor dried food (Curtis 1926:30–31).

A variation of this also occurred when a child was born. The woman was placed in a warm pit and covered with aromatic herbs and blankets. She was sung over and taught the lessons of womanhood, which included mother-hood, by shamans, by other religious officials, and by older women. These songs were among those that Moon had taught the people when she was on earth. Contained in these songs were instructions about how the girls should care for themselves at menstruation, information about the danger of the menses blood to things sacred and associated with male activities, especially economic, and general advice on the proper conduct of an adult woman; for example, laziness was bad, hard work was good.

A Cahuilla woman elder today says that "the periods of the Moon go with a woman's period. When the Moon dies you have to have your period. When it comes up you go and wash and clean up. You are a new person again. You gauge your period by the phases of the moon. When it doesn't follow that way, the person hasn't taken care of themselves. Now it doesn't work properly for women."

Since Moon was the symbolic representation of women—their special friend and mentor—when a woman died special songs regarding Moon were sung at her funeral. Contrariwise, when a man died songs regarding the Sun were sung. Thus, the male and female forces from which all power ultimately came in the creation were celebrated in these most sacred texts.

## Aspects of the Moon

Moon, like several other celestial phenomena, has more than one aspect. There is *Menil,* a *nukatem* (demigoddess), culture heroine, symbolic repre-sentation of that which is woman from the beginning of time; and there is the celestial phenomenon of moon. The celestial aspect began after Moon fled the world of the creator.

The various phases, or aspects, of the Moon were meaningful to the Cahuilla. The presence of new moon (*pangish*—the sliver) was celebrated as a sign of good health and long life. The people would shout and sing and take special baths in honor of the new moon and in anticipation of her continued good health and, thereby, theirs.

The position of crescents told the Cahuilla whether there would be rain or drought, an important signal since the Cahuilla lived in an area where the slightest change in water conditions could be critical for them. Moon also was associated with good luck in hunting. A full moon (*takchul menil*) is associated with good luck. Since it creates such a bright light, it is a good time for night-hunting. One culture hero, *kisily pewik*, was said to hunt at the new moon and he would always kill a new deer at that time (Hill and Nolasquez 1973:17).

On several occasions, the Cahuilla from various clans have recounted the various aspects of the moon. Hooper (1920:362) was told that there were thirteen moons and a lunar calendar listing fourteen months. Curtis gives twelve names for times approximate to our calendars. The Cupeno, a *kauis-iktim* Cahuilla sib, have given three lists (Hill and Nolasquez 1973: 111–12).

Two versions of the creation given by two Cahuilla brothers, each at different times, are cited above. Still another version (Hill and Nolasquez 1973:162) names five moons: full—"*menily yutaxwe*"; half moon—"*menily kwaanengaxwish*"; new moon—"*menily pangish*"; moon getting bigger—"*menil kaywaka*"; and moon completing—"*takchum milyuk.*" Other Cahuillas referred to "*sowl*" as "*muka*", meaning the moon is dead, and "*seva*" as "*pangish*", when the sliver begins.

Hooper was given a somewhat similar, but less specific, list of seasons based on the moon; they are "*to menyil*", "*tawe menyil*", "*seya menyil*", "*sa menyil*", "*menyil naa*", and "*menyil*" (Hooper 1920:362). There is here a suggestion of a bilunar system. The term "*menilyika*" refers to moonlight.

These variations of moon-naming suggest a close count or reckoning with the phases of the moon in order to keep track of important events. Since so many are recorded, it seems that a fairly accurate monthly reckoning of time was in use, based on phases of the moon—although some of these would not be regular.

Various associations with aspects of the moon are recalled—*U,* an upward crescent, suggested rain; *C* suggested a lot of babies would be forthcoming; and a full moon suggested good health and luck to all. Menses was sure to follow a full moon, that is, the death of the moon. In another aspect—for example, the crescent moon—drought or rain was indicated.

At the time of the new moon, *Menil*'s appearance was celebrated with much "shouting," dancing, ritual bathing, and other activities. Boys and girls raced toward a spring of water. It was, for the Cahuilla, an assurance of further good health and life.


# Eclipses


Lunar eclipses were considered to be dangerous times, since Moon was thought to have been eaten by animals of various sorts or the souls of those about to die. Eclipse ceremonies are recalled by the Cahuilla. Songs and/or dances to help Moon get well were commonly done so that Moon would not die. An eclipse of the moon or sun signaled the loss of Moon, which could signal the loss of all life. It created great fear. Consequently, it was not a time for hunting or other economic activities. All of the energies of the community were necessary for the defense of the group.

These eclipses, caused by spirits of the dead people or those about to die (apparently unsatisfied ones, or even evil spirits who were eating *Menil*), required community ritual. Since it could be the souls of people about to die that were eating the Moon, the death of someone would be predicted. Shamans watched carefully in order to determine who it might be that was dying so that their souls could be returned, their death prevented, and the threat to *Menil* removed. The eclipse is a reminder of the death of *Mukat*, the creator, and of the precariousness of power and life itself.

For the Cahuillas, eclipses represented an imbalance in the cosmo-logical system—an offense against order and the hoped-for predictability of life. Since an eclipse represented a definite imbalance to the universe, with potential death to all, it is not surprising that various forms of ritual activity took place at these times. Everyone shouted during an eclipse in the hope that the noise would drive off the particular beings devouring or hiding the object, thereby helping Sun or Moon to come back to life. With this great shouting and mayhem, many people hid, especially women and children, so as not to be harmed. They would awaken the children, saying that the Moon, the blood, is coming, so they would hide a long time. Pregnant women were in special danger.

Songs and rituals were organized to defend the Moon and the Sun (when it eclipsed) against attack by sending the power of man to help. As it was generally a man's place to restore order to the universe in the Cahuilla world, priests and shamans came together to combine their power with that of all persons in order to assist the cosmological mother and the Sun at a time of great need. By helping these parents, these male and female aspects of the universe, they helped to guarantee their own future.

## Another Role for Moon

Specific uses of the moon for timing of events, as with the stars, are only occasionally recorded in the published literature on the Cahuilla. Undoubtedly, the earliest account is that of an eagle-killing ceremony written by Warner, an early Anglo who settled among the Cahuilla. He recounts specific associations with aspects of the moon's appearance. A feast, or fiesta, was celebrated at a full moon, during winter, usually in December or January after the gathering of the "spontaneous" wild crops (Warner 1857:43–45). Shortly after the event, the annual funeral (*nukil*) ceremony celebrations were held. Those group members who had died since the last such ceremony were honored and their souls released to the land of the dead (*Telmekish*). In his account "Eagle Fiesta of the California Indians," a most important event signifying the everlasting nature of life, the continuance of spiritual power useful for the Cahuilla is described. An eaglet was raised and ceremonially "killed," and its feathers removed for use in ritual objects, in skirts, for example. The bird was buried with great dignity, not unlike a human.

Warner, who was one of the few non-Indians of his era (ca. 1856) to witness it, describes the eagle-killing ceremony as follows:

> Upon the approach of winter, and after the gathering of the spontaneous fall crops, at the full moon, this solemn and instructive celebration takes place. The inhabitants of the friendly villages, not only near but more remote, are ceremoniously invited to participate in the festivities of the occasion. Suitable preparations having been made, upon the designated day, the people who have received invitations arrive from the surrounding villages. A sufficient area for the accommodation of those who take part in the ceremonies, as well as for the spectators, having been enclosed, in the center of which a bright fire is kindled, the evening is spent in chanting and dancing. As the full orbed moon gracefully ascends towards the zenith, the performance becomes more animated. A short time previous to high moon, the officiating priest, bearing the heaven-bound messenger, makes his appearance. All is hushed in silence as he enters the enclosure and approaches the burning pile, displaying the immortal bird before the anxious and admiring multitude. Low-toned and solemn chants and ejaculations, inter-

spersed with benedictions, flow from the priest as with measured step he passes around the fire. Having in this manner introduced himself and subject to the congregated people, he informs them that if they have any thanks for blessings received, or petitions to send to the Great Spirit, to communicate the same; and then, directing his discourse to the eagle, recounts all the notable events, either of good or evil which they have enjoyed or suffered during the past year. The many anticipated wants for the coming year—the genial showers, the fruitful forests and fields, the abundance of game, and security from the enemies, are dwelt upon.

As the moon approaches her greatest altitude, the scene becomes exciting. The measured steps become quick, the low voice gives way to earnest entreaty and commands, until the speaker winds himself up to the highest physical and mental excitement. The imperial messenger is then charged in the most emphatic manner, to speed his way to the courts of heaven, and without fail to lay before the Great Spirit their combined thanks and petitions, while at the same time he is instructed to faithfully represent them before the giver of all good.

As the last words of this solemn and imposing charge dies away upon the still bosom of night, the spirit of this bird of Jove takes its silent and peaceful departure from the body, to wing its way to the source of all life. The moment the head of the bird is seen to droop in death, and while its spirit still lingers to take a last look, and receive the parting ejaculations, a deep and solemn suspiration breaks forth from the attending multitude. A silence, as if instantaneous death had fallen upon every person present, reigns without interruption, while the officiating priest, passing round the open area, displays to the people the lifeless body of the eagle, which has voluntarily resigned his life here to become the messenger and advocate of man at the celestial courts.

The large feathers of the bird are then plucked and carefully preserved for future use, and the body committed to the flames, where it is closely watched by every person present until the last particle of its body disappears in ascending vapor. The remainder of the night is spent in dancing, accompanied with singing and chanting. In the morning, presents, consisting of the proceeds of the summer and fall harvests, are divided among those guests which have been invited from other villages.

It is a common occurrence that the person who makes this feast, distributes the entire produce of his fields among his guests. None but the more industrious among the Indians, are able to enjoy the luxury of giving an eagle feast, and they are necessarily left destitute of food, and are compelled to attend similar feasts at other villages, where they obtain a more bountiful share in the distribution (Warner 1857:44–45).

## Other Accounts of Moon

Other than in the creation myth itself, Moon only occasionally appears in other Cahuilla stories of early times. She appears in a tale regarding people who went to see the Sun. In this tale, a young man who is staying with Sun is instructed not to wander around. Upon hearing a noise, the sound of Moon making *ollas* [1] (the slapping sound of the paddle on the coils), he went over to the house of Moon. He was restless, unduly curious, and not sufficiently mature to obey instructions given by elders. Since he did not have enough power to prevent it, the power of the Moon killed him. When Sun returned home and found the young man dead, he brought him back to life—but, again, his curiosity caused him grief. He wanted to know what was in the *ollas* that she made, and he again went to see, despite admonitions to the contrary. Moon had finished a jar and had filled it with materials (hermetically sealing it to reserve seed was commonly done). He took a hot rock to melt the tar off a sealed *olla*. Upon making the tar soft, he raised the lid and small, insectlike creatures flew out. He didn't notice at first, but then he saw many warriors standing behind him. They had come out of the *olla* and had been transformed. The warriors shot him with arrows and tore him to pieces. They threw the pieces away, scattered them about, and strung his guts on the bushes. When Sun returned, he put him back together and placed the warriors back into the *olla*.

This story, which presents the case of a disobedient person, goes on with other variations regarding careless handling of things of great power and tragic results, a common element in Cahuilla teaching, since power is dangerous to handle unless one has the requisite knowledge-power to handle it (Bean 1972 : 162).

## Magical Games

As Moon was associated with the joy of games, social life, beauty, art, and color, so she was also associated with magic or luck. Patencio (1943 : 111) recalls that the presence of the new moon was associated with luck in playing the Cahuilla gambling game, known as *peon*.

A significant social and recreational activity, *peon* is an activity more clearly understood as an intensely active, "magically" motivated game. It is, for the most part, an activity that only Indians engage in. To understand it at all, if you are not Indian, is considered a most remarkable feat. This game was usually played at night by firelight. A well-lighted night was advantageous to players—so that they could see opponents' faces and hand movements—as well as to viewers, who so enjoyed this most exciting gambling game, which was accompanied by very high wagers.

*Peon* is not unlike the hand game so popular throughout the West among American Indians. It involved guessing what combination of black and white sticks was hidden in the hands of four men who composed a team, playing against another team of four men. Each team was backed by a group of singers whose songs, overheard by the various players, could be sung to bring "power" to these players. Women, who occasionally played this game too, also sang. When it is played, competition is intense and wagers are high, as is emotional contagion. The game is played often and at recreational times, but while considered somewhat secular, its use of special knowledge and power causes a "win" over another team. Like bird songs, it is a rallying point for Cahuilla identity and associated with Moon (one of her contributions to Cahuilla culture).

## Moon Today

Older Cahuillas today are still concerned with the moon. It is a part of everyday life, although less directly and intensely so than in past decades. Younger Cahuillas may know little about traditional Cahuilla astronomy, yet they are advised of some matters. Older people can recall much of these matters and consider them significant. Older women are especially concerned that younger women are not familiar with Moon and its implications for proper female care and that this can cause various ailments: for example, cramps or difficult pregnancy.

Moon remains a symbolic representation of the past and of womanhood in particular. Her role as a teacher, the first basket maker, and the like are important identifying themes for reinforcing the status of Cahuilla women and Cahuilla aesthetic prowess as well as the value of hard work, carefulness, and attention to detail.

## Man in the Moon

A recent phenomena, man's landing on the moon, was perceived by the Cahuilla and some other California Indians as an example of non-Indian

cleverness and Anglo ability to do miraculous, powerful things with technology, rather than natural power, which "of course they do not possess to
the degree that Indians do." Cahuillas, as well as other North American
Indian shamans, have brought this to the author's attention. What they said
was almost an exact duplication of what Essie Parrish, a famous Pomo
Indian shaman, said to me as I was watching the event with her in her living
room. She noted, as did Cahuilla shamans, that since they had been to the
moon many times and seen it, its facade was not at all unfamiliar to them.
She noted that "white peoples had great power—were clever and could do
great things with their mechanical ways that Indians did with their natural
power." So, once again, the truth and power of the old culture—despite the
ravages of entropy over the last hundred or so years—was demonstrated to
all Indians.

Cahuilla men and women of knowledge were well versed concerning
their astronomical world. This knowledge was comparable in its complexity to that of other California groups and some agricultural societies. Such
knowledge was explained in an oral literature to which all Cahuilla had
some access, but a good part of it was secret or special knowledge that was
known only to specialists and passed down to others on a "need to know"
basis. Today, we know the least about the latter area of knowledge.

The richness of what is left is impressive, however, in its scientific,
practical, and poetic uses. It was carried through time in the form of an oral
literature enhanced by music and reflected in the visual arts, rock art,
basketry, and body-painting which adds to its interests culturally and
aesthetically. The Cahuilla system melded science and art. It was as systematic in this manner as all Cahuilla institutions.

The poetic and well-articulated philosophy explained these phenomena to the people in dramatic and exciting ways that were directly related to
human emotions and conditions. Whether the subject at hand was a great
sky adventure of heroic persons, or a compendium of mundane anecdotes,
the object lessons for the Cahuilla were clear: Don't be selfish; obey tradition; maintain order; value knowledge and secrecy; be respectful of the
aged; be careful of power and powerful peoples; and, if you are one who has
the mark of power (intelligence) and you have a commitment and a personality that others respect, you have an obligation to the community and
family to use it for the group. Enjoy the universe and use it, but respect
relatives and people of rank and knowledge. Remember, always, that it is
full of danger, of unknown quantities and qualities which must be experi-

mented with and tested very carefully before they can be used. The beings of power are both good and malevolent: They may help you, and they may be generous and friendly, yet they may change and, like the climate of the desert or the mountains, help you one year and fail you in another. Man is responsible for much of what happens in the universe, including the entropic nature of power. It is his task and obligation to learn, to observe, to pay attention to the signs provided, and to participate in and maintain the well-being of that universe. He must be cooperative with other beings and powers so that the universe remains in balance for the good of all.

All of these values and more are in the sky for the Cahuilla to see every day and night; the Cahuilla were reminded at special times, like ceremonies, eclipses, falling stars, celestial movements, and great and marvelous happenings which take place in the theater of the sky. This theater of supernatural operations is on view for anyone who watches, and it can be learned and predicted because of the knowledge with which the bright and attentive Cahuilla were rewarded. Because of the knowledge that he or she would receive, accolades and rank could be accrued and, most importantly, one could be of service to the community in ways beyond those displayed by ordinary people. Some knew of future happenings—when crops would be ready to plant or harvest, when animals were ready for capture, when weather conditions would change, and, often, when people would die. And because of the intimate association of Moon and women, Cahuilla women were not disenfranchised in the religious sphere. Rather, Moon's power was also women's power.

## Notes

1. *Olla*—Spanish for jar. It was hand-thrown using coils of clay; the paddle was used to smooth them.

## References

Bean, Lowell John. 1972. *Mukat's People*. Berkeley: University of California Press.

Bean, Lowell John, and Harry W. Lawton. 1973. Some Explanations for the Rise of Cultural Complexity in Native California with Comments on Proto-Agriculture and Agriculture. In H. Lewis, *Patterns of Indian Burning in*

*California: Ecology and Ethnohistory*, v–xlvii. Ramona: Ballena Press Anthropological Papers.

Curtis, Edward S. 1926. *The North American Indian*, vol. 15. New York: Johnson Reprint Corporation.

Drucker, Philip. 1937. Culture Element Distributions, vol. 5: Southern California. *University of California Anthropological Records* (Berkeley) 1(1): 1–52.

Harrington, John P. Fieldnotes

Hill, Jane H., and Rosinda Nolasquez. 1973. *Mulu'wetam: The First People; Cupeña Oral History and Language.* Banning: Malki Museum Press.

Hooper, Lucille. 1920. The Cahuilla Indians. *University of California Publications in American Archaeology and Ethnology* 16(6): 315–80.

Kroeber, Albert L. 1925. *Handbook of the Indians of California.* Washington: Bureau of American Ethnology Bulletin 78.

Patencio, Francisco. 1943. *Stories and Legends of the Palm Springs Indians.* As told to Margaret Boynton. Los Angeles: Times-Mirror.

Seiler, Hansjakob. 1970. *Cahuilla Texts,* with Introduction. Bloomington: Indiana University Language Science Monographs 6.

Strong, William D. 1929. Aboriginal Society in Southern California. *University of California (Berkeley) Publications in American Archaeology and Ethnology* 26(1): 1–349.

Warner, J. J. 1857. Eagle Fiesta of the California Indians. Reprinted in *Some Last Century Accounts of the Indians of Southern California,* ed. Robert F. Heizer. Ramona: Ballena Press Publications in Archaeology, Ethnology and History no. 6:43–45, 1976.

# 10

■■■■■■■■■

## *Racing* Simloki's *Shadow:*
## *The Ajumawi Interconnection of Power,*
## *Shadow, Equinox, and Solstice*

■■■■■■■■■

### JACK M. BROUGHTON AND FLOYD BUCKSKIN

*Jack Broughton currently makes his home in Seattle, where he is a Ph.D. candidate in physical anthropology at the University of Washington. Floyd Buckskin lives close to Simloki, where he continues learning the traditions of his Ajumawi people. In this chapter they draw upon Buckskin's knowledge and previous scholarship to explain the significance of some Ajumawi sacred geography and show how events predicated in the sky become both subject and object here on earth.*

Solstice and equinox observations in native northern California were widespread and appear to hae been frequently associated with the keeping of a calendar to regulate the timing of ceremonial, legal, economic, political, and social affairs (Hudson et al. 1979). The Ajumawi (a tribelet of the Achomawi), who inhabited the Fall River Valley in northeastern California (Olmstead and Stewart 1978 : 226), were apparently no exception although a survey of the Achomawi ethnographic literature (including Angulo 1926; Angulo and Freeland 1931; Dixon 1905, 1908; Kniffen 1928; Kroeber 1925; Merriam 1926, 1928; Olmstead and Stewart 1978; Voegelin 1942) reveals only the vaguest of references to these astronomical events. However Voegelin quotes an "Achomawi proper" (Ajumawi) informant as declaring, "know when shadow is at certain place sun is going to 'back up' and that it will snow" and "mainly watch shadow from Soldier Mt. ('it goes to Jim Hunt's place') for solstices" (1942 : 234). Additional insights into the details of Ajumawi solstice observations and sky watching practices have recently emerged through the work of Buckskin and Benson (Buckskin 1985; Benson and Buckskin 1987).

Buckskin is a native Ajumawi who lives with his family on ancestral land in the Fall River Valley. His knowledge of the traditional Ajumawi lifeway has been passed down from generation to generation. Buckskin (1985) has noted both the association of a particular triangular constellation (part of the European Northern Cross) with the manner in which Jamul (Coyote-man) staked out the triangular North American landmass in the construction of the world, and the alignment of the shadow cast by Soldier Mountain or "Simloki" (incorrectly spelled "Simlek" in Benson 1985) with winter and summer-solstice sunrises. It is our purpose here to expand Buckskin's brief notes on this relationship as well as the native practice of racing Simloki's shadow.

Unless specified to the contrary, all of the following data were obtained through tape-recorded discussions with Floyd Buckskin during the spring of 1988 in the Fall River Valley of northern California. The data pertaining to the equinox shadow/sunrise alignment were verified directly by both authors from the top of Simloki during March 19 and 20, 1988.

## The Significance of Solstices and Equinoxes to Ajumawi Life

The Ajumawi have been noted for their lack of ceremonialism (Dixon 1908:220; Kroeber 1925:313), and there were no official solstice or equinox ceremonies, but these occasions did serve as key landmarks in the calendar and were deeply integrated into several aspects of Ajumawi life. Specifically, the winter solstice marks the middle of winter; the vernal equinox marks the middle of spring; the summer solstice marks the middle of summer; and the autumnal equinox marks the middle of autumn. The forty-five days on each side of a solstice or equinox combined constituted the total ninety days of a season.

The autumnal and vernal equinoxes were dates of particular importance to the Ajumawi storytelling calendar, for these times marked the beginning and end of the storytelling season. Individuals who told stories after the vernal equinox or before the autumnal equinox might fall victim to any number of disastrous events, such as being struck by lightning.[1]

Solstices and equinoxes were occasions of particular significance to the Ajumawi doctors, as it was primarily during these times when their "power" was publicly displayed. Folks from throughout the valley gathered at sacred places to witness the incredible feats of the doctors. Without the public proof of power, an alleged doctor would not be believed. A doctor could demonstrate his or her power in a number of ways. Some of the more common ways involved eating fire or glowing coals, cutting each other's heads off and dancing around without heads, surviving falls from tall trees, pulling live animals or inanimate objects out of people's bodies, and bringing people back to life.

While the solstices and equinoxes may have had additional significance to the Ajumawi people, Buckskin recalls only the points discussed above.

## Simloki's Shadow

Simloki, or Soldier Mountain, is a conical, five-thousand-foot-high volcanic mountain that stands prominently at the western edge of the Fall River Valley, forty miles southeast of Mount Shasta. Beginning in the late afternoon, as the sun retreats toward the western horizon, Simloki's shadow first becomes apparent at the foot of its eastern slope. As the sun sinks, the triangular shadow stretches eastward across the Fall River Valley. Just before sunset, the point or apex of the shadow falls on the Big Valley Mountains on the eastern edge of the valley. Precisely where the shadow point falls on this horizon depends on the season. The time between the first appearance of Simloki's shadow (at its foot) and the time it reaches the Big Valley Mountains on the eastern horizon (ten to fifteen miles away) is approximately one and a half hours, though this, again, depends on the season.

At sunset on the winter solstice, the apex of Simloki's shadow points directly to the Little Hot Springs at the base of the Big Valley Mountains near the town of Day, in the northeastern corner of the Fall River Valley. This is also the location of the old Jim Hunt allotment (named for a native Ajumawi man) and the place where a number of Ajumawi mythological events of religious import took place; for example, the spirit-being Jamul, or Coyote-man, left his footprints there in rocks. Significantly, this is also the location on the horizon where the summer-solstice sunrise occurs (Fig. 10.1). Buckskin recalls that this phenomenon was pointed out to him by tribal elders during his childhood. The reference in Voegelin (1942:234), then, which states, "Mainly watch shadow from Soldier Mt. ('it goes to Jim Hunt's place') for solstices," can refer only to the *winter* solstice.

Buckskin has also observed a similar phenomenon at sunset on the summer solstice. At this time, the shadow cast by Simloki points directly to the position on the Big Valley Mountain horizon where winter-solstice sunrises occur (Fig. 10.1). Buckskin notes that there are hot springs at this location. He does not recall mention by tribal elders of this summer-solstice

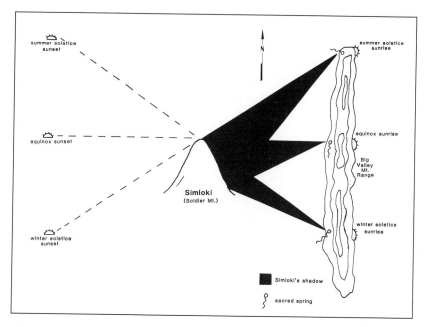

**Figure 10.1.** The dynamics of *Simloki's* shadow.

shadow alignment, as was the case for the winter solstice. He also notes that the shadow is quite long and more difficult to discern at this time of the year.[2]

While it was not mentioned in Buckskin's (1985 : 50) previous discussion involving the dynamics of Simloki's shadow, an additional alignment exists on the equinox. At sunset on the autumnal or vernal equinox the shadow of Simloki is cast (due east) directly to that position on the Big Valley Mountains where the sun rose that morning. This is a sacred location to the Ajumawi; there is a sacred spring here, and the area is inhabited by many spirit beings. Figure 10.2 depicts the progressive movement of Simloki's shadow across the Fall River Valley to the Big Valley Mountain range on the late afternoon of the vernal equinox. The apex of the shadow points directly toward the place where the sunrise occurred that morning.

More than a mountain, Simloki is a sacred entity to the Ajumawi, primarily as a male power place. Simloki's shadow carries much significance and is itself considered a spirit-being. Thus, the occurrence of the culturally relevant equinoxes and solstices are verified to the Ajumawi by a spirit-being, in the form of a shadow, who points to sacred locations on the

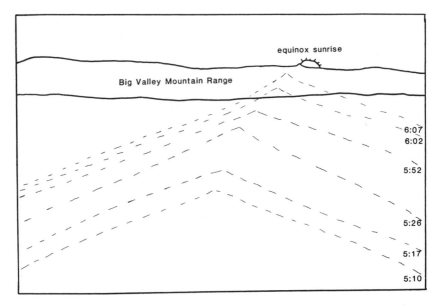

**Figure 10.2.** Progressive movement of *Simloki's* shadow on the afternoon of the vernal equinox. Morning sunrise is superimposed on the Big Valley mountain range.

horizon at these times. These points also represent the locations of key astronomical (solstice and equinox sunrises) and mythological events. The spirit-being makes sure the people do not miss the solstices by pointing to the same culturally significant point for several late afternoons in a row. While the solstices and equinoxes were verified to the Ajumawi by the location of the rising sun, an equally, if not more, important indicator of these events was the location of Simloki's shadow. Thus, Simloki's shadow may be considered a heirophony; it confirmed the sacredness of both these particular geogaphical areas and the occurrence of solstices and equinoxes.

## Racing Simloki's Shadow

The idea of racing Simloki's shadow came from the First People, specifically Kwahn, the Silver-Gray Fox-man, and Jamul, the Coyote-man. The origins of these dieties, who existed in the beginning when there was no land or light, is unaccounted for (Merriam 1928:vii). Both Jamul and Kwahn possessed mighty powers of magic, but they each had quite distinct personalities. Jamul was deceitful and a troublemaker. He lacked common sense and was conceited as well as a braggart. Kwahn, on the other hand, was honest, thoughtful, and wise.

Jamul and Kwahn were constantly in disagreement over most matters. Jamul always thought that he was the best: the real leader of the First People. An Ajumawi tale illustrates the competitive nature of the relationship between Kwahn and Jamul.

> Kwahn, the Silver Fox-man, and Jamul the Coyote-man, made the laws. Kwahn made good laws; Jamul changed them. One day Kwahn called the people together in the big roundhouse to make laws. Jamul was away. They wanted to hurry and make the laws, and also to name the trees and plants and everything before he came back, for they did not like his laws.
>
> Kwahn had made all the trees low, so women standing on the ground could reach the nuts and acorns and berries. He also made a law that a woman could kill bear and deer by pointing at them with her hand. Then she could drag them home.
>
> Jamul argued that this would be too easy, for women could then get along without men. Then he made the trees grow tall so the men would have to climb them to shake the nuts and acorns down. And he changed the law so women couldn't kill bear and deer by pointing at them—the men would have to hunt them.
>
> Kwahn made the first knifes; he made them of hard splinters of yellow pine. Jamul didn't like them, so he made his of black flint [obsidian].
>
> Kwahn had made a law that there should be four children in each family—no more—two girls and two boys, all made of white ocean shells.
>
> Jamul didn't like that. So he changed the law and now there are some great big families, and some with no children at all.
>
> Another time Jamul and Kwahn were arguing about Summer and Winter. Kwahn said Winter should have not more than four moons and Summer eight. But Jamul insisted that Winter should have ten Moons; Summer only two. So Kwahn told him to go up on Mount Shasta and try out having ten moons of Winter (Merriam 1928:145–46).

And so it was that Jamul and Kwahn forever quarreled over who should make the laws and who should be the leader. To decide, finally, who was to be the leader of the First People and who should command the ultimate power, Jamul and Kwahn decided to have a big race. The winner, of course, would receive the honor of chief leader.

With such a prize at stake, both Jamul and Kwahn began practicing and getting in shape for the big race. The primary aspect of this preparation was the racing of shadows. In the afternoon as the sun would begin to drop, Jamul, and particularly Kwahn, could be seen racing the shadows of large trees or mountains as they stretched across the valley. When race day came,

Kwahn would inevitably win as Jamul would stop, midrace, to wander off into the bushes to eat, sleep, copulate, or masturbate. Jamul would typically contest the outcome of a race and schedule a rematch.

This is how the Ajumawi got the idea to race shadows. And given the significance of Simloki, it is little wonder that the shadow of this mountain was the focus of their racing.

The racing of Simloki's shadow was reserved strictly for men. In the late afternoon, a man would wait for the shadow to first appear at the eastern foot of the mountain, at which time he would race off across the Fall River Valley to a location at the base of the Big Valley Mountains. The particular location at the base of this range would depend on the season. On the solstices and the equinoxes, the orientation of the shadow would align directly to sacred areas with springs, and to the solstitial and equinoctial sunrises. These were the most important times to race.

Like Jamul and Kwahn, the Ajumawi raced for "power" (*denahui*). Any man could race Simloki's shadow but only those who beat it would obtain power. (The term *power* is a simple English translation for a complex cognitive idea. In other words, the European notion of power is not directly translatable into the Ajumawi conception of *denahui* [Dreyer 1988]).

To the Ajumawi, a man without power is no man at all. Power gives you good luck in hunting, leadership, and reproduction. It gives you the ability to handle any kind of situation that might come up without being overwhelmed. Most men who were successful in beating Simloki's shadow received some sort of luck (including luck in gambling) or became good leaders.

Power was generally granted by spirit-beings who were either impressed or simply felt pity. An Ajumawi legend illustrates this concept: One man raced and raced, day after day and month after month, but he just couldn't seem to beat Simloki's shadow. Diligently racing by the Fall River one afternoon, he heard a frog speak to him. The frog said, "Get on my back. I'll give you some power because I really feel sorry for you; I've really taken a liking to you." So the man got on the frog's back, and the frog took him across the river and gave him the ability to beat the shadow. Symbolizing the acquisition of power, blood began to flow from his nose, ears, mouth, and eyes. This Ajumawi man, whose name was Hasting Lowe, raced and beat Simloki's shadow from that day on until well into his nineties. He died sometime in the 1950s.

While independent spirit-beings, such as the frog, grant the ability to beat the shadow, Simloki's shadow is a spirit-being itself, and is responsible for administering power as well. Thus, when racing the shadow you are actually racing a spirit-being. And if you should look back, while racing, to see how you are doing, the spirit-being would probably kill you on the spot. Consequently, the racers never looked back. If you impressed the shadow spirit-being by beating it across the valley, it would grant you power.

Because the spirit-beings grant an individual the ability to beat the shadow and because many of these spirit-beings inhabit the sacred areas at the base of the Big Valley Mountains (the same locations where the solstice and equinox sunrises occur), it is understandable that racing would be more significant on the days when Simloki's shadow would align to these areas. The days when this occurs, of course, are the solstices and equinoxes.

## Notes

1. Merriam (1928:iv) notes that the Modesse (Achomawi) "recite their religious history in the winter season. They begin during the first moon of December and stop about the 20th of March." We agree about the terminal date of the religious storytelling but dispute the date given for its commencement.

2. It should be mentioned that in Buckskin's (1985 : 50) initial brief characterization of this phenomena, several mistakes from transcription errors are present. "At winter solstice sunset, the shadow of *Simlek* aligns with the point where the summer solstice sun sets; conversely, at summer solstice the shadow falls at the point of winter solstice sunrise." In addition to the fact that the correct spelling of the Ajumawi word for Soldier Mountain is Simloki, rather than Simlek, the phrase "where the summer solstice sun sets . . ." should correctly read "where the summer solstice sun rises." An earlier version of this paper, noting such corrections, was presented in Farrer's course on ethnoastronomy at CSU-Chico in Spring 1988.

## References

Angulo, Jaime de. 1926. The Background of the Religious Feeling in a Primitive Tribe. *American Anthropologist* 28(2): 352–360.

Angulo, Jaime de, and L. S. Freeland. 1931. Two Ajumawi Tales. *Journal of American Folklore* 44 (172): 125–36.

Benson, Arlene. 1985. Preface to Racing Simlek's Shadow. In *Earth and Sky: Papers from the Northridge Conference on Archaeoastronomy,* ed. Arlene Benson and T. Hoskinson, 49–50. Thousand Oaks, Calif.: Slo'w Press.

Benson, Arlene, and Floyd Buckskin. 1987. How the Seasons Began: An Ajumawi Narrative Involving Sun, Moon, North Star, and South Star. *Griffith Observer* 51(7): 2–15.

Buckskin, Floyd. 1985. Racing Simlek's Shadow. In *Earth and Sky: Papers from the Northridge Conference on Archaeoastronomy*, ed. Arlene Benson and T. Hoskinson, 49–54. Thousand Oaks, Calif.: Slo'w Press.

Dixon, Roland B. 1905. The Mythology of the Shasta—Achomawi. *American Anthropologist* 7(4):607–12.

——. 1908. Notes on the Achomawi Indians of Northern California. *American Anthropologist* 10(2):208–20.

Dreyer, Bill. 1988. California Indian Conceptions of Power and Place. Paper presented at the Anthropology Forum, California State University, Chico, Spring 1988.

Hudson, Travis, Georgia Lee, and Ken Hedges. 1979. Solstice Observatories in Native California. *Journal of California and Great Basin Anthropology* 1(1): 39–63.

Kniffen, Fred B. 1928. Achomawi Geography. *University of California Publications in American Archaeology and Ethnology* 23(5):297–332.

Kroeber, Alfred L. 1925. The Achomawi. *In Handbook of the Indians of California*, 305–17. Washington, D.C.: Bureau of American Ethnology Bulletin 78.

Merriam, C. Hart. 1926. The Classification and Distribution of the Pit River Tribes of California. *Smithsonian Miscellaneous Collections* 78(3):1–52.

——. 1928. *An-nik-a-del: The History of the Universe as Told by The Mo-desse Indians of California*. Boston: Statford Co.

Olmstead, D. L., and O. C. Stewart. 1978. "Achumawi." In *California*, R. F. Heizer, ed., *Handbook of North American Indians*, Washington, D.C.: Smithsonian Institution.

Voegelin, Erminie W. 1942. Cultural Element Distributions: Northeast California. *University of California Anthropological Records* 7(2):47–252.

# 11

**■■■■■■■■**

# North Pacific Ethnoastronomy:
# Tsimshian and Others

**■■■■■■■■**

## JAY MILLER

---

*Jay Miller, editor and assistant director of the D'Arcy McNickle Center for the History of the American Indian at Chicago's Newberry Library, has published over four dozen articles and six sole-authored or edited books on various Native American peoples. We required an almost impossible task from him: summarize Northwest Coast ethnoastronomy. Although these several societies are both well-studied and well-known, there is very little known about their indigenous astronomical systems. Truly this is salvage work, for the systems are no longer intact.*

---

Overcast skies and steady rain may not seem conducive to astronomy, but along the North Pacific coast, observations made from fixed locations ("seats") played a vital role in these maritime societies. Families ranged widely between routine camps and towns at strategic locations on the landscape, using resource locations which were owned and inherited by members of a House, a feudal–like corporate group identified by heraldic emblems. The heads of households led the kin groups and towns, assisted by specialists like artists, environmentalists, and advisors. Foremost among these specialists were elders knowledgeable about the skies in terms of stars and planets, along with winds, tides, and other shifting indicators of time. Skylore had both practical application for the extensive navigation typical of the coast and cultural import for the ranks within society. In this region, members of the elite were and are believed to have a special rapport with nature. Their lives reflected the divine favor of Heaven, as indicated by peculiar combinations of social and environmental events. Thus, the summer birth of an elite baby might be accompanied by a brief snowfall, or the death of an old chief by a sudden squall. To predict and monitor such convergences, specialists watched the skies and seas to advise the leader of changes in nature that were both expected and spectacular.

Indeed, the American-Canadian Northwest remains justly famous for the complexity of its societies and the richness of its environment. Here, too, the sky is reflected on the earth, with varying degrees of intensity. More provocative than comprehensive, available data indicate the importance of the sky for understanding how and why things function on the earth. While early travelers, missionaries, explorers, and traders were quick to note a belief in a sky or heavenly God, they were not generally concerned with details of astronomical lore. Thus, our first reliable information was collected by some of the most famous early anthropologists as part of their general interest in recording ethnographic details. This paper briefly summarizes what is generally known of Native Northwest Coast astronomy before considering the Tsimshian in greater detail.

## Quinault

The most succinct statement on skylore for the region comes from the Quinault of the coast of Washington State, as summarized by Olson (1936:176–77):

> In a region where the winter season is one of almost continuous rain and storm one scarcely expects to encounter the reckoning of the winter solstice, yet the Quinault kept definite track of both solstices. At several villages there were "seats" (a stump or stone) where the old men watched both sunrise and sunset. Usually they sighted from the seat to a pole placed in the ground, or to a designated tree. [Note 70 adds that the sighting was done by marking on a stick placed horizontally the spot where the shadow of a certain tree fell at the moment of sunrise. One such mark indicated fifteen days until the solstice.] If the sun traveled farther north than in ordinary years(!) it was considered a sign that a good year with a heavy run of salmon would follow. If the solstice occurred during a waning moon it moved but little each day, indicating that it was heavily loaded (with food) for the year to follow. But after a solstice which occurred during a waxing moon the sun traveled far each day and indicated a lean year to follow, with sickness and famine certain to come. The winter solstice was called xa'Ltaanm (comes back, the sun). There was no name for the summer solstice but it was observed in the same fashion. It was believed that at the summer solstice the sun set four or five times at exactly the same place.

As indicated, observations of the sky were to mark both seasonal and nightly events. Thus, winter solstice was also the time for exceptionally high tides, when Quinault whalers made contact with their supernatural patron (ibid. : 177), drawing spirits, humans, and whales into a complex network of preparatory ritual and energetic sea hunts. Only a few star and constellation names were recorded. Bob Pope, a Quinault said to have been born in the 1830s, was able to identify the Evening and Morning Stars (regarded as chiefs), Pleiades, Orion(?), North Star, and Great Dipper. If someone were able to count all nine of the Pleiades, that person would become rich and a chief, presumably because such attention to detail and knowledge of the sky could be put to use for the greater good of the community.

Living on the outer coast and looking toward the western horizon, which other Salishan speakers called "the edge of the world," the sky filled the Quinault universe. Knowledge about it was pooled among the elders of the present (or the nobles of the past), who checked it against the periodic observations made from fixed locations. The movements of the sun played a major role in these systems, probably because it so dominated the day, when people were actively pursuing economic and social pursuits. For long-distance voyagers hugging the coast, some skylore also had navigational significance.

## Kwakiutl

For the Kwakiutl, living along the Inside Passage of British Columbia, the universe had four realms: the sky of immortals, the earth of mortals, the underworld of ghosts, and the undersea of wealthy immortals, which included the land of the salmon people on its rim (Boas 1935 : 125–40).

Of these realms, the sky had priority. A world like that of earth—except that its inhabitants, houses, and resources were all vastly more significant—the heavens were the home of the sun, moon, stars, Thunderbird, and ancestors who came to earth to found many of the tribal houses. The sky chief, associated with abalone and the sun, governed this realm. In some town histories, the sun is called his son and the clouds his daughters. In others, the chief, whose tribe is the stars, is called Post of Heaven, and he went down to earth along a copper pole to establish hereditary treasures and trails of benefit for human communities. In other instances, the ancestors of many of the Kwakiutl tribes were believed to have lived in the sky as birds, generally the Thunderbird and his younger brothers, who flew down to earth and assumed human form to become the founding ancestors of important Kwakiutl social units, called *numaym* in this native language.

Even now, some mortals can still go to the sky and stars during dreams in order to receive important revelations. Coming to various people at different times, such dreams are individual events, separate from the sacred histories which validate the claims of corporate houses to hereditary crests: inherited, heraldic art forms involving song, dance, design, and drama. Crests have two contexts for expressions, with winter ceremonials—dramatizing the rituals of ancestors holding sacred names—and potlatches when families give away food and wealth in honor of other, more historical names. Ancestors believed to come from the sky were described or impersonated during both of these events. Taken together, such dreams, winter ceremonials, and potlatches served to emphasize the importance of the sky for individuals, families, and towns.

## Bella Coola

According to Bella Coolas, the sky is the location of *Nusmatta,* the gigantic house of the Creator (Ałquntam), who was and is the first cause (McIlwraith 1948). It is from the sky that everything came and it is to the sky, specifically *Nusmatta,* that all return. The Creator sent the ancestors of various kindred families to specific locales on the earth, often wearing the skins of specific bird species when alighting on particular peaks. There, they removed the skin cloak, which went back to heaven and assumed human form. Ever since, the route between earth and sky via such a peak has been followed by the souls of members of the same family as each is born and dies. Named immortals made these passages and constituted the actors of the sacred history, which is transmitted through the families and households of their descendants, enabling each generation to perpetuate these immortal names.

At the beginning, the Creator set up a tally post in *Nusmatta* for every Bella Coola who would ever live. Since mythic names were and are hereditary, it seems likely that these posts represented ancestral names, rather than specific individuals, since each post is emblazoned with a crest (species cloak) of the first ancestor. When the person linked with the post becomes ill, the post leans. Shamans will sometimes go above to straighten it up, if possible, or to estimate the duration of that life by the precariousness of its angle.

Also in the beginning, the Creator set up an enormous wash basin with many little compartments holding water. Each one holds the water of life for a designated individual (or name), and shamans also may have gone to inspect these in ancient times. Even now, the washing of patients during shamanic cures seems to be related to the symbolism of this basin.

At death, a person divided into corpse, shadow, and ghost. The spirit becomes a ghost and travels back through its generations of ancestors until it reaches the spot where the first of them was sent to earth by the Creator, dons the cloak of the species it used to float to the mountain top, and ascends to heaven to live in *Nusmatta*. Existence above is like that on earth, but all personal skills and abilities are enhanced.

When a member of a secret society died, a drama was enacted to make it appear that the body itself was carried away through the smokehole by the ancestral crest, graphically representing the journey of the dead along its ancestral route back to the sky.

After the funeral, memorials were held, of which the most significant was the Bella Coola version of the potlatch, whose hallmark, setting it apart from that of their neighbors, is the central importance given to the dramatic enactment of the return of a deceased relative in the guise of a crest (McIlwraith 1948: 458). Equally unlike similar ceremonies by other tribes, there was singing but no dancing (McIlwraith 1948: 470). As described for the Bella Coola with unusual clarity during such rituals, the priority of the sky is expressed through the association of life, death, and immortality with *Nusmatta* and the Creator.

In contrast to the cognatic/ambilateral societies of Salishans and Kwakiutlans along the southern coast, those of the northern coast are matrilineal. Here the crests, lore, and offices belonging to a household are passed from mother's brother to sister's son.

## Tlingit

Among the northernmost of these nations is the Tlingit, where astronomical knowledge was also important, although we know little about it. In a fine collection of narratives, arranged as poetic verses, Dauenhauer and Dauenhauer (1987: 95, cf. 330) include within a sacred history of a clan house:

People who were elders
routinely
sat outside.

We used to call it "a.an."
Here they checked
the stars,
Venus
and
the Milky
Way.
They would check where they were now,
and where the moon was rising from
and where the sun was setting from.
They would check.
People used this as a map.
They used it also to work by.
That's what he would look at toward evening.

Thus, from opposite ends of the coast, we have accounts of elders at fixed seats checking the sky and stars. Presumably, they were watching the weather, the seasons, the winds, and the availability of resources which are influenced by these.

Probably all peoples in the Northwest shared these beliefs, but they have not been well reported in print. To suggest some of the richness of such knowledge in the past, I now consider the better known Tsimshian peoples of the Skeena and Nass Rivers, in addition to offshore islands, of northern British Columbia.

## Tsimshian

Among the Tsimshian, areas of knowledge were controlled by specialists acting as advisors to the royalty, the most elite members of the heraldic houses of their communities. Alas, the last of the traditionally trained sky watchers for the Tsimshian town where I have been most involved died two weeks before I made my first visit there. My information has been drawn, therefore, from conversations with his heirs and from the available literature.

The Tsimshian have had a complex development. Over ten thousand years ago, there were people living along the North Pacific Coast near the mouths of the Skeena River and trading for obsidian from the interior. Trails in this territory were part of an established trade network by five thousand years ago and have been in continuous use since then, now as paved roads. By three thousand years ago, prestige goods were traded within a ranked society like that of historic times. Graves indicate warfare as well as trade, with a trophy head cult that echoed the Old Bering Sea Complex of Alaska and Siberia and of Shang (1600 B.C.) China. Sites in Rupert Harbor show cedar-plank houses and towns gradually increasing in size and layout. By two thousand years ago, Tsimshian society stabilized, with resource areas claimed and utilized by uncontested owners. Members of Tsimshian Coastal towns wintered near Metlakatla in Rupert Harbor, went to the Nass River for spring runs of candlefish, and utilized tributary streams of the Skeena during the summer. These aboriginal patterns continued until Russian traders began modifying them about 1750.

While the complexities of Tsimshian culture and society have been difficult to grasp, the new generation of Tsimshianists has made significant contributions by building on the turn of this century work by native collectors like Henry Tait and, particularly, William Beynon, and by working together with scholars such as Franz Boas, Marius Barbeau, Viola Garfield, Wilson Duff, and others. My own work has been both community-specific and comparative so as to present a holistic model of the Tsimshian.

As now understood, Tsimshian society was consistently structured in terms of a series of fourfold divisions. Politically, there were the Coastal/Southern and the Nishka/Gitksan tribal–drainage–linguistic polities. Socially, there were four classes of royals, nobles, commoners, and slaves, with the freeborn classes having membership in the semimoieties of Blackfish–Wolf or of Raven–Eagle.

The most common associations of these fourfold divisions had to do with habitat zones associated with various immortals. The sources of greatest power are at the bottom of the sea or the height of heaven, with the life zones grading from sea to beach, to forest, to peak, to air, and to sky.

The basic unit of the overall system was the House, a feudal corporation localized in a cedar-plank building with interior space arranged by class, rank, and sanctity. Slaves stayed nearest the door, the most vulnerable location, and the ranking family lived at the rear beside the carved and painted screen that set off the compartment where the treasures (crests and wonders) were stored.

The House had four aspects: (1) an architectural building, decorated with heraldic art; (2) a corporation whose membership descended through females, a matrilineal descent group of householders from lineages, clans, semimoiety, and moiety half; (3) a repository for corporate treasures, inherited artforms such as songs, dances, designs, and outfits based upon sacred histories detailing the adventures of the primordial holders of the immortal names; and (4) real estate, the named sites of the House, seasonal camps, resource-gathering areas, and fishing places.

Families moved with the seasons to these hereditary resource areas, gathering together in fall camps for games and festivities before settling into the large plank houses, along sheltered bays and banks for the winter ceremonial period.

Tsimshian chiefs, those holding the immortal "great name" of a House—and with it a ranked position (a "seat") within the hierarchy of clan, community, and tribal houses—held two roles during a year. In summer, the season devoted to economic pursuits, the chiefs were known as "real people," who celebrated the successful harvesting of their resources at potlatches when House members hosted guests from other houses at feasts sharing their bounty while displaying and validating their crests in public. The most important crest of a House was usually a special hat, worn by the chief during the potlatch. During winter, the sacred or religious time, chiefs "put away" their crest name(s) and "put on" their wonder (*naxnox*) name(s), each associated with a mask.

All of Tsimshian society responded to these summer/winter, economic/religious, crest/wonder dualisms that subsumed the foursomes also permeating the society. Within each town, moieties were distinguished as Owner or as Other. The Owner moiety was descended from the immortal name who founded a House and used that place and territory. The House of the greatest name of the Owner moiety occupied the center of the town, with cadet houses on either side of it and the houses of the Other moiety farther along the row of buildings facing the beach or river.

This pattern was jumbled by Eurocanadian contacts and the movement of Tsimshians to the vicinity of trading posts and mission stations. It was in the newly settled neighborhoods at Port Simpson, Prince Rupert, and both Metlakatlas that most fieldwork before the 1970s was conducted. Members of all four of the semimoieties, various towns, and the full array of ranks and classes shared space there, complicating the data. Within this novel context, Tsimshian leaders sorted themselves out by staging elaborate events, called rivalry potlatches, whereby chiefs strove to outdo each other and assume a position in an overall ranking of town chiefs. These rivalry potlatches caught the attention and ire of government officials and missionaries, who managed to convince the Canadian government to ban potlatches and wonder displays in amendments to the Indian Act in effect between 1890 and 1950, when these were decriminalized.

The Wonder System was abandoned by the Tsimshian when they became Christians through the efforts of William Duncan, an Anglican lay missionary who devoted his life to their conversion and to the development of successful economic cooperatives in the model town of Metlakatla in British Columbia. After an argument with his bishop about dispensing communion, Duncan led his converts to an island near Ketchikan, Alaska, where the community continues in American jurisdiction.

The modern Tsimshian now celebrate potlatch–like feasts during the Christmas holidays when most family members are able to return home. Crests are still made and displayed, but Christian humility has somewhat muted prideful one-upmanship. Other vestiges of the ancient society also remain, and among these is a keen interest in the environment.

While the society has changed, its cultural underpinnings have been maintained. Tsimshian culture is based on an axiomatic tension of related oppositions (between open and closed, lenses and lids, wonders and crests) expressing the fundamental importance of Light as the source for existence.

In the beginning, the universe was in twilight and its apex was a deity called Heaven, who was very sensitive. If angry, pleased, or touched by humans, he sent radiant messengers ("shining youths") to earth, each accompanied by four flashes of lightning and four crashes of thunder. Several fathered human children and started royal lines. One such father, wearing a bright garment decorated with a rainbow with stars above and the sun or moon on either side, brought his sons back to earth (Barbeau and Beynon 1987 : 268–69). Alas, the design is only verbally described, so we have no idea whether the stars related to a specific constellation or the general symbolism of the sky.

One shining youth became contaminated by humans and grew ever more greedy and lustful, becoming Raven, the Tsimshian culture hero who eventually stole Light (sun, moon, and stars) from its primordial owner and released it over the earth while greedy for candlefish (eulachon). Ever since, light and dark have alternated. At that moment, Tsimshian learned to regard the sky, the movement of the luminaries, and the will of Heaven (Dunn 1978 : 57, #1102: LAXA; noun: heaven, sky, storm) as basic to their universe.

Though proverbs are rare among Native Americans, the Tsimshian have a saying:

Heaven looks down on him; said of a poor man who is suddenly favored by good fortune. Heaven is considered the Deity, and the man upon whom he casts his eyes is successful in all his undertakings. Therefore it is a common prayer of the Tsimshian: O Heaven, look down upon us, your children! (Morison 1889:285, #5).

As Heaven had his retainers and messengers, so too did every Tsimshian chief.[1] Although the same chief changed from summer crests to winter wonders by wearing different outer garments, his (rarely, her) staff was divided into seasonal specialties based on participation in the Crest or Wonder dichotomy. For example, there were separate artists for heraldic crests or for religious wonders. The first was concerned with natural phenomena and the second with Heaven in his majesty. A few members of the staff with general skills served year around, particularly the astronomers who advised the House and its members about the proper time for scheduling events involving resource harvesting or predicting the fate of various activities. Thus, during an expedition to counter witchcraft, disguised as a war party, the leader, after reversing the sorcery, called off the warriors.

> That night, Mediks who was a seer and astrologer, read in the stars and said, "I see a very bad omen for us. It is well we shall return and delay our attack on the Kitselas (Barbeau and Beynon 1987:154).

Although sometimes called an astrologer because of this ability to prophesy, the Tsimshian term is more precise.

> GYEMGAT. noun. astronomer (specifically, a moon reader, a person who can predict the food seasons) (Dunn 1978:31, #575).

The term means someone who is literally "moon-struck" (fixated, or obsessed), derived from GYEMK (verb intransitive: hot, warm; noun: heat, month, moon, sun. (Dunn 1978:31, #576) and GYEMGMAATK (noun: moon. [same: 31, #577]). As elsewhere, each astronomer used a fixed location from which to make observations. Some, often an old man, sat on a stump that was chopped out like a chair with seat and backrest (cf. Quinault and Tlingit). He visited his seat every day at the same time, usually just before sunset to observe where the sun went down. The horizon line of the Northwest is quite rugged so it is easy to trace the course of the sun as it moves north and south with the seasons to mark the yearly calendar.

While the sun was watched daily, and particularly at the solstices, it was the moon that defined the months, when particular resources and festivals were celebrated. Based on such observations, the astronomer advised the chief on the proper time for undertakings by house and community.

A comparison (Dunn n.d.) of seven versions of Tsimshian calendars indicates nine food moons divided into three seasons, along with winter, which had three recognized winds in the first of two stages. During the winter season of overcast skies, the astronomer relied on the winds, which were both obvious and seasonally specific: "Winds drive the cycle of the seasons" (Dunn n.d. : 4). By name, these three seasonal heralds were Leaf Scabber, a strong North wind bringing the first killing frost of the year; Mould Flusher, an ESE wind coming immediately after Leaf Scrubber to purge the streams of the fungus that grew on the bodies of spawned-out salmon; and Blizzard, a NNW wind with powder snow that marks the start of Famine Winter, the second, dreaded stage of that season.

In sacred history, everything has a human form under the cloak of its kind, with immortals being much more powerful than other species. Thus, Stars, Sun, Moon, and four Winds are all humanoid immortals living in plank houses in the sky. Sometimes vengeful, they used their powers to punish a boy who mocked the Stars by taking him into the sky and tying him outside their smokehole so sparks would fall on him (Barbeau and Beynon 1987 : 306–8). In stories, the four Winds are variously treated as men or as women. Confirming the calendars, North Wind was opposed by South Wind, whose allies were East and West Winds. The daughter of South Wind married the son of North Wind and nearly froze to death until rescued by her youngest brother. Together, South, East, and West Winds forced North Wind to confine himself to four months of the year (Barbeau and Beynon 1987 : 47–49).

Other famous sky dwellers, born to the son of the Sun and a woman who survived the massacre of her town, were the Heavenly Children sent down to earth with crests on their house fronts.

> On the house of the oldest was Sun; on the next were Stars; on the next Rainbow; the next, Sky-Above; and on the youngest's house, Mirage. They were all on the front of the houses, and were painted in bright colours. The paintings were as if they were alive and supernatural (Barbeau and Beynon 1987 : 263).

Ever since, their Tsimshian descendants have had the right to portray such designs on their own housefronts to represent their relationship to the original Heavenly Children.

In another legend, Heaven became angry at noisy children and sent down a pretty feather, which carried all of them into the air and dropped them to their deaths. A secluded girl survived and from her mucus were created wondrous children who restored the dead.[2] Her sons went on to marry the daughters of the women who controlled the Winds. North Wind's daughter was Northern Lights, South's was Cloud, East's was Ripener, and West's was Sunset (Barbeau and Beynon 1987:54–55). In general, each Wind had an associated season: North and Winter, South and Summer, East and warmth, and West and ripening.

In the same way that the chiefs of each house and town joined together every winter as members of exclusive secret societies or orders, their specialists also held periodic meetings upon an elevated peak far up the Skeena River, an interior promontory—remote from most Coast, Southern, and Nass communities—and ideal for their observational purposes because surrounded by mountain ranges on all sides.

Pierce (1933:152–53), the author of the following quote, was the son of a Tsimshian mother and an English father. Though a missionary noted for his strictness to Victorian ideals, his cultural and linguistic education as a Tsimshian obviously taught him the importance of such traditions, as he relates:

> Andancaul is situated on the right bank of the Skeena River, almost five miles below Kitzeguela village. It was formerly a large fishing camp belonging to the Kit-wun-gah tribe. Behind this camp is a very high hill— the highest on the Skeena.
>
> The name of this hill is Andimaul, meaning the "Seat of Native Astronomers." The top of this hill was a specially selected place for the astronomers belonging to the different tribes to gather on an evening watching the sun sinking away on the mountains. By watching the sun in the spring of the year, and again in the fall, they claimed to be capable of discerning just what the coming season would bring forth.
>
> In the spring, they could tell whether berries were going to be plentiful or scarce, and whether there would be a good run of salmon or otherwise. Also whether the summer would be hot or cold, wet or dry. In the fall, they knew what kind of winter to expect; whether severe or mild and whether a light or heavy fall of snow, also whether any epidemics would be prevalent.
>
> One branch of the "Grease Trail," extending from the Nass [River], led right past this seat on the hill, and along this route travellers were continually passing and repassing.
>
> Today any traveller passing by may see several little spots, here and there, which is claimed to have been worn away from constant use as seats by these astronomers in the olden days.
>
> When sitting there in consultation and each one agreed, then a messenger was sent to all the different tribes warning the people and telling them

what they might expect to happen. At the present time astronomy at Andimaul is a thing of the past. This place is now a fishing camp only for a few families from Kitzegeula who have made it their home, and as they joined the Salvation Army this is now a small Salvation Army settlement with an officer in charge.

It is fitting that the Tsimshian, one of the most complexly organized societies on the North Pacific coast, would also, as shown in the quote above, have one of the most sophisticated systems for coordinating astronomical observations. As each town had its "seats" at fixed locations for checking observations, so the nations had Andancaul, a hill still revered for its memorable links with the past.

All of the peoples of the North Pacific were mariners of a high order. As such, they had practical reasons for knowing and using the stars and sky, although their routes were within sight of shore rather than pelagic. Little of this practical knowledge has survived, although what did is sufficient to indicate that celestial observation involved several overlapping systems involving the sun, stars, winds, tides, salmon migrations, and seasonal harvests. Modern Canadian place names and landform charts now dominate marine travel, so the lore of crest displays and former wonders has now become the primary conveyor of traditional knowledge. In the past, such lore would have been subjected to complex interpretations passed on during the training of apprentices by family experts in various fields. What survives of this lore reiterates Heaven as high god and skyforms as beings, immortals having humanoid essences, living much like traditional humans. Throughout, the metaphor of the House pervades all; even the universe itself was considered one enormous dwelling.

But most important of all is the metaphor of "seats." The immortal names are treated as though they occupied fixed positions within a building. The present holders of these names, similarly, occupy fixed "seats" at potlatches and other public events. In a universe believed to be in constant flux, with concurrent movements in the sky, sea, and earth, it stands to reason that those with fixed points for observation would have a better view of the panorama of life, whether it was displayed in the sky or on the earth.

# Notes

1. While Tsimshians are now avowedly Christian, Heaven reflects ancient Native American beliefs in a high god (Miller 1980).

2. According to one Tsimshian, this story took place on Digby island where the Prince Rupert airport is now located. As an outer island of the harbor, it has unusually good sight lines for air traffic which might have also been beneficial to earlier sky watchers.

# References

Barbeau, Marius, and William Beynon. 1987. *Tsimshian Narratives*, vol. 1: *Tricksters, Shamans and Heroes*, ed. John J. Cove and George F. MacDonald. Ottawa: Canadian Museum of Civilization, Mercury Series, Directorate Paper 3.

Boas, Franz. 1935. *Kwakiutl Culture as Reflected in Mythology*. Memoirs of the American Folk-Lore Society, vol. 28.

Dauenhauer, Nora Marks, and Richard Dauenhauer. 1987. *Haa Shuka, Our Ancestors: Tlingit Oral Narratives*. Seattle: University of Washington Press.

Dunn, John. 1978. *A Practical Dictionary of the Coast Tsimshian Language*. Ottawa: Canadian Ethnology Service Paper 42.

———. n.d. The Tsimshian Calendars. Manuscript in possession of the author.

Hindle, Lonnie, and Bruce Rigsby. 1973. A Short Dictionary of the Gitksan Language. *Northwest Anthropological Research Notes* 7(1): 1–60.

McIlwraith, Thomas. 1948. *The Bella Coola Indians*, vols. 1 and 2. Toronto, Ontario: University of Toronto Press.

Miller, Jay. 1980. High Minded High Gods in North America. *Anthropos* 75:916–19.

Morison, O. 1889. Tsimshian Proverbs. *Journal of American Folk-Lore* 2 : 285–86.

Newton, Norman. 1975. On Survival of Ancient Astronomical Ideas among the Peoples of the Northwest Coast. *British Columbia Studies* 26: 16–38.

Olson, Ronald. 1936. The Quinault Indians. *University of Washington Publications in Anthropology* 6(1): 1–190.

Pierce, William Henry. 1933. *From Potlatch to Pulpit*. Vancouver, British Columbia: Vancouver Bindery.

# 12

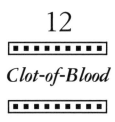

## Clot-of-Blood

ALICE B. KEHOE

---

*In these days of specialization, it is gratifying to find people such as Alice Kehoe, who is both a competent archaeologist and ethnographer. She has worked closely with the Blackfoot people and has published a major textbook on North American Indians. Here she shares some of her understanding of Blackfoot knowing, especially that concerned with treatment of in-laws and parents, as well as hunters and hunting. Not only is proper behavior patterned in the sky, but also it is painted on tipis for all to see and remember.*

---

In the night sky over the northwestern plains the Blackfoot see the Smoking Star dancing. Probably the Great Nebula in Orion (Wissler 1936:17), the Smoking Star is the transmigrated hero Clot-of-Blood, dancing forever as he danced long ago in the belly of the Wind-sucker down on earth. Flickering on top of his head is his bright flint knife.

Clot-of-Blood's story is a popular tale throughout the northern Plains. The Blackfoot version recorded at the turn of the century by Wissler with his half-Blackfoot collaborator Duvall (Wissler and Duvall 1908:53–58) and by the Dutch linguist Uhlenbeck is a well-structured quest narrative carrying our hero from miraculous birth to apotheosis as he slays monster after monster, leaving his legacy of spiritually potent tipis in the camps of the people. You may see them there today: the bear-painted and snake-painted tipis, microcosmoi with their black tops representing the sky, complete with the Pleiades and the Big Dipper on the smoke flaps and the Morning Star on the back, their central portions the earth with its patron creatures and the lower border of triangles or semicircles representing mountains or hills, sometimes with circles depicting the puffball fungus called "dusty stars" thought to be meteors fallen to earth (Kehoe in press).

There was once an old man and woman, say the Blackfoot, who suffered greatly at the hands of an unnatural man who had married all three of their daughters. Instead of honoring his parents-in-law with the choicest meat, as a man should, this monstrous fellow forced his aged father-in-law to go out each morning to drive herds of bison to the pound where the younger man waited at his ease to shoot the fat cows. When the women, his wives, would skin and butcher the cows, their husband would forbid them to give anything to the old couple. Only the youngest daughter dared to disobey, throwing bits of good meat surreptitiously into her parents' tipi.

One day, as the old man was chasing a herd he noticed a clot of blood on the trail. He recognized it to be a fetus aborted by a panicked cow. Bending down, he picked up this edible scrap and put it into his only receptacle, his quiver, hiding it from his rapacious son-in-law. Arriving back at his tipi after the hunt, the old man gave the clot of blood to his wife to cook. To their amazement, when she put it into the pot to boil, it began crying. It was a baby boy! The old woman took the child out and wrapped it in a swaddling blanket.

The monstrous son-in-law heard the crying and told his wives to find out whether it came from a baby girl who could grow up to be another wife for him, or from a boy; if a boy, it was to be killed. The wives reported they had a new sister. That night, the child instructed the old woman to hold him to each of the lodge poles in turn, beginning with the pole at the East, the doorway. When the old woman had completed the sunwise circling of the lodge, the boy jumped down, grown.

Clot-of-Blood was hungry. The old woman told him, "Oh, my boy, your brother-in-law over there is starving us." Our hero's career of rectifying evil began: taking the old man out before dawn to run a herd to the pound, Clot-of-Blood killed a fat cow and skinned it himself, telling the old man to rest. By this time, the monstrous son-in-law was up, looking for his father-in-law, enraged that he would dare go out ahead, telling the old woman in her tipi, "I have a mind to begin by killing you." When the son-in-law reached the pound, Clot-of-Blood heard him threaten the old man, "That one eating is living the last of his life." Our hero jumped up and shot the evil man dead.

Leaving the old couple to be cared for by their loving youngest daughter, Clot-of-Blood went up the river valley to a camp with many lodges. Instead of going to the tipi of the leading man as ordinary visitors would,

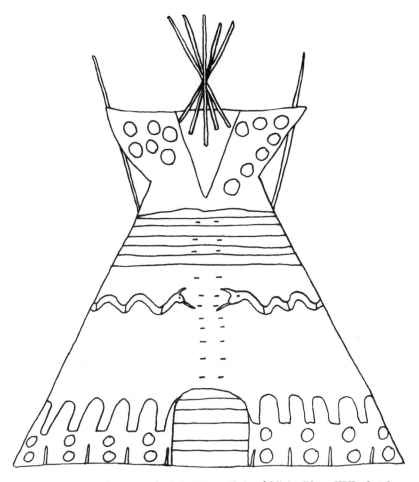

**Figure 12.1.** Snake-painted tipi. (From *Painted Tipis*, Plate XVI, Southern Plains Indian Museum and Craft Center, Andarko, Okla. 1973)

Clot-of-Blood went into a tipi of old women. "I am an old woman's child," the miraculous youth told them. The old women explained that a family of bears lived in the camp, terrorizing the people, taking the women and the meat from the corral. Clot-of-Blood went out in the morning to the corral, slaughtered the fattest cow, and distributed the choice back-fat to the old women. As they predicted, the bear cub ambled up to take the delicacy from them. Clot-of-Blood faced the bear cub and slashed him across the face.

The cub ran home, crying. His parents came toward the corral, stretching as bears do in threat. Clot-of-Blood stabbed each of them, then went into their lodge and killed all the bears but one, a young female. She he let escape, to repopulate her tribe. Giving the potent bear-painted lodge to the people, Clot-of-Blood continued his journey.

The next camp was terrorized by rattlesnakes. The biggest of them lay in his tipi surrounded by the women he had forced to serve him. Clot-of-Blood repeated his actions of seeking the hospitality of a lodge of old women, then in the morning slaughtering a bison cow for the people in their corral. While the abused people ate, he boldly entered the snakes' lodge, helped himself to the cup of berry-flavored drink standing ready for the big snake's refreshment, and struck the monster with his flint knife. Awakened, the big snake and all the snakes in the tipi reared up and rattled. Clot-of-Blood slashed at each of them, decapitating all but one young female whom he let go to carry on her tribe.

Giving the snakes' painted lodge to the old women, Clot-of-Blood went on, looking for the Wind-sucker that the old women warned him waited to eat passers-by. Pretending to be sucked in by the wind, Clot-of-Blood jumped into this monster and found its belly full of people, some already dead and others passively waiting to die. "We shall dance," announced Clot-of-Blood. He tied his flint knife on top of his head like a dance ornament and began leaping up and down. Soon, the flint knife had cut down the monster's heart hanging above its bellyful of people. Clot-of-Blood used his knife to cut an exit between the dead monster's ribs and freed its victims.

Now that he had conquered four monsters abusing camps of people, Clot-of-Blood turned to ridding the world of evil creatures preying on lone travelers. First, he was enticed by a woman inviting him to join her in the amusement of sliding down a rope as otters slide down a riverbank. Clot-of-Blood correctly surmised that this woman would kill those she seduced; he turned her trap against her by asking her to show him how to slide, then cutting the rope as she swung out, dropping her to death in rapidly flowing Cut Bank Creek. Next was a young man who suggested they wrestle together as young men like to do. Clot-of-Blood noticed a flint knife sticking up beside the trail. Our hero overcame this evil one by throwing him upon his own hidden knife. Farther on, Clot-of-Blood was approached by a woman who proposed they play with Sioux women "a game of catch." [1] Clot-of-Blood insisted on throwing the ball first, and smashed the seducer's head with it. The hero then returned to the old women's lodge, announced,

"I killed all those that treated you badly," and left the camp, accompanied by a new comrade.

After traveling a long way south, the two young men came to a large lake where the comrade told him that many people had been killed. A monster Blood-sucker lay on the shore. Clot-of-Blood awakened it by touching it with his flint knife. Slowly, the monster crawled into the water. Clot-of-Blood followed it, telling his comrade to expect to witness his death. The water of the lake rose high in turmoil as good and evil fought, the water turning red with blood. At last Thunder rolled over, rumbled and threw lightning, and completed Clot-of-Blood's mission by flinging the monster onto the prairie. The lake was no more, and on its dry bed—which can be seen today with blood-red rocks (Black Boy 1973 : 70)—were Clot-of-Blood's bones. In the night, his spirit is seen with the spirits of all the dead people, all the myriads, all stars.

In the Blackfoot universe, the tale of Clot-of-Blood is an account of events that is presumably true; that is, the Blackfoot do not oppose history to myth (Wissler and Duvall 1908 : 17). Truth resides in the authenticity of meaning, more than of events. Clot-of-Blood is benevolence personified and located in the interdigitation of the Above world and the mundane earth. Above live Sun, Moon, their son Morning Star, and the multitudinous spirits we see as stars. On earth we see beings in the form of animals, humans, meteorological phenomena, sometimes even rocks; all the temporary manifestations of almighty spirit. Bison were the embodiment and symbol of the good life, of benevolent Power; the most crucial resource for the Plains peoples, bison furnished the bulk of their food, lodge covers and bedding, and raw material for a variety of storage containers and tools. Clot-of-Blood, the bison fetus miraculously born as a man, is benevolence personified.

Clot-of-Blood quests for evil in order to destroy it. He kills a bad human, the human-like powerful bad bears, the creepingly inhuman bad snakes, and then the bad amorphous tornado (Wind-sucker). For each type of people killed—human, bear, snake—he leaves alive a young female, making it clear that not the species, but only the evil among them, are to be eliminated. After progressing from a family horror through larger horrors to the howling sucking wind, Clot-of-Blood turns from these open threats to slay veiled evil, the danger of lust, heterosexual and homosexual.[2] Finally, he returns to the larger scene for his apotheosis. The lake is the home of a Great One so awesome it is not directly named.[3] In translations, such Great Ones are called water-bears—the more literal translation—or water-bulls. His final adventure pits Clot-of-Blood against nameless dread itself, the embodiment of evil force. In the cosmic battle, climaxed by Thunder's intervention, both die. The human comrade walks away, back to the people who now can live freed of so much evil.

The cosmic significance of the tale is so underscored by noting the wider occurrence of some of its motifs. Robert Hall notes that the constellation we call the sword of Orion is known to the Crow and Hidatsa, Siouan-speaking northern Plains neighbors to the Blackfoot, as the severed hand of the mythical personage Long Arm, owner of an all-seeing powerful ax (Hall #1977:506, 510–11), links Long Arm with the Aztec Tezcatlipoca, whose obsidian "smoking mirror" makes him all-seeing. That the Blackfoot identify the nebula in Orion's sword as Clot-of-Blood's flint knife and call it the Smoking Star may reflect an association between its flickering and the glancing of light off stone blades held by powerful deities. The possibility that some elements of the tale were borrowed from Hidatsa suggests that there is a significance to old women in the Blackfoot story, derived from the Hidatsa's Old Woman Who Never Dies, Grandmother Earth (cf. Kehoe in press). Old Woman's Grandson is a Hidatsa culture hero, and Clot-of-Blood specifically says of himself, "I am an old woman's child." The monster met in the final battle appears to be a Blackfoot version of the Siouan underwater panther that roils the waters and eats people.

More important than the sources from which elements may have been borrowed is the integrity of the tale itself. The basic form of the tale, a starving old couple finding a miraculous babe that grows to manhood overnight and then sallies forth to rectify evil, is widespread (Thompson 1957, vol. 5:396–97, motif T540). The Blackfoot version, especially as told by Tatsey to Uhlenbeck, is aesthetically pleasing (cf. Wissler and Duvall 1908:17, for Blackfoot valuation of this aspect): Clot-of-Blood is born in a pot of boiling water and dies in a lake of roiling water; there are four antagonists abusing camps of people, then four against our hero alone (four is the ritual number for the Blackfoot). The well-structured tale incarnates life-giving spirit symbolized by bison in the form of a human nurtured by old women, whose longevity coupled with women's innate reproductive power earns them deep respect in Blackfoot society (Kehoe 1976).

The cosmic significance of the tale of Clot-of-Blood has not been appreciated by earlier ethnographers, in part because none realized the hero is a bison. Uhlenbeck and Wissler were gentlemen of their culture, unfamiliar with such raw facts of reproduction as the appearance of an early-aborted fetus. Because I suffered a miscarriage, I know such a fetus looks like a clot of blood. Reading the story of Clot-of-Blood, I was struck by the likelihood that he was produced by a cow in the herd run in by the old man. I checked the meaning of his name, Kutoyis, and knew my hunch was correct when I learned *kutoyis* refers only to menstrual blood and the placenta.[4] Bison meant life to the Blackfoot: the tale is an epic myth about life battling death.

The real theme of the Clot-of-Blood myth is the beneficence of the Almighty. Pitying humankind, it provides life-supporting bison and, at the same time, curbs the tendencies of other creatures to abuse us. When Blackfoot see younger couples honoring their parents by supporting them as well as possible, when they see bears and snakes and tornados keeping proper distance from human settlements, they can remember how these well-regulated relationships were enforced by the old woman's child, life-supporting spirit incarnate. When Blackfoot are tempted to stray from the path of virtue, they may recall how Clot-of-Blood exposed the danger inhering in beckoning seducers. These lessons are vivid in Blackfoot consciousness because they can see on earth the dry lakebed with its blood-colored rocks, Clot-of-Blood's deathbed, and in the sky at night they can see the flickering of his flint knife, there in the bright constellation we call Orion's Sword.

## Notes

1. "Sioux women" catching balls is a double entendre on "ball," which among the Blackfoot as in English, refers also to testicles. The ball game is also called "Cree women" (Wissler 1911:58), and Cree are famous among the Blackfoot for their love charms.
2. Grinnell's (1892:36) version describes the wrestler as a "handsome woman," as do Wissler and Duvall (1908:57), but in the 1940s the Blackfoot storyteller Cecile Black Boy (1973:70), like Uhlenbeck's narrator Joseph Tatsey, gives it as a young man.
3. Allan R. Taylor notes (personal communication, November 15, 1985) that the Blackfoot word for *bear* is not etymologically descended from the common Algonkian word for *bear*, and elsewhere he has mentioned the prevalence of innovative descriptive or metaphorical terms in place of standard forms in Alberta Assiniboine and Sarcee as well as in Blackfoot (Taylor 1983:34).
4. Personal communication, Hugh A. Dempsey, October 22, 1981.

## References

Black Boy, C. 1973. Blackfeet Tipi Legends. In *Painted Tipis by Contemporary Plains Indians Artists*. Washington: U.S. Dept. of the Interior Indian Arts and Crafts Board.

Grinnell, G. B. 1892. *Blackfoot Lodge Tales.* New York: Charles Scribner's Sons.

Hall, Robert L. 1977. An Anthropocentric Perspective for Eastern United States Prehistory. *American Antiquity* 42, no. 4:499–518.

Kehoe, A. B. 1976. Old Woman Had Great Power. *Western Canadian Journal of Anthropology* 6:68–76.

———. In press. Ethnoastronomy on the American Plains. In *Ethnoastronomy of the Americas,* ed. V. D. Chamberlain and M. J. Young. Thousand Oaks, Calif.: Slo'w Press.

Taylor, A. R. 1983. Old Vocabularies and Linguistic Research: The Case of Assiniboine. *Na'pao* 13:31–44.

Thompson, Stith. 1957. *Motif-Indx of Folk-Literature.* Bloomington: Indiana University Press.

Uhlenbeck, C. C. 1911. Original Blackfoot Texts. *Verhandelingen der Koninklijke Akademie van Westenschappen te Amsterdam. Afdeeling Letterkunde* n.r. deel XII, no. 1.

Wissler, C. 1911. The Social Life of the Blackfoot Indians. *American Museum of Natural History Anthropological Papers* 7, pt. I:1–64.

———. 1912. Ceremonial Bundles of the Blackfoot Indians. *American Museum of Natural History Anthropological Papers* 7, pt. 2:65–289.

———. 1936. *Star Legends among the American Indians.* American Museum of Natural History Guide Leaflet Series 91.

Wissler, C., and D. C. Duvall. 1908. Mythology of the Blackfoot Indians. *American Museum of Natural History Anthropological Papers* 2, pt. I:1–163.

# 13

## On the Necessity of Sacrifice in Lakota Stellar Theology as Seen in "The Hand" Constellation, and the Story of "The Chief Who Lost His Arm"

RONALD GOODMAN

*As an instructor in the Lakota Sinte Gleska College, Ronald Goodman found he was in turn being instructed in aspects of Lakota ethnoastronomy. Those experiences led to a recent monograph on Lakota astronomy. His sensitivity to the Native view and his adherence to their requests cause him to summarize where others have been able to quote directly. Nonetheless, what follows is an eloquent affirmation of the continuing importance to Sioux people of the Sun Dance and its relation to the sky and its native beings.*

The Lakota story "The Chief Who Lost His Arm," together with the Lakota constellation called "The Hand," (Fig. 13.1) communicates a sacred teaching, which describes both the sacrificial origin of the world and the necessity of sacrifice each year when life on Earth needs to be renewed.

Generosity is a cardinal Lakota virtue. In the story, the Chief's selfishness, his unwillingness to make any meaningful self-sacrifice, is shown to be not only self-defeating, but also a threat to cosmic order.

The Lakota understand the stars to be "the holy breath of God," the *woniya* of *Wanka Tanka*. Thus, the Lakota constellations in the night sky represent sacred utterances—holy speech, whose specific meanings are transmitted through stories and ceremonies in the oral tradition. The Lakota interpret the annual disappearance from the night sky of The Hand constellation in the spring as a divine signal of the impending loss of the Earth's fertility. Therefore, the disappearance of The Hand (which represents the arm of the Chief in this story) is also a summons to the whole Lakota nation. In the context of Lakota culture, it means that a willing sacrifice of blood is necessary.

Today, as in traditional times, the annual Sun Dance, which occurs in midsummer, provides the opportunity for Lakota men and women to participate in the cosmic renewal of life by shedding their own blood for the sake of all life. Their generosity in pledging to dance in the Sun Dance stands in contrast to that of the Chief's selfishness. Self-sacrifice is primal for the Lakota, as it is involved in the very creation of life as we know it. The spiritual intention behind the voluntary shedding of blood during the Sun Dance can be found in Lakota oral tradition. According to James Walker's version of the Lakota creation myth (Walker 1983), the original creation of this world occurred when the first of the superior gods, *Inyan,* "The Rock," gave his own blood to create the Earth and sky. Here is a key portion of the story:

### Rock and Earth

Inyan (Rock) had no beginning for he was when there was no other. His spirit was "Wakan Tanka" (The Great Mystery), and he was the first of the superior gods. Then he was soft and shapeless like a cloud, but he had all the powers and was everywhere. "Han" was then, but she is not a being; she is only the black of darkness.

Inyan longed to exercise his powers, but could not do so for there was no other that he might use his powers upon. If there were to be another, he must create it of that which he must take from himself, and he must give to it a spirit and a portion of his blood. As much of his blood would go from him so much of his powers would go with it, for his powers were in his blood and his blood was blue. He decided to create another as a part of himself so that he might keep control of all the powers.

To do this, he took from himself that which he spread around about himself in the shape of a great disk whose edge is where there can be no beyond. This disk he named *"Maka"* (Earth). He gave to Maka a spirit that is *"Makaakan"* (Earth Goddess). She is the second of the superior gods, but she is part of *Inyan.*

### The Waters, the Sky, and the Great Spirit

To create Maka, Inyan took so much from himself that he opened his veins, and all his blood flowed from him so that he shrank and became hard and powerless. As his blood flowed from him, it became blue waters which are the waters upon the earth. But the powers cannot abide in waters, and when the blood of Inyan became the waters, the powers separated themselves from it and assumed another shape. This other being took the form of a great blue dome whose edge is at, but not upon, the edge of Maka (Walker 1983 : 206–7).

The first creation was accomplished through self-sacrifice in the shedding of one's life-force: blood. Contemporary Lakota Sun Dancers are participating in the renewal of life. Mircea Eliade writes that human actions gain their fullest meaning "by reproducing a primordial act, repeating a mythical example . . . Reality is a function of the imitation of a celestial archetype" (Eliade 1952:4–5). In order to do this, the Lakota imitate the conduct of Inyan, who provides a sacred archetype or pattern. As Inyan sacrificed his blood to create the world, so the Sun Dancers voluntarily sacrifice their flesh and shed their blood in order symbolically to re-create the world and renew life on Earth each year.

Joseph Epes Brown has written about the necessity of sacrifice in his article on the Sun Dance:

> When man in awful ceremony is actually tied to this Tree of the Center by the flesh of his body, or when women make offerings of pieces cut from their arms, sacrifice through suffering is accomplished that the world and all beings may live, that life be renewed, that man may become who he is.
>
> The Sun Dance, thus, is not a celebration by man for man; it is an honoring of all life and the source of all life, that life may go on, that the circle be a cycle, that all the world and man may continue on the path of the cycle of giving, receiving, bearing, being born in suffering, growing, and so finally to be born again. So it is told that only in sacrifice is sacredness accomplished; only in sacrifice is identity possible and found. It is only through the suffering in sacrifice that finally freedom is known and laughter in joy returns to the world. (Brown 1978:12)

As so often happens in life, lessons are learned only through inappropriate behavior. The lessons of Inyan and the Sun Dance are reinforced through the negative example of the Chief Who Lost His Arm.

Two Lakota versions of the story exist. The first was told by Black Elk to Neihart in 1944 (De Mallie 1984); the second version was given in 1986 by Ollie Napeshni, a contemporary storyteller, at Sinte Gleska College in Rosebud, South Dakota, where it may be examined in the archives.

Black Elk's version can be paraphrased as follows:

## The Chief Who Lost His Arm

Fallen Star announces that he is planning to marry a woman in a nearby village. When he speaks to the woman, who is the daughter of a chief, she tells him that the Wakinyans, or "Thunder Beings," have torn away her father's arm. She will only marry the man who is able to recover it.

Fallen Star goes in search of the arm. As he travels from village to village, he meets spirits who give him special powers. He gains a sinew and a live coal, an eagle plume, a swallow feather, a wren feather, and words of power. These gifts will enable him to change his shape, and also to escape from the Wakinyans once he finds the chief's arm.

As he goes from village to village, he sometimes seems to be in the area of the Black Hills, but at the same time he also appears to be traveling through the star world. He travels through three villages of "star peoples," and it is said that his son will have to visit the other four.

Fallen Star reaches the Wakinyans and by changing into a man he is able to outwit the Wakinyans and Iktomi and recover the chief's arm. By using the other powers he was given, he is able to flee successfully. He restores the arm to the chief, marries the daughter and they have a son (DeMallie 1984:404–9).

Like many Lakota stories, "The Chief Who Lost His Arm" initially describes how not to behave. Lakota listeners understand implicitly that the chief had been selfish, and that his selfishness threatened to interrupt the cosmic cycle. Continuation of life requires the renewal of self-sacrifice. Because the Chief apparently refuses to make any offering of himself, divine intervention becomes necessary. First, "The Thunders," the Wakinyans, tear off his arm and hide it. Second, Fallen Star (who has a human mother, and a father who is a star, that is, a spirit) must complete the process by struggling with the Thunders and regaining the arm.

Implicit in this story is the Lakota understanding that the Wakinyans take away the fertility of the Earth every year. They also take away each year the masculine power to fertilize the Earth, which the arm symbolizes. This is an essential function of the Wakinyans in the annual cycle of life, death, and renewal. The power to generate life is gained, lost, and regained each year, but only through sacrifice.

The cosmic cycle is presented on the narrative level as a typical hero story that even includes elements of kingly succession. The Chief does not voluntarily give his arm to the Thunders. He represents the old year. That is why restoring his arm does not really restore him. Fallen Star has earned the spiritual right and the generative power that the arm symbolizes. Fallen Star represents the new chief and the new year. He has proven himself worthy of marrying the Chief's daughter. The daughter is homologous with a young and fertile Mother Earth. The son born to Fallen Star and the Chief's daughter stands for the emergent life-forms of a renewed earth. The fact that Fallen Star is sometimes in the sky and sometimes on earth symbolically links the two and reinforces the importance of people living according to precepts set forth in the sky.

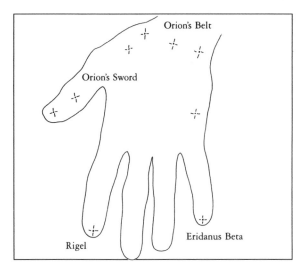

**Figure 13.1.** The Hand constellation. It occurs in Orion and represents the hand that the Chief lost when he lost his arm. The belt of Orion is the wrist, and the sword is the thumb. Rigel makes the index finger. The little finger is the northernmost star in Eridanus, Eridanus beta.

What the old chief loses involuntarily, the sun dancers also symbolically vow to recover. They overcome chaos, death, and the earth's infertility by doing as Inyan and Fallen Star had done. Thus, as Inyan created the world by shedding his blood, the sun dancers hope to renew the world by voluntarily sacrificing their blood.

The Hand constellation (*nape*), which was identified for me by William Red Bird of the Rosebud Sioux Reservation in 1986, occurs in Orion, and represents the hand that the Chief lost when he lost his arm (Fig. 13.1). The belt of Orion is the wrist. The Sword of Orion is the thumb. Rigel makes the index finger. The star for the little finger is the northernmost star in Eridanus, *Eridanus beta*.

Years ago, *nape* had its heliacal setting a short time before midsummer. This was the period when summer solstice occurred in *Matotipila,* "The Bear's Lodge," a Lakota constellation consisting of eight stars around Gemini. As stated earlier, the Lakota regard the disappearance from the night sky of The Hand constellation as a divine signal of impending loss of fertility. This necessary annual loss is represented in the story by the Wakinyans who tear off the chief's arm. It is also an announcement that sacrifice will be required to recover the power to fertilize the earth again.

The reappearance in the night sky of the *nape* constellation occurred in autumn. It then approached the meridian shortly before winter solstice. Thus, at one time, the *nape* announced the imminent onset of the two great divisions of the year: the summer and winter solstices.

The reappearance of The Hand is a cosmic affirmation that the blood sacrifice during the Sun Dance at summer solstice has been effective and successful. In the dead of winter, the Lakota know they have helped to make life possible again in the coming year. They have reenacted the archetypal sacrifice of *Inyan*. They have recovered the Chief's arm as Fallen Star had done, thereby helping to renew life on Earth. By following sacred precepts limned in sky and story, the Lakota affirm their way of living and practicing ritual not only as proper but also as essential for the continuance of the very universe.

## Notes

1. As the stars slowly precess, they change both their positions with respect to the geographic pole and their time of helical rise and set.

## References

Brown, Joseph Epes. 1978. "Sun Dance," *Parabola* 3, no. 2 : 12, 15.
Eliade, Mircea. 1952. *The Myth of the Eternal Return*. Princeton, N.J.: Princeton University Press.
DeMallie, R. 1984. *The Sixth Grandfather*. Lincoln: University of Nebraska Press.
Walker, James. 1983. *Lakota Myth*, ed. Elaine A. Jahner. Lincoln: University of Nebraska Press.

# 14

■■■■■■■■■

## The Chief and His Council:
## Unity and Authority from the Stars

■■■■■■■■■

### VON DEL CHAMBERLAIN

*Both an astronomer and the director of the Hanson Planetarium in Salt Lake City, Von Del Chamberlain has recently been working with Navajo ethno- and archaeo-astronomy. He is, however, best known for his work with Pawnee ethnoastronomy, a subject he pursues here as well. In this essay he demonstrates how a constellation charters human action, giving it both proper form and substance.*

Probably nothing is more symbolic of the American Indians than the image of a chief. Even more impressive is a gathering of chiefs, sitting in council to unite the concerns of many groups. This representative procedure for making weighty decisions might well go back to prehistoric times, and it continues in the modern world. Nations—even groups of nations—have adopted it, and it is the essence of modern consensus management. Leaders gather together to share information and opinions, and decisions flow out of such gatherings to influence the lives of the represented groups.

For the Skidi Band of Pawnee Indians (Fig. 14.1), the principle of Chiefdomship was found in the sky. The "star-that-does-not-move" (Polaris) was considered by the Skidi to be the Chief Star, which watched over its heavenly band to be sure that they continued to follow their prescribed paths. This star also looked down upon the people and set the pattern for their government.

Not far from the Chief Star is a circlet of stars which the Skidi and other American Plains groups called the Chief's Council. This group has been identified as the stars commonly known today as Corona Borealis (Chamberlain 1982:137–41). As we shall see, the Skidi associated these stars with both abstract and concrete factors that involved their deities,

**Figure 14.1.** A group of Pawnee headmen. (Photograph by William H. Jackson, Loupfork Village, Nebraska, 1871. Smithsonian Institution, National Anthropological Archives neg. no. 1228.)

their leaders, and even their homes. All of these factors can be brought together in the Skidi concept of the importance of being united.

Almost opposite the Chiefs in the sky, there is another group of stars which, to the Skidi, also represented the principle of unity. This is one of the best known groups in the entire firmament—the Pleiades.

## Skidi Cosmic Traditions

Skidi Pawnee cosmology elaborates traditions based upon objects and phenomena of the sky (Chamberlain 1982). This is a most unusual set of beliefs

focused on stars rather than on the more common Native American orientation to Earth and Sun. Indeed, the Skidi obsession with planets and stars
contrasts rather sharply with the solar, lunar, and terrestrial deities of many
other tribes.

In order to place concepts relating to the Chief Star, the Council of
Chiefs, and the Seven Stars in perspective, the highlights of Skidi cosmology are briefly reviewed here. This material comes from what George
Dorsey (1904: xxiii) referred to as "cosmogenic" traditions—those dealing
with ideas of origin, ritual, and ceremony. Thus, we are concerned here
with beliefs, rather than with less serious lore.

The Skidi did not identify *Tirawahat,* the supreme god, with any
object, unless it was the entire sky. They thought of him as residing at the
zenith, with his influence radiating over everything. The other sky gods,
carefully placed by *Tirawahat* in their proper positions, assisted him in
planning and accomplishing creation of Earth and people, and then in
providing for the people who had been created. The sky gods, headed by the
unseen *Tirawahat,* were the supreme first council held at the time when
*Tirawahat* assigned the others to their stations and gave them instructions
about what they should do (Dorsey 1904: 3–14).

From that time onward, everything was planned in the East, the
masculine direction, where all the gods of heaven would make their appearance and where the dawn would burst forth each day. Here the red Morning
Star, first of the gods to be created by *Tirawahat,* presided over a great council of all the star gods. At this council, the creation of people was planned.
The great white star of the West, the Evening Star, opposed the plan. It was
in her domain, the western, feminine side of the sky, that the plan must be
carried out, for she ruled over all of the powers of fertility, birth, and
renewal of life.

The male gods of the East courted the beautiful White Star of the
West. None was successful until the Red Star determined to travel west in
order to realize the council's decision. Thus, Morning Star made a difficult
legendary journey to the abode of the Evening Star. En route, he encountered and conquered dangers, and finally mated with the female star,
bringing about the birth of the first human, a female child who was placed
on earth. This westward movement of Morning Star, the conquered dangers, and the successful courtship of Evening Star have extremely interesting astronomical interpretations that I have explored elsewhere in detail
(Chamberlain 1982: 52–90).

The first male child was the offspring of Sun and Moon, and from the union of the girl and boy came the first group of people. As these primal people lived their lives, they encountered other people and found that they could understand each other. Each group paid homage to a star which had given them a sacred bundle, along with ceremonies needed for successful life. The patron stars were some of those which sat together in the original councils in the sky. The various groups of people began to realize that the powers of their bundles and associated rites might be amplified through unification of all the bundles.

Thus, following the pattern which had been set in the heavens, the groups met in the first great council on Earth. Coming from different directions, they established their camps on Earth in positions that mirrored the pattern of the patron stars in the heavens above. Each of their individual bundles and accompanying ceremonies was bonded into a great round of ceremonies of far greater power than could be realized from any of its parts alone. Thus, the outcome of the unification council was the formation of the Skidi Band, a confederation of groups previously separated. The principle of council lies at the very core of Skidi cultural identity, and objects and phenomena of the sky are primary theological as well as natural elements of their worldview.

## The Chief

Modern people are most familiar with the North Star as the navigational star. To the Skidi, the way-finding principle of this star was more one of leadership than of geographical orientation. The records we fortunately possess of Skidi traditions tell us how important this star was to these people. Again, we turn to the cosmogenic tales recorded by Dorsey, which explained the relationships between stars, natural phenomena, and people.

> Tirawa spoke to the gods, and said: "Each of you gods I am to station in the heavens; and each of you should receive certain powers from me, for I am about to create people who shall be like myself. They shall be under your care. I will give them your land to live upon, and with your assistance they shall be cared for" . . . "You" (pointing to *Karariwari*, Star-that-does-not-Move, North-Star) "shall stand in the north. You shall not move; for you shall be the chief of all the gods that shall be placed in the heavens, and you shall watch over them." . . . Then Star-that-does-not-Move was told that in

after time, when the people should be upon the earth, he should communicate with the chief of the people, so that the people should have a chief among them, who should resemble the Star-that-does-not-Move presiding over his people (Dorsey 1904 : 3–4).

The pole star, then, was a symbol of stability, leadership, and guardianship. This concept was deeply ingrained in Skidi society. The North Star was, to some extent, representative of *Tirawahat*, the creator god who was never seen as the other gods were. Murie (n.d.) refers to the North Star: "It is the chief. It sits just like the Father who sits above . . . It imitates the Father sitting in the heavens." The Pawnee thought of *Tirawahat* as residing at the zenith, always directly overhead. The Chief Star, always present in the sky, represented all of the leadership qualities that *Tirawahat* bestowed to the people through the chiefs.

The Skidi people once possessed a bundle given to them by the North Star. It was said that the bundle contained, among other things, a heavy stone which had come from the Chief Star. They kept a lance, covered with feathers, with the bundle. This seems to have been a kind of effigy of the Chief Star. "It looks like a spear, but is covered with all kinds of birds. It has all kinds of birds flocking around it . . ." (Chamberlain 1982 : 106). The feathers might have been symbolic of birds as messengers between the people and the stars—thus, messages between the chiefs on the earth and the Chief in the sky.

The Skidi society of chiefs emulated the qualities they recognized in the Chief Star. They painted their faces as they had been directed to do by the star; they wore the downy feather on their heads; and they did not dance and sing, but maintained rigorous control over their actions, voices, and temperaments, attempting to emulate the stars. They did all they could to keep the type of order among the people which they perceived in the constant and consistent movements of the stars.

The North Star, the Great Chief in the sky, always visible in the night, was the supreme example known to all the Skidi and clearly related in their thought to their own chiefs. The people looked to these leaders to be like the celestial prototype and to guide them in smooth, consistent, and repetitive paths. They would perform needed ceremonies; they would plant and hunt and in all ways live in a well-ordered sequence. They would repeat the sequence each year, just as the stars of heaven repeat their seasonal aspects relative to both Earth and Sky. In this sacred way, under the guidance of both heavenly and earthly leaders, the Skidi believed that their lives should be spent as the sky gods had intended.

## The Council of Chiefs

The Skidi Pawnee people were comfortable in living in either of two houses. They spent much of the year hunting on the open plains, under the roof of the sky. But they always returned to their villages, where they planted gardens to supplement what they gleaned from the bison herds. Here, they resided in earth lodges (Fig. 14.2) that were constructed to resemble the great lodge of the world.

The earth lodges were home and observatory as well as the confirmation of Skidi life and practices.

> We have no full data as to the precise methods of observation, that being part of the professional knowledge of the priests; but it is said that the usual method was to note the positions of certain stars at their first appearance after sunset and again at the time of year when they could be first seen upon the horizon of dawn. Observations were also taken through the smoke hole of a lodge, by taking a seat west of the fire at sunset and noting what stars could be seen (Murie 1981 : 41).

Details of the observational possibilities of a Skidi lodge are explored elsewhere (Chamberlain 1982 : 134, 163–83). Here, we will concentrate on the symbolic elements of the lodge, focusing on the groups of stars considered in this chapter.

People entered these structures through eastward-facing doorways, just as the Sun, Moon, and stars appeared over the eastern horizon. The fireplace in the center was symbolic of the Sun, which gave warmth and light to the world. There was a very sacred place in the West, opposite the entrance, which was dedicated to the Evening Star, mother of the first human child. Four intercardinal posts provided the primary support for the dome-shaped roof, and these posts were symbolic of four primary stars that supported the dome of the sky. Finally, directly at the center of the roof was the circular smokehole, which represented a circular group of stars that passed nearly overhead in the sky—the stars called "the Council of Chiefs."

> This council circle corresponds to the circle of stars just overhead (Corona Borealis), called by nearly all of the Plains tribes "the camp circle." By the Skidi it is spoken of as the "Council of the Chiefs," over which the North-Star presides (Dorsey 1904 : 340 n. 121).

In the collection of George Dorsey's field notes (Dorsey n.d.; Chamberlain 1982 : 158–61) in the Field Museum in Chicago, there is a small ledger containing the handwritten account of the building and dedication of one of the last Pawnee lodges. The account, told by Buffalo Skidi, dated

**Figure 14.2.** Pawnee earth house constructed on the fairgrounds at St. Louis, 1904. (Smithsonian Institution, National Anthropological Archives neg. no. 15–498.)

April 30, 1905, briefly relates the story of the very first lodge made to protect the first human children of the stars.

It was *Tirawahat* himself who determined how the lodge should be built, so that the children of the stars should have a house like the heavens (Chamberlain 1982 : 156). He did this, as always, through the sky gods. Each star was to furnish a post to stand in the proper direction representing the star. *Tirawahat* himself marked the very center by causing an ash tree to grow there. Then, the Circle Stars overhead sat in council and decided how the fireplace should be made. They commanded the Sun to send down fire from heaven to burn the tree, establishing the place of warmth at what would be the heart of the lodge, standing directly beneath the place of *Tirawahat* and honored by the direct light of the Council of Chiefs as they passed overhead.

The lodge, which was constructed according to the blueprint established in this supposedly ancient story, had just two openings. One faced the East, the direction where thinking was done, where planning took place, and where warmth and light originated. The smokehole faced the Above, the direction of origin of all things, the place of the light of wisdom and original instruction. It was here that smoke would exit the lodge to carry messages to the celestial gods. Chiefs of the people sometimes would sit around the coals, which were believed to obtain their light from the

Morning Star and the Sun; while overhead, the celestial Council of Chiefs would pass nearly in conjunction with the direction of *Tirawahat* himself. The chiefs of the people could look up and see all the things that reminded them of the source of wisdom, authority, and unity.

The Council of Chiefs, then, was symbolic of the very principle of council which was of such great importance to the Skidi. In this concept, we see relationships to *Tirawahat,* whose station was the zenith. He remained at the zenith, not partaking of the motion of the star gods. At the zenith of the lodge was the opening shaped like the Council of Stars, which could be seen through the opening, and each of which was a chief: all relating to the great unseen, supreme, Chief residing at the zenith of the sky.

There are many other probable symbolic relationships. The chiefs among the people received their authority from the stars. Even the fire, believed to contain power from the Sun and stars, seemed to represent authority from the gods, and they could use that fire to burn sweet grasses, sending prayers mingled with the smoke which moved upward through the top of the lodge toward the top of the great sky lodge.

For present purposes, the shape of the group of stars is most important. The circle is, of course, the ideal arrangement for a group of people to deliberate effectively as equals. It is the arrangement which the Skidi considered appropriate and which they believed was prescribed by the stars.

> The chiefs sat in a circle in the lodge, imitating the circle of the stars right straight up in the heavens in the night (Dorsey, n.d. box 8, "North-Star bundle ceremony": 2).

Perhaps the Skidi thought of the smokehole as being the opening through which *Tirawahat* and the star gods watched over them, as well as the place to ventilate smoke. It is consistent with what we know about the Skidi to suspect that they might have considered the smokehole to be the symbolic orifice for the flow of unifying power from the stars into the Skidi residence.

The concept of council was found throughout Skidi traditions.

> The circle of stars over head, Corona Borealis, is known as the Council of Chiefs, Lesaru. This council is symbolic of, and is to remind the people of the original council of stars presided over by the Morning Star (Dorsey, n.d., box 7, "Religion/general": 104).

These important stars, then, represented the great mythical councils as well as the councils to be held on Earth.

The Chiefs in Council were immensely important to the Skidi. Their dimness in the sky was more than compensated for by their conceptual brilliance. They are referred to with great frequency in the field notes and publications on the Skidi.

For example, Dorsey (1904:65–68) recorded a story about a poor, ugly boy whom the people despised. Pitying himself, he went to the top of a high hill to die. A handsome man dressed in a fine buffalo robe came to him and magically transported him to a lodge where other men were seated in a circle with one standing by the fireplace. The boy was informed that the men in the lodge were the Circle of Chiefs he could see in the sky from his village. In empathy, the leader of the group told the boy that he could choose which of the group he wished to resemble. The boy made his choice and was sent back home with the instruction that he must make four successful raids, each time following with an offering to the Star Chiefs at the hill where they found him. Only then should he take a wife. If he did not do as he was told, he would return to his former self.

The now handsome boy, who seemed a stranger in the village, was highly favored, especially by unattached females. In his new strength, he failed to follow the counsel he had received in the Star Chief's lodge, and once again he became ugly and lame.

The boy returned to the hill where he was met again by one of the Chiefs who simply told him that they would pity him no more, for he thought more of women than of what the Celestial Chiefs had attempted to give him. He was sent home to be content as the scabby, blind, dirty, and poor person he truly was.

Although this is a story intended to teach a moral, it also illustrates the significance of the Council of Chiefs in Skidi tradition. Such a council was considered to flow from the heavens; the council of chiefs within the village was empowered with the authority of the stars. It was foolish in the extreme to disobey such direction. One could become great through the wisdom of the chiefs, but without such wisdom, or acting contrary to it, one would be, and would remain, loathesome.

## The United Stars

The Skidi associated another group of stars, which they called simply the Seven Stars (Pleiades), with the zenith. These, too, could be observed through the smokehole of the earth lodge, but at times in opposition to the culmination of the Chiefs. The two groups, Chiefs and closely clustered Seven Stars, could be critically observed as key elements of the Skidi calendar in order to determine appropriate times to begin ceremonies.

> The priests noted the position of the seven stars (Pleiades). At a certain hour of the night or dawn, the exact procedure is not known to us, a priest sat by the fireside and looked up through the smoke hole. If he could see the seven stars directly above, it was time for the planting ceremonies (Murie 1981:76).

The observations of both groups of stars could be made from the same place in the lodge at the two key observational times of day. In early February, about one hour before sunrise, the Chiefs would be seen through the smokehole, high in the sky. At the same time of year, the Seven Stars would appear in almost the same place seen through the smokehole but at the end of evening twilight. So we see that these two important groups of stars filled a most interesting calendrical role.

Furthermore, we find that both stellar groups symbolized unity to the Skidi. Writing about these stars in her well-known treatment on the Hako, Fletcher (1904:151—52) translated a Pawnee song to the Seven Stars:

> Look as they rise, up rise
> Over the line where sky meets the earth;
> Pleiades!
> Lo! They are ascending, come to guide us,
> Leading us safely, keeping us one;
> Pleiades,
> Teach us to be, like you, united.

Perhaps no more beautiful idea has ever been associated with these clustered stars. It is an idea clearly embedded in Skidi Pawnee philosophy.

The closely clustered appearance of the Pleiades makes them a natural choice for a symbol of unity. The fact that they are nearly opposite to Corona Borealis and that both groups of stars suggested unification to the Skidi implies a well-constructed observational system, tested over many years of time. Although the observations were made by simple methods, they were very effective. Built-in redundancy included critical observations of several groups of stars and careful notation of the behavior of plant and animal life (see Chamberlain 1982:116—22, 163—83, for details on Skidi observations).

These observations were part of a well-established system of calendrics used by the Skidi. Nothing was more basic to order, and therefore to unification, than an effective calendar. Knowing when it was safe to plant, when herds could be found grazing on the prairie, when it was time to harvest the wild and domestic crops, and when ceremonies should be conducted, was essential to trust in the authority, knowledge, and wisdom of leaders. The Skidi seemed content in the system of living they had derived, and the appearance of the seven united stars guided them both in scheduling and in unifying their efforts.

The conceptual relationships among the three celestial entities of Chief Star, Chiefs in Council, and Seven Stars, combined with the great *Tirawahat* at the zenith of the sky and the smokehole at the zenith of the earthlodge, all neatly embedded in the cosmology of the Skidi, reveal great philosophical and observational depth. These ideas, coming from a people once thoughtlessly called *savage,* present a powerful sociological lesson in the political, domestic, and consensus-management significance of a council.

The alignment of the place of *Tirawahat* above, the opening of the lodge to the sky through which the celestial Council of Chiefs and the unified Seven Stars would be seen and down to the fire within the lodge radiating life-preserving warmth, are symbolically powerful conjunctions of observable elements. In addition, the principle of chiefdomship symbol-ized by the star–that–does–not–move as an example to those who would be responsible for the welfare of the people. Both the fire within the lodge and the people who resided therein received their life-force from the an-cestral stellar gods. Things of greatest importance to the Skidi seemed to have their counterparts in the sky.

The Skidi people made and used a wonderful artifact that symbolized some of the ideas discussed here (Fig. 14.3). A chart of the heavens, drawn on animal skin, portrays the star gods of the Skidi. One side shows the glow of sunrise and the male stars of the East. On the opposite side is found the yellow light of evening, the Moon and the beautiful Evening Star. Between these are important groups of stars, and the Milky Way (pathway of de-parted spirits) splits the chart.

The Chief Star is shown very large on the chart, reflecting the great importance of the star. Likewise, the Chief's Council is more prominent than one might expect from the relative dimness of its stars in the sky. The Seven Stars are there in a tiny cluster, not really resembling the appearance of the cluster in the sky but very easy to find (see also Chamberlain 1982 : chap. 5).

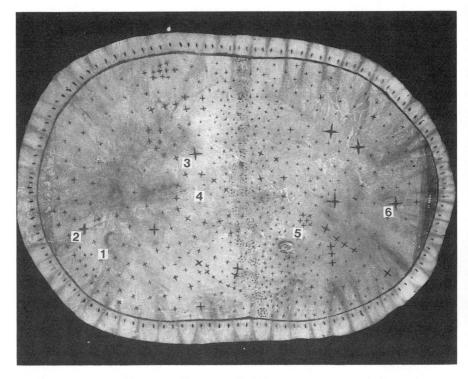

**Figure 14.3.** Skidi Pawnee chart of the heavens. Objects of importance are (1) Moon, (2) Evening Star, (3) Chief Star, (4) Council of the Chiefs, (5) Seven Stars (Pleiades), and (6) Morning Star.

Looking at this unique artifact, we can be reminded of many ideas of significance to the Skidi—ideas that are of importance to most other groups as well. The Sun, Moon, and stars have always provided the calendrical information from day to day and year to year that is needed for the survival and development of cultural identity and strength. To the Skidi, the stars also provided patterns for political, religious, and moral guidance. Every individual within the Skidi Band could identify the principles of unity patterned within the stars. They felt an unusual identity with these stars, for they believed them to be their ancestors as well as their gods. Indeed, the Skindi Band derived its strength from the ceremonial and political system that resulted from the confederation of small families tracing lineage to particular stars. As a group, they had become united through their stellar-derived beliefs, rituals, and seasonal activities. In every way, they believed themselves to be the children of the stars.

## Epilogue

One item concerning the Council of Chiefs has particularly puzzled me over the years. More than one line of evidence describes them differently than we see Corona Borealis in the sky.

> Right over head there is a circle of stars, this is the council; in the center of this circle is one star, that is the servant of the chief, cooking over the fire (Fletcher n.d. : 95).

> My son, the men of this circle are what your people call "chiefs sitting in the heavens;" we are the stars that you see circled in the heavens; the errand man you see yonder is the central star in the heavens (Dorsey 1904 : 66).

And, in a published myth, Dorsey (1906 : 45) mentioned twelve sticks that are referred to as representing "the twelve stars in a circle above the heavens who sat as chiefs in council." The Skidi chart of the heavens clearly shows eleven prominent stars composing the figure representing the Chief's Council.

I often looked at Corona Borealis and was puzzled by these descriptions mentioning a dozen stars and the idea that there should be one in the center. Then, one night when camping out with my son, I had an experience that answered these perplexing questions.

Nestled comfortably in my bedroll beside a stream, I fell asleep watching the stars. During the night I opened my eyes, perhaps more asleep than awake, and there were the Chiefs, just as they should be. Even the Errand Man was there at the fire inside the circle. All my previous wondering about this puzzle brought me completely awake. What was I seeing? Was there an artificial satellite passing through Corona Borealis? No, it remained. Had I discovered a nova (a star which suddenly becomes much brighter than before)? As I pondered this, I carefully identified the stars in that part of the sky. The realization I had been striving to achieve over several years suddenly came. I was not asleep! I was not seeing a transient phenomenon. I was seeing the Council of Chiefs as the Pawnee probably saw them.

I had often reminded myself, and others, that we must be careful not to step into the trap of not being able to see things differently than the ways we have been taught to see them. But Corona Borealis seems so very well defined. It is a partial circle of stars, each of about the same brightness. Had someone not already familiar with the stars attempted to identify the Chief's Council, they might have been more successful than I. Now, on this wonderfully clear night, my less-structured, half-asleep mind had allowed

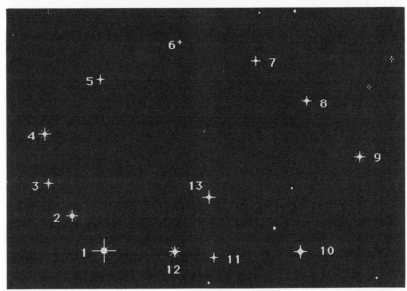

**Figure 14.4.** The Council of Chiefs consists mostly of stars in the constellation Corona Borealis, plus two stars in Bootes. *Top:* an actual photograph of the stars. *Bottom:* identification chart: (1) Alpha Corona Borealis, (2) Gamma Corona Borealis, (3) Delta Corona Borealis, (4) Epsilon Corona Borealis, (5) Iota Corona Borealis, (6) Rho Corona Borealis, (7) Kappa Corona Borealis, (8) Zeta 2 Corona Borealis, (9) Mu 1 Bootis, (10) Delta Bootis, (11) Eta Corona Borealis, (12) Beta Corona Borealis, (13) Theta Corona Borealis.

me to see beyond my inhibitions. The Council does consist of about a dozen stars, and there is one fairly bright one tending the fire inside the circle (fig. 14.4). The Fire Tender is actually one of the stars of the crown. The other stars of the circle are somewhat dimmer—too dim to be picked out easily unless the viewing conditions are good. When the sky is clear and dark and when the Chiefs are located near the zenith, the picture is just as it was described by the Pawnee informants working with Fletcher and Dorsey. Dimmer stars continue a curved line started by some of the stars of the Crown into a larger circle than that partly defined by the Crown. This throws the star at one end of the Crown into the larger circlet: the Fire Tender, or Errand Man.

I suppose that the fun would go out of this type of research if all of the questions were nicely answered. Now I am puzzled why the Skidi chart of the heavens does not show the Errand Man inside the circle of stars. The dim stars that are there are like the others which are just randomly scattered over the chart. Perhaps one of them was intended to be the assistant to the Chiefs. I wonder.

# References

Chamberlain, Von Del. 1982. *When Stars Came Down to Earth: Cosmology of the Skidi Pawnee Indians of North America*. Los Altos, Calif., and College Park, Md.: Ballena Press and Center for Archaeoastronomy.

Dorsey, George A. 1904. *Traditions of the Skidi Pawnee*. Boston and New York: Memoirs of The American Folk-Lore Society, 8.

———. 1906. *The Pawnee: Mythology*. Washington, D.C.: Carnegie Institution of Washington Publications, 59.

———. n.d. Original manuscripts and associated notes, on file in the anthropology archives, Field Museum of Natural History, Chicago.

Fletcher, Alice C. 1904. The Hako: A Pawnee Ceremony. *Twenty-second Annual Report of the Bureau of American Ethnology*, part 2. Washington, D.C.: Government Printing Office.

———. n.d. Field notes on the Pawnee and correspondence with James R. Murie (Manuscript no. 4558, 1, 2, 93, and 95), on file at the National Anthropological Archives, Smithsonian Institution, Washington, D.C.

Murie, James R. 1981. Ceremonies of the Pawnee, part 1: The Skiri, ed. Douglas R. Parks. *Smithsonian Contributions to Anthropology 27*.

———. n.d. Transcriptions in Pawnee and translations in English from gramaphone recordings of the Skidi Pawnee priest known as Scout. On file in the anthropology archives, American Museum of Natural History, New York.

# 15

■ ■ ■ ■ ■ ■ ■ ■ ■ ■

## *The Conjurer's Lodge:*
## *Celestial Narratives*
## *from Algonkian Shamans*

■ ■ ■ ■ ■ ■ ■ ■ ■ ■

### THOR CONWAY

---

*Thor Conway's earlier vocation as an archaeologist with the Canadian government led him to interact closely with Ojibway residents of Canada, where he met several shamans, well versed in traditional ways. Those experiences led Conway to study Ojibway lore and rock art. Why is the land the way it is and what does that have to do with shamans? These questions were addressed by Conway's consultants as they limned movements of their people from the sky to the earth, where structures and narratives receate what they once lived in the heavens.*

---

The Ojibwa and related Algonkian bands of the upper Great Lakes area once scheduled their ritual year in reference to celestial events. A special group of medicine men, the *Wabeno* or "White Light of Dawn" shamans, taught a cycle of interrelated celestial legends to their apprentices through formal instruction. This carefully transmitted lore defined the Wabeno's sphere of influence by providing the perceptions and expectations that regulated the timing of seasonal-change rituals, fertility rites, and the renewal of food resources.

The recent ethnographic fieldwork I have conducted with the few surviving Wabeno shamans has resulted in the recovery of their formerly private, celestial narratives (Conway 1985, in press). These legends include the previously unpublished story "Descent of the Ojibwa from the Moon," a complete version of the "First Burning of the Earth" tale, and segments of the "Origin of the Culture Hero/Trickster Nanabush." These stories establish the Hole in the Sky motif as the basis for advanced shamanic-trance experiences, while reinforcing the spirit world's influence on earthly events.

The aboriginal inhabitants of the upper Great Lakes include many widespread Algonkian groups whose descendants survive today. Various names, such as Ojibwa, Chippewa, Cree, Algonquin, and Ottawa are used to identify the people who call themselves Anishinabe. The folklore presented here is the result of personally financed anthropological fieldwork done between 1980 and 1988 among various bands of northern Algonkians living in the boreal forest north of Lake Huron and Lake Superior in Ontario, Canada. Several individuals who retained detailed knowledge of celestial beliefs were interviewed on repeated visits to their homes or on field trips to sacred sites. In each instance, the elders were shamans from families with a long history of shamanism extending back to the nineteenth century or earlier (Conway and Conway 1990).

The transmission of private, shamanic knowledge often follows family lines among the northern Algonkians. This trend was evident with two of the elders in this study, who were, respectively, the grandson of Schoolcraft's main Lake Superior Ojibwa informant and the son of Speck's Temagami Algonkian primary informant and interpreter (Figs. 15.1 and 15.2). Personal visions and access to spirit helpers were passed along within family lines. For some related shamans, ritual items such as birchbark prayer scrolls could be transferred from master to apprentice. While anyone could become a shaman in Algonkian society by obtaining basic skills for interacting with the supernatural, powerful shamans developed their advanced spiritual knowledge by building upon the personal experiences of their fathers or, especially, grandfathers. Recent genealogical research indicates a trend toward direct transmission of personal names from grandfather to grandson. Similarly, several elders reported shamanic apprenticeship to their grandfathers rather than their equally skilled fathers. The full implications of this generational jump are now being investigated.

Several ancient forms of shamanism are preserved among the Ojibwa and neighboring Algonkian bands. Extensive studies of the Midewewin, or Grand Medicine Society, suggest that shamanism continued to evolve and become specialized in the northern Lake Superior and Lake Huron basins throughout the protohistoric and early historic periods (Hoffman 1891; Landes 1968). At least four major types of shamanism existed among the Ojibwa (Conway in press), but only the Wabeno shamans were intimately involved with celestial matters. The other shamanic specialities included the emerging priesthood of healers in the Midewewin, the trance-seeking Djiski-Inninik shamans, and the Mushkiki herbal doctors. The Wabeno shamans were both feared and respected, as they were capable of misusing their love medicine and hunting magic for malevolent purposes. For example, some shamans engaged in the dreaded "bear-walker" form of destructive witchcraft, which is widely recognized among the Ojibwa. Bear-

**Figure 15.1.**    The noted Lake Superior Ojibwa shaman Fred Pine. (Photograph by Thor Conway)

**Figure 15.2.** Kush Kush Michael Paul, a highly respected traditionalist from the Temagami band, being interviewed by the author.

walking, which formerly served as beneficial hunting magic under the control of Wabeno shamans, became corrupted for personal revenge and destruction. However interesting sorcery and the black arts may be, Wabeno astronomical knowledge concerns me in this chapter.

The Wabeno were responsible for celestial and lunar time-keeping, using calendar sticks and related notational devices. Under Wabeno direction, a series of seasonal transition rituals occurred at specific intervals, including the solstices and equinoxes. These public or corporate-level duties were concerned with the harmonious balance between man, the animate landscape, the spirit world, and the band's food and medicinal resource needs. The Wabeno's private functions related to human and animal fertility and prophecy (Redsky 1972).

Only fragments of the northern Algonkians' native astronomy have survived into the late twentieth century. There are several reasons for this. Native lifeways suffered the effects of warfare, disease, and rapid cultural changes created by the advent of European immigrants. Much of the starlore was directly tied to magic and ritual, which the missionaries despised as pagan beliefs. In addition, starlore often had dual levels of interpretation. The more public aspects of celestial folklore dealt with weather forecasting, the identification of constellations with figures from well-known folktales, and the timing of seasonal movements within the band's territory. Most of the celestial folklore collected in the past century has been this secular material. Fewer members of the northern bands shared the sacred, more private aspects of skylore. Even in the late nineteenth century, an anthropologist noted that starlore specialists, the Wabeno shamans, were difficult to locate. Only two Wabeno shamans could be found in a population of fifteen hundred Ojibwa residents of northern Minnesota (Hoffman 1891:156–57). In the 1980s, on a reserve in northeastern Ontario with over fifteen hundred band members, a single Wabeno shaman survived. According to other shamans and elders interviewed, he was the last Wabeno in the eastern Lake Superior area. The paucity of published ethnographic sources for Wabeno astronomical beliefs is not surprising (Angel 1987). My field research supplies some of the cultural contexts and interpretations offered by the Wabeno shamans I interviewed.

## The Peopling of the Earth—An Ojibwa Narrative

Most societies carry origin legends that often reinforce their mythic ancestry. The northern Algonkians attribute their beginning to Nanabush, a giant trickster hero. Algonkian folklore can be divided into two levels, the sacred and the secular. Most of the common tales are widely known by all members of Ojibwa society.

According to Ojibwa traditionalists who retain a more archaic form of their language, the word Anishinabe can be translated "From Where We Came Down." Thus, Anishinabe makes an oblique reference to the Hole in the Sky. The root word *Anish* denotes a "male originator" or "primal male." The concept is also understood as a veiled reference to the first people who came down from the star world by way of the Hole in the Sky. Some Ojibwa believe that this descent of man happened in stages.

The following celestial origin story was collected in English and Ojibwa, on several occasions, from Fred Pine, a resident of the Garden River Indian Reserve near Sault Sainte Marie, Ontario, Canada (Fig. 15.1). Mr. Pine, also known as Sahkahodjewwahgsah, "Sun Rising over the Mountain," is a member of the Shingwaukonce, the "Little White Pine" family. He was trained in starlore at the beginning of this century by several individuals. Born in 1897, Fred Pine learned the following account from the Garden River band storyteller, Wabmaymay, "The Dawn Pilleated Woodpecker." Blind in his later years, Wabmaymay was a formal storyteller or Muhzhinahway.

The solar references in Mr. Pine's and Wabmaymay's personal names indicate their training in celestial knowledge and, more specifically, their status as Wabeno shamans. These folktales were learned verbatim over many retellings. Mr. Pine, who as a child was kept nonliterate in order to prepare for his shamanic training, never alters the sequence or the contents. He fondly recalls sitting under a tree with other children sometime prior to 1910, offering the blind elder Wabmaymay the traditional tobacco gift which was then hung on a tree branch while the legend was told.

The paragraphs are numbered for reference in the analysis of the following myth. The cadence of the narrative and frequently repeated key words remind us that the Algonkian story cycles were not created as written forms. The oral culture's origin as performance art, told by skilled story-tellers, is preserved in the text.

    1. "Here's another story. I knew in my younger days that I had some-thing in my head. I took in everything that I heard. The reason that I can tell these stories is study. I worked on it. It's a gift that you don't get for nothing. I dreamt for my gifts. At the same time, I have the experience of talking to many Indians. The Indian, nobody knows where he came from. But he came from the moon. They lived up there. That's where the Indian was put in the first place. Indians used to talk about that story years and years ago. The

Indian people originally lived on the moon, but the atmosphere dried out. There was no more rain there. The moon was once like here. The earth breathes. It gives off moisture. The plants catch the moisture."

2. "Everything had dried up on the moon. Everything was dried out, and the animals were starving and dying out. The animals were bigger than they are today. Great big creatures. The Indians would go out and hunt these animals, but all of the game was dead from the drought on the moon. All of these animals were friends to the people. You see, the animals were raised with the people. Indians understood the animals. So, the people were starving. Out of desperation, they even ate lichens off the rocks. The medicine man said, 'We'll have to do something. We can't live here anymore.'"

3. "But up on the moon there were huge animals. A spider was as big as an elephant. But the Indians were friends with them. At that time, the Indian could touch the animals. They were friends with all the animals where they were living."

4. "The medicine man saw that there was no more life left in the moon; he thought, 'I got to do something else to save my tribe.' The Holy Spirit came to the medicine man. He said, 'Look around.' The spirit said, 'You'll find a place for these Indians, your tribe.' The medicine man strolled across the rocks of the moon, all around, until he found a big hole. The hole went right through the moon like a ravine."

5. "And the medicine man looked down this hole, and he saw North America. Paradise. 'Green, everything is green. Lakes, beaver, other animals, and everything.' He said, 'This is the place, the place for my tribe.'

6. "Now the medicine man couldn't bring all of the people down, so he picked out the best people. The ones that obeyed everything. Spiritual people. Wise men. You're looking at one right now."

7. "You know how he got the Indians down here? The medicine man used a huge spider. The medicine man hired the spider to let them down with the web. A spider never runs out of web. That's why I'm here now."

8. "When the first Indians arrived on the earth, the animals were different. They had ribs on top of their skin, or they had heavy scales. The Holy Spirit told the Ojibwa to destroy these things. 'I didn't put them on the earth,' he said. 'Somebody put those creatures into the sea.' Later the holy spirit changed the oceans to salt water. When the salt water came in, all of these terrible animals went inland. They started to eat roots, tearing up trees and destroying the land. So the Holy Spirit told the Ojibwa, 'I want you to destroy these creatures because they will eat you up.' That's when the Indian

started to make arrows out of flint. Flint is hard. It will go through the scales on the animals. The Indians killed some of the animals."

9. "That star with the long, wide tail is going to destroy the world some day when it comes low again. That's the comet called *Genondah-wayanung* [Long Tailed Heavenly Climbing Star]. It came down here once, thousands of years ago. Just like a sun. It had radiation and burning heat in its tail."

10. "Before the comet came, life on the earth was easy for the Indians. The moon never died [waxed and waned] at that time. There were no cycles of more food and less food. No seasons, until that comet burnt up the country."

11. "The comet burnt everything to the ground. There wasn't a thing left. Indian people were here before that happened, living on the earth. But things were wrong, a lot of people had abandoned their spiritual path. The Holy Spirit [*Chimanitou*] warned them a long time before the comet came. Medicine men told everyone to prepare."

12. "Things were wrong with nature on the earth. All of these big animals were tearing up the trees, fighting one another. These creatures were even eating one another. They would have destroyed the forests; then nobody would survive. So the Holy Spirit said, 'Go in there, someplace in the swamp. Roll yourself in there. And stay there for so many days.' The Spirit told the good Indians to hide in the muskey [bog], or crawl into holes in the ground. That's why they survived. He was going to send that *chianungnah-way* 'Long Tailed Star' that year. That's a comet. They were warned a long time before. The women said, 'We want to prepare. We are going to get rid of these evil creatures.' Animals were even eating one another."

13. "The Indians rolled up in mud to get protection from the heat. That's why they survived. They had educated people [medicine men who fasted], and they knew what to do. For survival, the Indians took the air sac [air bladder] from a sturgeon. It's white and long like a tube. They swallowed that tube, and breathed through it under the swamp or laying under the mud. That's how the Indians breathed when the fire went through. Some of the Indians were caught by the comet's fire and destroyed, the bad ones. That's what happened there a long time ago. I'm talking about way beyond two thousand years ago."

14. "Then that *Chigahnunnahway Anung* went through here. The comet had a long, wide tail, and it burnt up everything. It flew low, so the tail scorched the earth. It was just so hot that everything, even the stones, were cooked. The giant animals were killed off. You can find their bones

today in the earth. It is said that the comet came down and spread his tail for miles and miles. That's what I was told. *Ozhohwah.* A tail."

15. "Even, you see, the Indians in those days were hairy. That's where they got some of their hair burnt off. They were like an animal in the start. Then they cross-bred to make a human being. That's the reason why today pure Indians have very little hair on them. They got no hair. And those Indians got baked in the mud. They had brown skin after that. They were like a tribe. They tried to cross-breed to see what they could come up with. It took quite a few years before they could get to be like Indians. This was before Nanabush came along. After that comet, new animals were put on the earth. Where they came from, I don't know. That's when the horse first started. That's how you see the horse showing on the rock [pictographs]."

16. "That comet made a different world. After that, survival was hard work. The weather was colder than before. But soon after the comet, the holy spirit send Nanabush along to teach the people how to live. He was a spiritual man that came from the morning star. I told a story about him. Indians are living on the Early Morning Star, Wabanung, that comes up with the sun. They're big people, and that's why Nanabush was so big. He came from there originally. Even the animals are big there."

17. "Nanabush never came to earth until the trees were grown after the fire. Nanabush and Muhdjikewiss finished making the people more human. They took the hair off of them. All the animals were large in those days. Nanabush shrank them to their present size so they wouldn't be so powerful. Like the weasel, he's fast. The weasel was too powerful."

18. "At that time, people never slept. They were just like insects, always awake and moving around. Always awake. And they would crawl around. So Nanabush told the people, 'I'll give you a rest.' Nanabush shot them in the head. Knocked them out. They were asleep for maybe ten or twelve hours. That's why we sleep today, from then on. Sleep is like that. And after that, people could talk. When the people woke up, they were talking. Before that, people were all like beasts. They followed one another like dogs. They mated like animals. Muhdjikewiss came before Nanabush. He was a spiritual being, a spokesman, an advisor. A lot of people don't believe this, but I believe it."

[Several sexually explicit segments are omitted.]

19. "Nanabush was alone on the earth except for his grandmother, but he knew there must be people elsewhere. He was sent under spiritual guidance. The Spirit told Nanabush to keep walking. So Nanabush roamed around. He searched the country that is our home, from western Lake

Superior as far as Hudson's Bay, to see if there were any living souls in this North America. He kept walking. Everytime he took off, he carried his grandmother on his back. But he couldn't find any people. Oh, he knew everything. Nanabush set trip cords made from basswood bark. If anyone was around, they would trip on the line, and Nanabush would hear them fall. He would go over to the spot and meet them."

20. "Nanabush knew there were other Indians too. He searched all over North America. He reached the ocean. That's when he got swallowed up by a whale."

[The whale story and several exploration tales are omitted.]

21. "That's the story, but that's just the beginning. These rocks are all burnt. One time before the fire went through here, the rocks were all solid. There was no broken rock. But the rock was cooked. And it tumbled down out of the mountains. Then the big cracks opened up. And this metal, like gold and copper, it melted. It ran across these cracks, you see. It might run for miles and miles. Maybe you'll find that mineral here. Or maybe you'll go thirty miles to find it. The reason why these lakes are all black is the comet burnt everything. Like the Montreal River north of here on Lake Superior. It is the first black river."

22. "You see, all the minerals run south. Every vein you see is south. The lakes are black. That's where the mineral is. The reason why they are black, whenever it cooled off the mineral, that lake never cleared up. You'll see the rocks in the black river. All black. They're all black from being burnt and from the ashes. There's a big ore deposit some place here because tons and tons were taken out from the veins of minerals. Not the main lode. The miners just took what was in the vein. But our belief is not to bother with that copper."

23. "After the comet came, the earth was bare. There were no trees. Just sand and gravel. It was people that fertilized the country with their feet. And I really believe that with all of my heart. They heard a voice, 'Trample the earth all over.' Their bare feet helped to spread the ashes and nourish the soil. All of the animals mated, and something was put on their feet. They walked on the bare earth. In two years time, everything started to grow. Their feet spread fertilizer all around the country. Old Nanabush came after that fire. The rocks were still soft from the heat. There are places today where you can see his footprints in the rock, or where Nanabush sat down on the rock near Kensington Point."

24. "When the comet went through here, it burnt this country down flat. Flat. When the land around Lake Superior was flat, there was nothing

here. It burnt right to the ground. Everything burnt. After the fire the medicine men said, 'Let's get this star to pull up some rocks.' The land was too flat. The land was flat when Nanabush found it. No mountains or anything. So all the people got together. They said, 'We will ask the spirits to protect the animals so they can accumulate.' They asked for rough land to shelter the animals. Animals can't live on perfectly level country. They need protection. They need a place to hide. That's when the Gravity Star came down and pulled up the hills and mountains. It formed the shape of this country. The Gravity Star could do anything. Lift mountains up, and make rough country. It is so powerful."

25. "If you walk the land, there's the story. What do you want? It's there. Everything is there. The creek is running. There's mountains there. There's a deer track there. A bird flies away. A rabbit is over there. There's your story. That's where the stars come in. Every thing on this earth is influenced by a star. Rocks, flowers, animals. Everything has its own star."

26. "What happened with the comet was a long time ago. I'm talking about way beyond two thousand years ago. There is a prophecy that the comet will destroy the earth again. But it's a restoration. The greatest blessing this island [earth] will ever have. People don't listen to their spiritual guidance today. There will be signs in the sun, moon and stars when that comet comes down again. That's the story, but that's just the beginning."

The tale continues with Nanabush's adventures, his treks across the landscape, and occasional foolishness. The first flooding of the earth follows with Nanabush reestablishing the world, restoring it to its present condition. Nanabush teaches the Indians about medicinal plants, and people learn about survival from the animals. Puckewis, Nanabush's brother, becomes transformed into the first beaver. He started the cycle of reincarnation. These and many other episodes completed the long Algonkian narrative. The more complete sources for these continued adventures include the Ojibwa and English texts in Jones's (1919:531—59) monumental work and the tales of the Wisconsin Ojibwa (Barnouw 1977:13—92).

## Algonkian Folklore Studies

The northern Algonkian people occupied a huge part of North America, extending from the northeastern United States across the upper Great Lakes and well into northern Canada. A considerable amount of Algonkian folklore has been collected. A few of the basic collections which pertain to the northern Great Lakes area include the works of Schoolcraft (1851–57), Skinner (1912), Speck (1915), Jones (1916, 1917, 1919), Jenness (1935), Densmore (1929), and Redsky (1972). Barnouw (1977) presents his collections along with an analysis of folk motifs. The earlier works of Reichard (1921) and others, especially Fisher (1946), provide important overviews.

Oral narratives offer carefully honed insights into particular cultures. Taken out of their cultural contexts, these tales would be far less meaningful. Recent studies have explored the metaphorical and structural insights offered by Native American oral narratives (Harkin 1988).

The Ojibwa and other northern Algonkian bands divide their oral narratives into two distinct categories: Atisokan, or tales about events having a historical basis; and Tcibatchimowin, which refers to more mythic stories. The Atisokan stories are characterized as accounts personally experienced by the narrator, his relatives, or ancestors. In northern Ontario, numerous Atisokan-style stories have been collected relating to the late seventeenth-century Ojibwa–Iroquois wars (Conway 1982). The Tcibatchimowin group of native legends preserves ancient accounts of the activities of ordinary and supernatural beings. These tales are filled with examples of expected behavior and lessons for proper spiritual living.

"The Peopling of the Earth" narrative presented in this chapter has a logical, counterpoint structure, which alternates between destruction and renewal. The moon's resources died out; while the medicine men discovered a paradise on earth, violence and moral decay developed on earth leading to the comet-induced destruction. Then, the first people fertilized the earth while receiving guidance from the culture hero Nanabush; at the same time, the first Indians remained primitive, so sleep was introduced and they were transformed physically into modern people.

In later sections of the Algonkian origin tale, Nanabush's brother Myeengun, the wolf, became the first creature/person to die. His other brother, Puckewis, transformed himself into the sustaining food animal the beaver. This led to the reincarnation of souls. The same duality continued with Nanabush's lax stewardship of the land, causing the first great flood. Again, global destruction was followed by the creation of a better world.

The underlying themes of death/destruction and rebirth/renewal in the narrative are based on the same shamanic experience of gaining enhanced power through a deathlike transformation. Algonkian shamans suffer and "die" on their starvation-induced vision quests, leaving their bodies to visit the spirit realm above the sky. Similarly, these shamans must leave the physical body for soul flights to find cures for their patients. The soulless body is described as a "dead" shell, and precautions are taken to avoid disturbing the entranced shaman.

The need for spiritual living is another theme found repeatedly in the tale. Algonkians believe that the souls of every animal, tree, and rock require appeasement, if the resource is disturbed or utilized. This principle developed into a series of thanksgiving rituals. For example, offerings were made to a plant's spirit before picking an herb. Hunters often placed painted and decorated animal bones in trees to send the animals' souls off to harmonious reincarnation.

Each episode in the original tale offers insights into the organization of the Algonkian universe and its inhabitants. The implications of the comet lore and the first burning of the earth in episodes 9 to 15 have been discussed in detail (Conway 1985). The reappearance of Halley's comet offered celestial confirmation of cyclic events beyond man's contol, while illustrating a theme in the burning of the earth story. The "First Burning of the Earth" is not directly linked to Halley's comet. All comets and meteors were regarded as serious omens requiring interpretation by Wabeno shamans.

The individual episodes of the Algonkian origin tale gradually lead from the general to the specific. At first, the landscape is defined as North America. After the comet's destruction, local landscape features in the northern Great Lakes area start to appear, such as the Montreal River in episode 21 and Nanabush's armchair in episode 23 (Fig. 15.3). In later segments not presented in this paper, many more specific lakes, rock shrines, and mountains are named, setting the basis for band territories and religious cycles. The characters also become individuals as the story progresses. Nanabush, his grandmother, his brothers Puckewis and Myeengun, and others become the main subjects as the story unfolds.

Most Algonkian folklore collections contain stories naming Nanabush as the first Indian, or as the first supernatural leader sent to help the struggling Indians. Apparently, fewer examples of episodes 17 and 18, which mention the spiritual advisor Muhdjikewiss, survived into the nineteenth and twentieth centuries. A first earth story collected from the Minnesota Chippewa mentions a similar spiritual messenger who arrives to teach the suffering first Indians at a time before Nanabush's arrival (Densmore 1929:98).

The development of humor in the origin tale is delayed until Nanabush starts to explore the earth and learn about the mysteries of the natural world. Numerous episodes relating Nanabush's comic adventures appear in the later sections of the narrative. These episodes are well known to most Algonkians. They form the public or secular component of the story.

**Figure 15.3.** The Devil's Armchair is located on eastern Lake Superior. The Ojibwa regard the rock as a place where Nanabush once sat. (Photograph by Thor Conway)

The model theme that man is a somewhat passive player, subject to the effects of greater forces, continues throughout. By the last half of the tale, the events are small-scale, commonplace encounters, such as Nanabush getting his head stuck in a moose skull, rather than global disasters that descend on the entire race of people.

The storyteller's personality enters the origin tale at several points: e.g., in episode 6, in a humorous aside that refers to the narrator as a wise man. It is meant to be funny, as well as to establish the narrator's status as an experienced shaman. The convention of inserting brief humor into a serious discussion characterizes the traditional Algonkian personality. Band elders often make jokes about their past misfortunes and hardships. Among Algonkian shamans, the occasional use of humor during interviews about sensitive, spiritual topics appears to serve as a mechanism to release tension. The discussions of spiritual matters, such as the function of the Hole in the Sky, are formal events structured by various sanctions. Just as direct questioning is an impolite action for Algonkians, direct naming of a spiritual being in conversation calls upon or alerts the spirit. It would be a potentially dangerous action.

As the narrator mentioned in episodes 9, 13, and 26, the origin legend

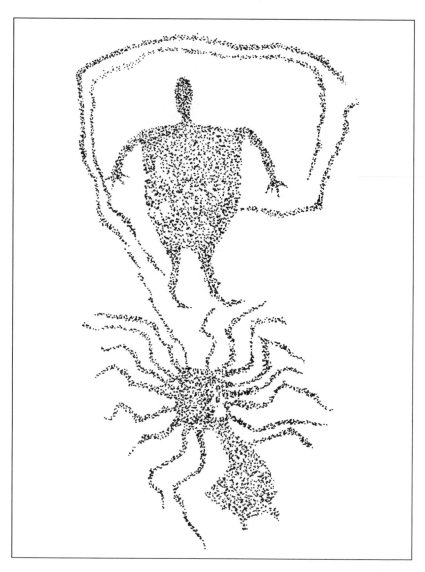

**Figure 15.4.** Among the several thousand northern Algonkian pictographs, only one painting shows a human figure connected to a spider. The panel may illustrate the tale "Descent of the Ojibwa from the Moon."

refers to events in mythic time long ago. The combined evidence of archaeology and rock art provides clues for the antiquity of the "Descent from the
Moon" story segment. A painting of a human attached by a long line to a
spider decorates the wall of a small cave at the Burnt Bluff pictograph site on
the north shore of Lake Michigan (Fig. 15.4). This rock-art panel, which in
all probability depicts the lowering of the first Indians from the moon, is
the only known example of a human connected to a spider at any of the
numerous northern Algonkian pictograph sites in the upper Great Lakes
(Lugthart 1968). The use of a cave (hole in the ground) can be interpreted as
a shamanic metaphor for the Hole in the Sky (M. Paul, personal communication). Algonkian shamans perceive caves and rock fissures as passageways
similar to the Hole in the Sky, useful for soul travel.

The Hole in the Moon leads to the discovery of the Hole in the Sky.
Unlike the Hole in the Sky, which appears repeatedly in Algonkian
shamanic accounts, the lunar opening is not mentioned outside of the
"Descent from the Moon" origin tale. The Hole in the Moon is not recognized by traditional Algonkians as a visible surface feature on the lunar
landscape. Some prominent lunar craters form a pattern seen as an Ojibwa
boy holding water pails, and the phases of the moon have cultural analogies.
The crescent moon represents spirit horns floating in the night sky.

The Burnt Bluff site is one of the very few caves with rock art in the
northern Algonkian culture area. Excavation of the cave floor revealed
numerous broken projectile points that had been fired at the rock art in an
offering ritual. The same ritual survived into the historic era with bows and
arrows and, later, rifles. The projectiles at Burnt Bluff were dated to the
Middle Woodland period around the second century A.D.

Although the myth presented in this chapter has entertainment value
within Algonkian society, it is also a prolonged metaphor that establishes
the basis of human nature, personalizes the physical landscape, and presents
methods of interacting with the spiritual landscape. The descent through
the Hole in the Sky is one theme/metaphor that can be examined in light of
recent ethnographic accounts.

## Hole in the Sky Tales and Concepts

The Hole in the Sky concept defines the primal, shamanic function of the
opening between the spirit world and the world we inhabit. To understand
this shamanic passageway, we need to combine knowledge from folklore
and Algonkian astronomy with an understanding of the conjurer's lodge.

Hole in the Sky is translated literally as Behgonay Ghizig, or alternately, as "Coming in Through the Sky," Pindegay Ghizhik. Despite occasional use of the term, *Hole in the Sky,* as a personal name or its presence in several folktales, most shamans interviewed for this study voice the term with great reluctance. This situation often inhibits the collection of Hole in the Sky lore. Most traditional Algonkians fear that the direct use of spirit names will elicit misfortune. It is essentially a Pandora's box theme. By directly naming a spirit or the Hole in the Sky spirit passage, an Algonkian shaman actively calls upon these powerful forces. When this action is done outside of a purposeful, ritual context, it is considered an annoyance to powerful spirits—the manitous. In collecting much of the ethnographic data for this chapter, several rituals were observed by the shamans and the interviewer. These activities included placing offerings at rock shrines and burning certain sacred plants to appease the resident spirits. Participation in these rituals followed a vision in which Mr. Pine was instructed to share his traditional knowledge with seekers of wisdom. These events made the publication of this narrative possible.

Part of the secrecy surrounding the Hole in the Sky concept is due to its direct connection to the conjurer's lodge, a formal structure built for shamanic trances. One group of Algonkian shamans, known as Djiskiinninik or Soul Men, performed public rituals requiring transformation from the physical body to the spirit mode within the conjurer's lodge.

At some point in Algonkian prehistory, Wabeno and Djiskiinninik shamans may have been undifferentiated. By the nineteenth century, each group had developed very formal specialities. The Wabeno shamans interviewed in this study displayed all of the powers and abilities of the Djiskiinninik such as soul flight, trance states, sucking tube healing treatments, and a working knowledge of sorcery. Yet no Wabeno shamans are recorded performing the shaking-tent ceremony. By contrast, the Djiskiinninik do not share the Wabeno skills such as sunrise ceremonies, fertility rituals, lunar time-keeping, making love medicines, or interpreting celestial omens.

From these interviews and historical accounts, I conclude that the Djiskiinninik shamans evolved from a more general form of Wabeno shamanism long ago. In other words, all Wabeno shamans retain Djiskiinninik powers, but no Djiskiinninik have Wabeno powers. Over time, the Wabeno specialist became more private as the Djiskiinninik enhanced their public roles.

Another clue to the Djiskiinninik origins comes from the conjurer's lodge. The Pleiades star group served as a symbolic pattern for the construction of the shaman's conjuring lodge. Originally, most or all shaking tent structures were built with seven poles to replicate the Pleiades constellation. Through time, the number of poles varied as the conjuring-lodge practice became more widespread.

Today, very few Djiskiinninik recognize the conjurer's lodge as a model of the Pleiades, even though these shamans ascend to the Pleiades/Hole in the Sky. In the early decades of this century when Speck (1915) and Hallowell (1971) conducted their fieldwork, the true origins of the shaking-tent/conjurer's lodge were also poorly understood by the Djiskiinninik. Then, as now, more emphasis was placed upon using different species of trees for the lodgepoles.

Ever since the earliest Europeans entered the Great Lakes area, travelers have recorded accounts of the conjurer's lodge or shaking-tent ceremony (Hallowell, 1971:14). The conjurer's lodge is a barrel-shaped enclosure built with several stout poles driven into the ground (Fig. 15.5). Horizontal supports bind the lodge together, with a birchbark and/or canvas covering completing the immovable structure (Fig. 15.6). The term, *shaking tent,* originates from events during the trance, when the conjurer's lodge often moved violently back and forth as the spirits entered the structure. Since conjurer's lodge performances were public events performed for members of the band and occasional nonnative guests, the lodges were constructed within villages and campsites.

The Hole in the Sky has been described by contemporary Algonkian shamans as an opening that breathes the transmission of spiritual power back and forth from this world to the star world. Whenever a shaman needs to recharge his or her power, soul-flight travel is used to reach the Hole in the Sky and cross the barrier to the spirit realm. The shaman's soul leaves the conjurer's lodge by way of the open top, which originally imitated the shape of the Pleiades/Hole in the Sky constellation (Fig. 15.7).

The shamans interviewed for this study regarded the Pleiades/Hole in the Sky constellation as the only opening between the star world and the earthly plane of existence. They viewed the sky as an otherwise flat, impenetrable barrier. Only the underside of the sky can be seen. Its upper surface is like the earth, but a more perfect world (Jenness 1935:28).

Because of the need for a cosmic connection to the Hole in the Sky/Pleiades constellation, as established in "The Peopling of the Earth" tale, shaking tent performances were only done at night. Important information regarding the Hole in the Sky was collected from the Temagami band of Algonkians whose homeland is located near the Ontario–Quebec border. In the tale of the girls who married two stars, an old-woman guardian spirit was described sitting over the Hole in the Sky during the day. She moved off

**Figure 15.5.** A typical shaking tent, or conjurer's lodge, was a conical structure with a pole framework. This lodge on the Long Lake Ojibwa, photographed in 1916, has a third horizontal support row under construction. (National Museums of Canada, neg. no. 36683.)

**Figure 15.6.** An Ojibwa conjurer, Kebegizik, entering the completed shaking tent. Birchbark and cloth cover the frame. (National Museums of Canada, neg. no. 36717.)

**Figure 15.7.** The position of the shaman in the conjurer's lodge is demonstrated in this uncovered example from Lake Abitibi in northeastern Ontario. The original six poles have been reinforced by additional, smaller poles. The opening at the top of the lodge mimics the Hole in the Sky. (National Museums of Canada, neg. no. 74140.)

the opening at night, allowing the sounds of shamanic activity on earth to reach the star world (Speck 1915:48). This account appears to imply a birth from the sky metaphor while reaffirming the nighttime access to the Hole in the Sky.

Inside the conjuring lodge, the shaman made a powerful connection to the star world. A typical experience was collected from an Ojibwa at Fort Hope. He reported that "the shadows of the conjuring tent reached to heaven and in the shadow I saw spirits moving back and forth" (Skinner 1912:154).

Wabeno shamans and Djiski shamans recognize the Pleiades as the physical and spiritual foundation of the conjuring lodge. "The Peopling of the Earth" legend provides an ancestral connection between the two worlds, while it also describes a more powerful, more perfect original condition. For thousands of years, the hunters and gatherers of the remote northern forests have been building replicas of a constellation on the ground in a quest for power beyond the stars.

To the Ojibwa, the knowledge preserved in the origin tale can be seen and interpreted daily in the surrounding landscape. At night, they see their history in the stars.

ACKNOWLEDGMENTS

The insights into Algonkian shamanism and folklore found in this study are the result of extended conversations with Fred Pine and Dan Pine, Sr., of the Garden River band; Michael Paul of the Bear Island band; and Chief Norma Fox of the Cockburn Island band. Fred Pine patiently retold the origin tale on many occasions. Working with Fred Pine, while sharing in his wisdom and humor, has been one of the highlights of my anthropological career. The narrative in this chapter is part of his legacy and a gift to all people who look to the sky for knowledge. I am grateful for the assistance of these elders over the years. My wife, Julie Matey Conway, first edited this paper and provided the illustrations.

# References

Angel, Michael. 1987. The Wabeno: Indigenous Indian Ceremonial or Euro-American Creation? Paper presented to the Society for Ethnohistory Conference, Berkeley.

Barnouw, Victor. 1977. *Wisconsin Chippewa Myths and Tales.* Madison: University of Wisconsin Press.

Chamberlain, Alexander. 1888. Notes on the History, Customs and Beliefs of the Mississauga Indians. *Journal of American Folklore* 1 : 150—60.

Conway, Thor. 1982. *Temagami Oral History Relating to the Iroquois Wars.* Toronto: Heritage Branch, Ontario Ministry of Culture and Recreation.

————. 1985. Halley's Comet Legends of the Great Lakes Ojibwa. *Archaeoastronomy* 8 : 98—105.

————. In press. Canadian Ojibwa ethno-astronomy. *Proceedings of the First Conference on Ethnoastronomy.* Thousand Oaks, Calif.: Slo'w Press.

Conway, Thor and Julie Conway. 1990. *Spirits on Stone: the Agawa Pictographs.* San Luis Obispo, Calif.: Heritage Discoveries.

Densmore, Frances. 1929. *Chippewa Customs.* Smithsonian Institution Bureau of American Ethnology Bulletin 86.

Fisher, Margaret. 1946. The Mythology of the Northern and Northeastern Algonkians in Reference to Algonkian Mythology as a Whole. *Man in Northeastern North America,* ed. F. Johnson, 226—62. Papers of the Peabody Foundation for Archaeology.

Hallowell, Irving. 1971. *The Role of Conjuring in Saulteaux Society.* New York: Octagon Books.

Harkin, Michael. 1988. History, Narrative, and Temporality: Examples from the Northwest coast. *Ethnohistory* 35 : 99—130.

Hoffman, Walter. 1891. The Midewiwin or Grand Medicine Society of the Ojibwa. Washington, D.C.: *Seventh Annual Report of the Bureau of American Ethnology, 1885—1886,* 143—300.

Jenness, Diamond. 1935. *The Ojibwa Indians of Parry Island, their Social and Religious Life.* Canada Department of Mines, Bulletin 78, Anthropological Series no. 17.

Jones, William. 1916. Ojibwa Tales from the North Shore of Lake Superior. *Journal of American Folklore* 29 : 368—91.

————. 1917, 1919. *Ojibwa Texts.* Publications of the American Ethnological Society, vol. 7, parts 1 and 2.

Landes, Ruth. 1968. *Ojibwa Religion and the Midewiwin.* Madison: University of Wisconsin Press.

Lugthart, Douglas. 1968. The Burnt Bluff Rock Paintings. The Prehistory of the Burnt Bluff Area, ed. James Fitting. *Anthropological Papers, Museum of Anthropology, University of Michigan* 34 : 98—115.

Redsky, James. 1972. *Great Leader of the Ojibwa.* Toronto: McClelland and Steward.

Reichard, Gladys. 1921. Literary Types and Dissemination of Myths. *Journal of American Folklore* 54 : 269—307.

Roemer, Kenneth. 1983. Native American Oral Narratives: Context and Continuity. *Smoothing The Ground,* ed. Brian Swann, 39–54. Berkeley: University of California Press.

Schoolcraft, Henry. 1851–1857. *Historical and Statistical Information Respecting the History Condition and Prospects of the Indian Tribes of the United States.* Vols. 1–5. Philadelphia: Lippincott, Grambo and Co.

Skinner, Alanson. 1912. Notes on the Eastern Cree and Northern Saulteux. *Anthropological Papers of the American Museum of Natural History,* vol. 9(1):1–179.

Speck, Frank. 1915. *Myths and folklore of the Timiskaming Algonkian and Temagami Ojibwa.* Canada Department of Mines, Geological Survey Memoir 71, Anthropological Series no. 9.

# 16

██████████

## *Asking the Stars:*
## *Seneca Hunting Ceremonial*

██████████

### THOMAS McELWAIN

---

*Thomas McElwain, a Seneca, is docent at the University of Stockholm, where he also earned a doctorate in comparative religion, after having studied in France and worked on the New York Seneca Reservations as a native language consultant for the Education Program. He has authored two books and several articles. This chapter, on Seneca hunting and life and their evocation in narrative, is metacommunicative in that its structure reflects the structure of ongoing Seneca belief and practice. These are not beliefs that once had currency in a less sophisticated world. Rather, they are vital teachings with import today. The sky beings cannot be divorced from those who they influence on earth any more than the hunter and the hunted can be separated. All form a living, interacting whole—one sustained breath.*

---

The Seneca people belong to the Iroquoian linguistic family and speak a language closely related to Cayuga, Onondaga, Oneida and Mohawk. At the time of the advent of the European colonies, the Senecas were a hunting and agricultural people in what is now central New York. They were then aligned politically with the great Iroquois League, from which large factions broke away in the last century to form scattered groups, among them the Seneca Nation in western New York, which provides most of the data for the present study. Ethnographic and historical information can be gleaned from the *Handbook of North American Indians* (Trigger 1978), as well as from Fenton (1936, 1947, 1968), Morgan (1962), Parker (in Fenton 1968), and Wallace (1969), among others.

The general relationship between hunting ceremonial and sky spirits of different kinds has long been recognized. Archaeological evidence for such beliefs in the northeastern area goes back for many millennia (Mc-

Elwain 1986:37–43). In recent years, a number of scholars (Chafe 1961; Foster 1974) have noted a progression from earth to sky in much public ritual, not only among the Senecas but also among other Iroquois people as well. It is my purpose to examine details of hunting ceremonial gleaned from Seneca narrative, which give precision to the relationships conceived to exist between sky and earthbound spirits. I draw upon both my own fieldwork and narratives collected by others.

The kind of ceremonial I am talking about is that of the individual hunter. Published documents of public ritual, as well as of secret-society ritual, give only scant clues about these ceremonial practices. Nor is it likely that the kind of ceremonial reflected in late nineteenth-century narrative is the same that occurs today. Hunting ceremonial of some kind exists among all hunters ancient and modern, Iroquois or not. Hunting ceremonial exists among Seneca people today, but the contents of this study should not be construed to describe it except in specifically mentioned details.

Having found an interesting reference in one of the stories collected by Jeremiah Curtin in the later half of the nineteenth century, I have taken as my major source material the references to Genonsgwa (*kẹ:nọ:skwa'*), or the Stone Coat, a narrative figure appearing in the story in question. Work with Curtin's material is hampered by the fact that it exists only in English. Nor is it certain that Hewitt's editing of Curtin's manuscripts is always useful to the systematic researcher. Since the aim of this study is not linguistic description, the use of the material may give definite results providing its weaknesses are remembered and accounted for.

The following summary, which is the result of my own reediting, provides the basis for the study to follow. The original published source, which is a good deal more extensive, provided as it is with Hewitt's explanations and quaint King James Bible language, is found in Curtin and Hewitt (1918:106–11).

### A Hunter Pursued by Genonsgwa

Four warriors decided to go hunting. They had to go up a large stream in canoes. It is said that these were the people who invented canoes. When they arrived at Kingfisher's Place, the eldest said for each one to do his best, and observe the usual fasts and injunctions.

[5]       On the following morning the eldest besought the stars, moon, and sun to aid them. They soon had plenty of game.

One of the hunters decided to go farther than usual. The leader warned him to be careful. Too stubborn to listen to advice, the man

went farther than he intended, following an elk. Night fell and he
[10] camped by a stream. Two women and a nursing baby appeared on the
other side of the stream and called out to him, asking how he had
crossed. Being suspicious that they were not human, he told them to
ford just below his camp. They eventually found a footbridge up-
stream, however. As they were crossing, the hunter ran downstream
[15] and forded, so he was still across the water from them when they
arrived at his camp. The women were angry and called for him to come
to them. He demonstrated his skill with tomahawk and bow and
arrow. Seeing that, one of the Genonsgwa women said, "It seems we
have met Hinon, the Thunder. Nevertheless, I intend to kill him."
[20]      The man was forced to hide in the center of the stream all night.
When it was light enough to see, he started running toward his
friends' camp with the women chasing him. At midday he heard her
voice saying she had almost caught him. At every sound of her voice he
fell to the ground from the effects of her orenda.
[25]      The man decided to hide in a tree. He had just hidden himself in
the top of the tree, when the elder of the women came to the tree.
Being a Genonsgwa she could not look up because of her stoney
clothing. The younger woman also stopped beneath the tree to nurse
the baby. Taking a small, animate finger from her bosom, the elder
[30] woman placed it in the palm of her hand and asked it where the man
was. The women were puzzled when the finger stood straight up. At
that moment the man slipped down from the tree, snatched the magic
finger, and fled. The women pleaded with him to return it. But he
went on swiftly under its power, leaving the women far behind.
[35] Without the finger they could only travel at a slow run.
     The man consulted the finger to know where and how far away
his friends were. When he had found his friends, rested and eaten, he
told them what had happened.
     The chief said they must leave the place the next day. They were
[40] just pushing off from shore when the elder woman appeared on the
bank and said, "Give me back my finger." The chief told the man to
give the finger back. Placing the animate finger on the palm of his
hand, the hunter held it out as far as he could over the stream toward
her. In reaching over the water she lost her balance and fell into the
[45] stream. That was the end of the Stone Coat woman.
     The young hunter retained the finger, and ever afterward con-
sulted it when hunting. He always had whatever game he wanted to
kill, plenty to eat as well as fine furs and feather robes.

The following chart illustrates the opposing pairs from abstract to
concrete and particular. The relationships between the upper and lower

members of the pairs can be noted in the seven episodes of the story. The episodes of the story correspond to the stages in the dynamic relationship between sky and earthbound spirits.

| Guardian Spirits | Sky Beings | Stars, Moon, Sun, Hinon |
|---|---|---|
| (Abstract) | | (Concrete and particular) |
| Helping Spirits | Earthbound Beings | *Genonsgwa* |

The hunters move between guardian spirits and helping spirits in the following seven episodes of the story: (1) hunting expedition planned; (2) petition of Stars, Moon, and Sun; (3) hunter goes further than intended and is stranded alone at night; (4) contest with Stone Coats; (5) the potent finger is acquired from the Stone Coat; (6) the Stone Coat is rendered harmless; and (7) the hunter is endowed with hunting success.

The particular narrative episodes of the story "A Hunter Pursued by Genonsgwa" correspond to the following general stages in earth–sky relations: (1) precision of the goal; (2) petition of sky-world guardians; (3) confrontation with the unwilling earthbound helper; (4) the guardian imposes upon the helper for aid through contest; (5) help is given to the human; (6) the hostility of the helper is rendered harmless; and (7) the goal is achieved.

I shall now examine each of these stages and episodes in detail.

## Precision of the Goal

The narrative goals that can be established to determine helping and guardian spirit relationships tend to be very stereotyped. The narrative expressions tend to be more or less symbolic in character, even in stories considered to be historical legend because of their references to particular people (line 2) and places. Hunting stories giving identifiable detail, such as the destination Kingfisher's Place, are considered as historical legend by Converse (1908) and Parker (in Fenton 1947). Because of the importance of mythical material imposed on historical places and characters, recent students of religion have referred to such stories as mythological tales (McElwain 1978). Native classification of "A Hunter Pursued by Genonsgwa" is that the story is true.

Stories classified as not true and showing an even greater proportion of symbolic elements tend to establish slightly different goals. They refer not to particular people, but to people in particular relationships: for example, a boy and his mother's brother, a brother and sister, or two brothers. The destination emphasizes directions with a symbolic character. Such symbols may give us clues to the meaning of hunting ritual that is missing from such stories as "A Hunter Pursued by Genonsgwa."

An important example of symbolic explanation of hunting ritual is precisely such directional indication. Seneca mythical symbolism of direction falls into two categories: (1) directions involving the tutelage of the sun; and (2) directions avoiding the sun. Sun directions are "where the sun rises" and "where the sun sets," with the latter often translated as Southwest by Hewitt (1903), who takes into consideration the fact that hunting excursions tend to take place in late fall. These directions are symbolic of the predictable course of lifeways. Such lifeways are symbolized by the goals of acquiring tobacco or chestnuts, on one hand, and a spouse, on the other. Some stories include both acquisition of sustenance in the first move of the story and a spouse in the second. Apparently, the use of chestnuts as a symbol of food source or sustenance comes from the fact that the word originally refering to corn or maize has been transmitted through faulty hearing as *chestnut*. The two words are easily confused in Seneca, *chestnut* being *'o:nye'sta'* and *corn* being *'o'nista'*.

The sun-avoiding directions are found in stories with a plot going North and South. These refer to unpredictable happenings, the encounter with witches and sorcerers, rather than the day-to-day ordinary course of life. The goal of the story generally can be predicted by the directions stated, even when a character starts northward ostensibly to hunt, obtain food, or find a spouse. The normal word for *North* in Seneca means "where it is cold." There is, however, a narrative word for North, *te'kä:hkwä:hkǫh*, meaning "the sun isn't there."

The presence and motion of the sun is extremely important in Seneca life. Action performed in daylight before the sun has reached the zenith differs qualitatively from action performed at other times. This is expressed, for example, in the masks in the Seneca False Face Society being painted red when made in the morning and black when made at other times. The face of the mythical prototype is considered to be red in the morning from the reflection of the sun, and black against the sun in the afternoon. The qualitative importance of the forenoon is seen in the limiting of the celebration of certain ceremonies, such as the annual dances and the recitation of *kaiwi:yo'*, the Good News of the Seneca prophet Handsome Lake, to the forenoon. In narrative, the sun in its presence and motion relates to the course of ordinary life, birth, growing, agriculture, marriage, hunting, and warfare. Exceptional activity, that of witches and sorcerers (*kahaih*), is performed in avoidance of sky beings, among whom the sun is most notable. That is why *kahaih* usually takes place at night. Such activity tends to be dependent on the relation between people and earthbound spirits or beings only. Eastward or westward movement can therefore be interpreted as an appeal to the sun's tutelage and by extension to sky beings generally.

Any proposed activity must presuppose either an attitude of appeal to sky spirits or a desire to avoid them. This may or may not be expressed in narrative. It may be expressed, as in "A Hunter Pursued by Genonsgwa" (line 5), by an appeal to the sky being. It also may be expressed merely in a symbolic direction. Directional symbols carry a connotation of appeal or nonappeal to a sky being for a person having grown up with Seneca narrative.

## Petition of Sky-World Guardians

The story "A Hunter Pursued by Genonsgwa" is unique in mentioning (lines 3–6) all of the ceremonial procedures to begin hunting. There are four such procedures. The first is the command to "do your best," probably *ja:kɒh* in Seneca. This command is often a narrative appeal to the use of personal *orenda,* defined by Hewitt as "mystic power" (1902). Exerting *orenda* seems to be something interior, and the command itself is the only thing that might be construed as ceremonial. Personal hunting preparation might include the care of weapons and clothing, activities perhaps not strictly ceremonial. It might be remembered that from the native point of view all such actions are functional. Students of culture call actions ceremonial when they appear to be nonfunctional in their own world view. The application of herbal "medicine" to a weapon might be a case in point. It is ceremonial and is culturally distinctive. But it is considered by every hunter to be functional, because it is supposed to reduce alarming scents. The command to "do one's best" is, in fact, a preparation for appeal to sky beings as the source of *orenda.* But the command is even more a preparation and warning for the confrontation with potentially dangerous earthbound helping spirits.

The observation of fasts is mentioned (line 4) in preparation for hunting. Fasting may also have very practical, functional effects on the physical demands of hunting. But fasting is well-known throughout much of North

America as a means of initiating communication with sky beings. It is difficult to see how the hunting fast could be separated, at least in origin, from a belief in, and appeal to, sky guardians thought to be an aid in hunting. The fast triggers culturally determined visionary experiences, in which the hunter may encounter the sky being in some anthropomorphic or other form. Prayers associated with fasting tend to appeal to the guardians' sense of pity for the fasting hunter and his discomfort in hunger.

The third aspect mentioned in the story "A Hunter Pursued by *Genonsgwa*" is other "injunctions" (line 4). These injunctions apparently refer to practices, also generally thought to involve the manipulation of scent, which have at least a ceremonial aspect. In addition to sexual regulations and practices, these include diet regulations or the avoidance of particular foods considered taboo to the individual, and the ceremonial purification of the body. In practice, hunters could purify their bodies by taking an early morning swim in the river. Moving water is considered essential for proper purification.

Although both fasting and "injunctions" may have some effect on the relationship between the hunter and game, I have a tendency to think that fasting also relates strongly to the hunter–sky spirit relationship, whereas the "injunctions" relate more to the hunter–earth spirit relationship. A good example in this story is found later on, when the relationship to the Genonsgwa is established in part by spending a night submerged in running water. Although earth spirits are not always feminine, as in this story, sexual abstinence may have been a way of reducing the jealousy of the earth spirit whom the hunter is attempting to control. Incidents of sexual activity between hunter and earthbound spirits are common in Seneca narrative. An example in the Curtin–Hewitt collection refers even to sexual activity between the lone hunter and Genonsgwa (Curtin and Hewitt 1918:555).

The last ceremonial preparation for hunting is the one that is of most importance in this study, the actual petitioning of sky beings for aid (lines 5–6). Such petitions were made in the story "A Hunter Pursued by Genongswa" on the morning following arrival at the hunting destination, Kingfisher's Place. The importance of morning actions as distinct from actions at other times has already been mentioned. No doubt both the effectiveness and appropriateness of morning petitions are factors in the hunter's choice of timing. Such effectiveness and appropriateness for morning prayers make the rule, but exceptions are found. An example of petitioning in late evening is found in Curtin and Hewitt (1918:683). This late-evening petition is especially interesting since the earthbound beings involved are also Stone Coats. The context is one of warfare rather than hunting, of crisis rather than planning and preparation. Hewitt's translation of the petition is as follows.

> The chief of the little party remained silent, thinking over the situation. Finally he said: "By means of a sacrifice we must ask Him who has made our lives to aid us in the coming battle. Moreover, we shall use in the sacrifice of prayer native tobacco, which I shall now cast on the fire." Then he took from his pouch native tobacco, which he cast on the fire with the following words: "Thou who has made our lives, give most attentive ear to the thing I am about to say. Now we are about to die. Do Thou aid us to the utmost of Thy power. Thou, ruler, it was Thou who gavest us this native tobacco; it is this that I am now employing. Here, take it; it is offered to Thee. Thou has promised us that Thou wilt always be listening when we ask in prayer by sacrifice. Now, it matters not whether Thou Thyself shall stand here, or whether it shall come by way of a dream, do Thou tell us fully what we must do in this crisis which Thou knowest confronts us so closely. Now I finish my tale. So it is enough. Now, moreover, we will lie down to sleep."

Some researchers who have depended more or less entirely on literature for their knowledge of Iroquoian religion ignore the fact that visionary experience does occur frequently among these people. The important role of the dream has suggested to such people that the dream has entirely usurped the role of the vision. As this text points out, both occur. I have collected many vision accounts on the Allegany Reservation in New York in the 1970s and 1980s. Visionary experience associated with hunting is especially prevalent. The most prominent figure is an enormous white stag, which is invulnerable to bullets.

The petition of stars, moon, and sun in "A Hunter Pursued by Genonsgwa" (lines 5–6) is most certainly a tobacco invocation similar to the one quoted above. Burning tobacco with its rising smoke is typical of sky-spirit petitions. Tobacco offered to another type of being is generally not burnt in Seneca narrative. The choice of sky beings to whom tobacco invocations may be made is quite broad. In the invocation quoted, the petition is limited to the Creator, addressed incidentally with both terms, *shǫkwatyę:no'kta'ǫh* and *hawęni:yo'*, the former being the term presently used by the so-called Longhouse Pagans and the latter by Seneca Christians. This terminological distinction is of late appearance and has been absolute only in the present century.

Foster (1974) has shown a structural correspondence between Thanksgiving addresses and the range of beings from earth to sky for the Cayuga.

Chafe's (1961) Seneca texts show a similar correspondence. I have found a similar structure in Christian prayers, which differ from the Longhouse prayers in omitting the four beings or messengers to the prophet Handsome Lake from the hierarchy of sky beings, and in avoiding the name *shǫkwatyę:-no'kta'ǫh*, while retaining the older term *hawęni:yo'*, translated as "ruler" by Hewitt. The following beings may be invoked by hunters: *takwanǫ'ę:yęt* (whirlwind), *hi'nǫ'* or *hatiwęnotatye's* (thunder), stars, moon, sun, and the Creator. It appears to me that tobacco invocations for hunting could be made to *shakotyowehko:wa:h* (also a wind being) or *'oshata'ke:a'* (dew eagle), but I have never found indications that such is the case in the communities with whom I have worked in western New York. Both of these are addressed in Seneca medicine societies today.

Some of these beings are addressed in kinship terms. It is precisely this Native American habit that suggests anthropomorphism to non-Native observers. Although it is possible to use the terms *being* or *spirit,* these are likely to give a wrong impression of the Native perception, which emphasizes relationships despite the tendency in translation to describe anthropomorphic beings. The thunder is addressed as grandfather, the moon as grandmother, the sun as elder brother, and the stars and wind in either masculine or feminine terms. I have not found particular individual stars, with the exception of the Morning Star, to be addressed in invocations of hunting.

The constellations most familiar in Seneca life are mentioned in the creation story (Hewitt 1903:227, 228). These include *hatitkwa'ta:'* or *teonǫtkwęh,* the Pleiades; when this constellation rises just after dark, it marks the winter solstice and the time of the midwinter ceremonies. The first term means "a cluster is present" and the second "they are dancing." The story of the Pleiades is well documented in many sources, but I have described its changing social and religious significance elsewhere (McElwain 1978:106–10). The Pleiades are accompanied by Orion, called *yenyohsyo:t,* "she is sitting." The constellation *nǫkakya'kǫh ka'sä:tǫh,* "spread beaver skin," or the Little Dipper, is watched when traveling at night.

The origin of a number of constellations is told in stories in which a group of people rise into the air. The Pleiades are dancing children who imitated their parents by making a feast and dancing one night. The Big Dipper is made up of hunters following a bear, the star on the lower outside corner of the Dipper (Curtin and Hewitt 1918:276).

There is an interesting episode in a Curtin story (Curtin and Hewitt

1918:468): a man beseeches the Morning Star for control over the water monsters (earthbound beings used by a witch grandmother to catch him).

> While looking around for some avenue of escape he saw the Morning Star shining brightly in the east. Remembering that the Morning Star had promised him in a dream in the days of his youth to help him in the time of trouble or peril, he prayed that the Morning Star would hasten the coming of the day, for he believed that with the advent of daylight the waters would subside and he would be saved. He cried in the anguish of his mind; "Oh, Morning star! hasten the Orb of Day. Oh, Morning Star! hurry on the daylight. You promised when I was young that you would help me if I ever should be in great peril." Now, the Morning Star lived in a beautiful lodge, with a small boy as a servant. Hearing the voice of the hunter appealing to him for aid, he called out to the servant, "Who is that shouting on the island?" The small boy replied, "Oh, that is the husband of the little old woman's granddaughter. He says that you promised him in a dream when he was young that you would help in the time of trouble." The Morning Star answered, "Oh, yes! I did promise him to do so. Let the Orb of Day come at once." Immediately daylight came, and the water on the island subsided.

The following aspects are prominent in the passage just quoted: (1) the cooperation of star and sun to control earthbound monsters; (2) the guardian relation of the Morning Star to the hunter; (3) the Iroquois acquisition of a guardian (in this case, the Morning Star) through the medium of dreams or visions; and (4) the controlling aspect of the sky beings over the earthbound beings during the time of the ascent of the sun. The stranded man is saved from the monsters only when the sun appears and the water subsides. Although the stranded man's early-morning petition of the Morning Star is in the context of crisis, a hunter's petition of the Morning Star is an early-morning event in any case, fully coherent with the rest of the ceremonial described in the story "A Hunter Pursued by Genonsgwa."

The tobacco invocation calls the attention of the sky being to the weakness of the hunter and his need of aid. Hunting anecdotes, to be heard in all of the communities I have visited, reflect this attitude. The hunter usually tells stories not of his own prowess, but of the amazing cunning of game animals. Boasting of hunting prowess is likely to alienate sky beings, who would no longer take pity on the hungry hunter. One should not infer that modern hunters consciously relate to such sky beings in that way. Probably, the attitudes associated with older ritual practices continue among many today from a mere sense of propriety.

## Confrontation and Contest

At this point, some theoretical understanding of the Iroquois concept of *orenda* is essential. *Orenda* is philosophically far more complex than Hewitt would give us to understand in his definition as "mystic power" (Hewitt 1902). The seventeenth-century Jesuits were only partly right when they suggested that both god and religion of the Iroquois were the dream, although the importance of the dream not only in Seneca ritual, but also in the acquisition of *orenda* through dream communication with sky beings is not to be underestimated. *Orenda* is the key word in Iroquois religion, philosophy, world view, and ordinary common sense. It appears that one of the Seneca cognates of the word *"orenda," 'oenǫ'*, refers to song, dance, or medicine society. In effect, *orenda* refers more to relationships than to entities.

*Orenda* presumes a balancing of relationships, a reciprocity if possible. It is not far from the attitudes that attend both ceremonial and economic exchange in aliterate societies around the world, or from the attitudes that attend a written contract in literate societies. Everything in confronting the earthbound helper ought to be seen in its role toward establishing these kinds of relationships, or *orenda*.

Two events intervene between the hunter and the game animal: the sky-world guardian and the earthbound helper. The approach to the guardian has already been seen. The second phase is the approach to the helper.

Contact with the helper is potentially disastrous. When it occurs in the etymological meaning of our English word *disastrous* (unstarred), that is, without a sky-world guardian involved, there is no hope for survival. A good example of such contact is found in the Morning Star story quoted above. When the witch grandmother herself is left stranded on the island, she appeals to the Morning Star. "The Morning Star replied, 'Oh, no! I never had any conversation with her. I never made any promise to her.' With these words the Morning Star fell asleep again and slept on, letting the Orb of Day come at its own time. The water on the island kept rising and rising until it had reached the top of the pine tree, when the inhabitants of the lake ate up the little old woman" (Curtin and Hewitt 1918:469). There can be no balanced relationship between human and earthbound helper without the cooperation of a sky being.

In the Genonsgwa story under consideration, the earthbound helpers involved are of course the Stone Coats, Genonsgwa, or in modern phonemic notation *kę:nǫ:skwa'*. Their earthbound nature is emphasized in this case by the weight of their stone clothing.

The encounter is particularly dangerous because it occurs at night (lines 10ff.), when the sky beings apparently have less control over the helpers. Evidence of this can be seen in the Morning Star episodes already noted, in which the coming of the sun is vital. There appears to be evidence, even in this Genonsgwa story, that the lone encounter at night is somehow advantageous. Disobeying a command to stay near the group, the disregarding of a narrative taboo, is known to be typical of the liquidation of lacks, to use Dundes's (1964) vocabulary. The fact that the chief of the hunting party expresses the prohibition (lines 7–8), rather than indicating that the lone encounter should be avoided, in fact suggests just the opposite: that a lone night encounter with the earthbound helper is precisely what the hunter seeks. My explanation of this is that the practice is a bait for the helper. The hunter tries to make contact with the helper by creating a situation in which the helper hopes to gain an advantage. The expression of the taboo itself is part of the subterfuge. The hunters hope the earthbound helpers will overhear and make an appearance. The real indications to the hunter are passed down through narrative tradition in the frost time, when the earthbound beings are less likely to overhear. Belief that earthbound beings will overhear conversation is still very much alive on the reservation today. People refuse to talk about such beings or tell stories about them in the summer months for fear of offending them and causing snakes to appear around human living areas.

Typical of the encounter is contest and dissimulation. The lone hunter gives false directions for crossing the stream (lines 12–13). There is *orenda* contest in the banter of angry words (line 16). The display of prowess with tomahawk and bow and arrows is an oblique appeal to *hi'nǫ'*, the Thunderer, who is, of course, a sky being (lines 18–19). Hiding in the stream until daylight has ramifications I have already noted in hunting ceremonialism (line 20). The course of the encounter shows clearly how well the lone hunter has prepared for the encounter by preparatory ceremonialism and appeal to sky beings. The hunter made an earlier appeal to stars, the moon, and the sun. Now he appeals to sky beings during the encounter as well, this time to the Thunder. Display of martial or hunter prowess is part of the ceremonial event of communication with some sky beings. This is particularly apparent in the Sun Dance, reported by Parker (Fenton 1968: 103), where hunters shoot a volley of arrows into the air three times during the ceremony. The Moon Dance includes a peachstone gambling game, reminiscent of many an *orenda* contest with sorcerers. In narrative, the peachstones are thrown up through the smokehole and turn into geese before coming the same color up into the bowl. The bird figure reveals the reliance of the hunter on sky beings in his contest with the sorcerer. The use of war dances is typical of the Thunder Dance, and the display produced by the hunter here is probably to be associated with the war dance.

It is not certain what the narrative actually implies about hunting practices now, at the time of the telling, or in earlier times. It seems safe to say, however, that hunters have expressed, through ceremonial actions, an awareness of the necessity of turning potentially dangerous forces to their advantage. This awareness must strongly color the world as seen by the hunter alone in the woods at night.

Causing people to fall by the mere voice (lines 23–24) is typical of contest in general, and appears most often in witchcraft and sorcery. A motif serving the same function is the beating of face-paint in a mortar. With every thud of the pestle the victim falls to the ground. Both of these are manifestations of *'otkǫ'*, or evil power. A good example of the latter in connection with acquisition of power over game animals is found in a Seneca story in which a young man is in contest with the keeper of game. He steals the small white deer from the keeper, whereupon all of the keeper's belongings follow him as he tries to escape. The keeper begins pounding face-paint. At every thud on the mortar, the young man falls fainting to the ground (Myrtle Peterson 1976).

The most typical contest is the footrace (line 21–22). This is found in many hunting stories with other characters such as the Great Bear and the Buffalo Man. In every case, a sky being helps the hunter to win the contest and derive hunting luck from the helper. These stories and figures all refer to single hunters and their attainment of hunting luck, generally for themselves alone when the *kęːnǫːskwa'* is involved, but often for the whole group when the Great Bear or Buffalo Man are involved.

Seneca medicine society ritual involves group relations to helpers, notably in the Dark Dance with its tutelary in the Little People. In this case, a stable relationship is maintained with reciprocal rights and obligations in society ceremonial. The individual hunter may participate by leaving nail trimmings in crevices of the rocks for the Little People, who use these in preparing their own hunting medicine. In return, they help the hunter. I was shown the place where these Little People, or *jokęǫ'*, are thought to live in Rock City, near the Allegany Reservation. The sky being invoked in this case is usually the Creator himself.

At this point, it might be mentioned in passing that a guardian–helper pair generally associated not with hunting but with agriculture is, in fact, the Thunderer, *hi'nǫ'*, and various serpentlike beings. The pair does occur in a hunting context, however, in the case of Curtin's story "The Woman Who Became a Snake From Eating Fish" (Curtin and Hewitt 1918:111).

When the contest takes the form of chase, often the appeal to a sky being is expressed in the direction stated or, even more overtly, in changing direction. This is lacking in Curtin's version of the story, "A Hunter Pursued by Genonsgwa," but would no doubt have been included had Hewitt been the collector. It is sometimes difficult to say whether Curtin's method of recording stories as he heard them is a better method, or that of Hewitt is to be preferred with its constant questioning and editing, a practice unfortunately calculated to destroy the natural storytelling situation and to elicit expected responses rather than natural ones. Such directional indications are given in stories of chase by the Great Bear, with a direction change from East to Southwest, indicating the aid of the sun, although not the aid of the Thunders in other stories. The story "A Hunter Pursued by Genonsgwa" has a direct appeal to the Thunders in the episode of the chase, and this appeal may explain the lack of directions. People appeal to the Thunder in an upward direction, and the chase takes a turn in favor of the hunter when he finally climbs a tree (line 25).

## Help, Escape, and Hunting Luck

At this point in the story of "A Hunter Pursued by Genonsgwa," all of the events that should have been triggered by ritual preparation have fallen into place. The hunter has supplicated the stars, the moon, the sun, and the thunder. Contact and contest with the earthbound potential helper has been instigated, despite the fact that the helper has realized that a sky being is cooperating with the hunter. At this point, the hunter should receive a token of hunting luck from the helping spirit. This is, in fact, what happens.

When the hunter slides down the tree and snatches the magic finger from the Genonsgwa (lines 32–33), hunting *orenda,* or luck, is transferred from the helper to the hunter. This is expressed in the story by the fact that the hunter is now able to (1) run faster than the Genonsgwa, (2) ascertain directions, and (3) regain his companions. On the other hand, the Genonsgwa people are no longer able to chase effectively. This characteristic explains the general unwillingness of helpers to aid hunters. The helper tends to lose *orenda* in direct proportion to the hunter's gain.

Narrative symbols of loss and gain in hunting *orenda* can be gleaned from the body of Seneca stories. Loss of hunting *orenda* is often symbolically expressed by loss of dogs or loss of eyeballs. A little common-sense imagination will immediately reveal why eyeballs and dogs are functional equivalents in Seneca narrative. It is because they are functional equivalents in the hunt itself. Dogs are lost by being caught and eaten by some earthbound monster or colorful renegade from the sky world, such as a whirlwind. In a few stories, dogs may be turned to stone. Eyes are stolen by competitive humans, usually for a witch mother-in-law.

Gain in hunting *orenda* may be symbolized by several things. The ability to run fast is typical, especially in connection with aid from the wind or thunder. In such situations, the hunter generally gives up use of the bow and arrows and uses only the war club for hunting. He is able to do so because of the supernatural powers of running he has been given. There are instances of the hunter of this type being aided by a crow rather than by running ability. The crow cooperating with the hunter makes it possible for him to knock down deer with a club.

Knocking down game with a club is still considered evidence of direct intervention of a sky being. In 1974, Effie Johnson told me the following story on the Allegany Reservation. She and her daughter were driving in the car when they saw a deer by the road. They stopped the car, but the deer did not move. They went over to the deer and hit it on the head. It fell down and they dragged it to the car. There it jumped up again. They hit it once more, this time killing it. They were then able to put it in the car and take it home. They hung it in a tree. When her husband came home from hunting, he said, "Where did that deer come from?" She said, "I just hit it on the head."

The cooperation of a pair is typical of Iroquois thought. Hunting is also dependent on the cooperation of a pair. Often the pair involved will be male and female. In Effie Johnson's story, the idea of the cooperation of the male and female pair is noticeable. The success of the woman's hunt is in relation to the man's lack of success. The man came home empty-handed, but the hunt was not futile. The story implies that the deer responded to the advance of the woman in the way it did because she was part of a hunting complex, including her husband and all of the sky guardians and earth-bound helpers participating in that particular hunting event. Although awe is not uncommon among Iroquois hunters, humor of this kind is a typical response to such situations. The story itself reaffirms belief in the configuration. Such stories often include a phrase suggesting that the Creator (a sky being) put the animals here for our use.

Another symbol of the increase of hunting *orenda* is to be found in a bone fetish. Contest with the Great Bear results in the whole hunting party gaining hunting *orenda*, symbolized by a bone taken from the burnt monster once it has been overcome. There are no narrative indications of how the bone is used, but it appears that the strength and prowess of the Great Bear participate in the hunter's activity through the medium of this fetish.

Finally, the story of "A Hunter Pursued by Genonsgwa" employs the symbol of the magic finger (line 29). Although the Thunder imparts the ability to run, the central symbol of increased *orenda* is the Genonsgwa's magic finger, which may be consulted for direction and distance. The magic finger also gives the ability to run fast. The magic finger points in the direction of the game indicated and, by rising from the palm, shows the approximate distance at which the game animal is located. This is why the Genonsgwa women were mystified when the finger stood on end (line 31).

In some stories, the hunter reaches a balance with the Genonsgwa by sharing meat in exchange for hunting luck. This balance does not usually last because of the jealousy between Genonsgwa and Seneca men over Genonsgwa women. Genonsgwa women, of course, always side with Iroquois men in such cases, in fact helping them to kill Genonsgwa men attacking in their fit of jealousy. Even then, the results are eventually ill fated.

"A Hunter Pursued by Genonsgwa" is a story typical for its successful conclusion, which is the annihilation of the Genonsgwa after hunting luck has been obtained from them. Genonsgwa men are annihilated by thrusting a burning log of basswood into their rectum. Genonsgwa women are disposed of by luring them into a stream where they are drowned. In any case, the goal is achieved. The earth and sky have cooperated in giving human beings the necessities of life. It is no doubt the Iroquois awareness of that cooperation which is their wisdom. Narrative indicators show that such awareness is heightened not only by storytelling, but by the ceremonial practices associated with hunting.

A summary of the configuration of Seneca belief suggested by narrative follows. The basic item is that hunting, for example among human activities, is dependent not only on human prowess and strength, but also on the cooperation of the environment.

A hunting event is the cumulative result of a chain of *orenda* events or pairs. The whole chain is not always expressed in any one story, and parts of it may be assumed. But the chain may be summarized as follows:

(1) A man and wife, or hunting partners.

(2) A hunter communicating with a sky being such as the stars, moon, sun, thunder or wind, or Creator.

(3) A hunter in contest with a potential earthbound helper, such as Genonsgwa, Great Bear, Little People, or another.

(4) A sky being imposing upon an earthbound helper on behalf of the hunter.

(5) A hunter successfully meeting and killing game animals.

A Western observer might suggest that this ordering is far more complex than awareness of stars for movement, of the effect of sun and moon on the habits and availability of game animals, and the wind in terms of scent—and all of these on the round of seasons, warrants. On the other hand, the criticism cannot be taken seriously until the world view that produces it produces also a mythology that as successfully integrates the hunter with the world of his interaction in terms of continuing life, rather than setting the hunter apart from the world as heroic because his hand is against it, its animals, its earth, and its sky.

# References

Chafe, Wallace. 1961. *Seneca Thanksgiving Rituals*. Bureau of American Ethnology Bulletin 183.

Converse, Harriet. 1908. *Myths and Legends of the New York State Iroquois*, with an introduction by A. C. Parker. New York State Museum Bulletin 125.

Curtin, Jeremiah, and J. N. B. Hewitt. 1918. *Seneca Fiction, Legends, and Myths*. Bureau of American Ethnology Annual Report 32.

Dundes, Alan. 1964. *The Morphology of North American Indian Folktales*. FF Communications no. 195, Helsinki.

Fenton, W. N. 1936. An Outline of Seneca Ceremonies at Coldspring Longhouse, *Yale University Publications in Anthropology*, vol. 9. New Haven, Conn.

———. 1947. Iroquois Indian Folklore. *Journal of American Folklore* 60.

Fenton, W. N., ed. 1968. *Parker on the Iroquois.* Syracuse, N.Y.: Syracuse University Press.

Foster, Michael K. 1974. *From the Earth to beyond the Sky.* Mercury Series Publication no. 20, National Museums of Canada, Ottawa.

Hewitt, J. N. B. 1902. Orenda and a Definition of Religion. *American Anthropologist* 4.

———. 1903. *Iroquoian Cosmology,* Bureau of American Ethnology Annual Report 32.

McElwain, Thomas. 1978. *Mythological Tales and the Allegany Seneca.* Stockholm Studies in Comparative Religion, vol. 17.

———. 1986. The Archaic Roots of Eastern Woodland Eschatology: A Soul-dualism Explanation of Adena Mortuary. In *Cosmos: The Yearbook of the Traditional Cosmology Society,* vol. 1, Edinburgh.

Morgan, Lewis Henry. 1962. *League of the Iroquois,* Chicago: Corinth Books.

Trigger, Bruce G., ed. 1978. *NORTHEAST. Handbook of North American Indians.* Washington, D.C.: Smithsonian Institution.

Wallace, Anthony F. C. 1969. *The Death and Rebirth of the Seneca.* New York: Random House.

# 17

[■ ■ ■ ■ ■ ■ ■ ■ ■]

## *Epilogue: Blue Archaeoastronomy*

[■ ■ ■ ■ ■ ■ ■ ■ ■]

## CLAIRE R. FARRER AND RAY A. WILLIAMSON

In a recent work Aveni (1989:3–12) describes the interdiscipline of archaeo-astronomy as being composed of two major segments; the segment names, Green (for Old World archaeoastronomy) and Brown (for New World archaeoastronomy), are multivocalic. Green is both the color of the land cover in most Old World sites and the cover color of the volume dealing with Old World sites from the 1981 Oxford II Conference on Archaeoastronomy. Green archaeoastronomy primarily concerns megaliths and their alignments, plus statistical and evolutionary arguments based on premises deduced, or induced, from Green work. By contrast, Brown is the cover color of the volume from that same conference that dealt with the New World, especially the artifactual residue of the great Mesoamerican and South American Indian civilizations. Brown archaeoastronomy, while also somewhat concerned with earth-surface phenomena, delved into the dirt—physical dirt resulting from archaeological digs and scholarly dirt from the layers of dust one had to endure while searching documents, for Brown archaeoastronomy is dependent not just upon alignments but also upon the linkages given life in ethnohistoric and historic documents.

While Green and Brown serve well for the majority of those who work in the interdiscipline, the terms do not equally well include those who work with living people and their traditions. Archaeoastronomers must content themselves with long-dead people whose traditions survive, if at all, in enigmatic structures with alignments to be discovered; in epigraphy that must be decoded; in art that requires interpretation; or in the scribal offerings of the conquerors that must be weighed on the scales of history and political exigency. In the Old World there is no evidence of direct, living descendants of those who built the magnificent megaliths; in the New World archaeoastronomers are more fortunate in being able to argue from documents, primarily from the Spanish, and ethnographic analogy from those living who are known to be the descendants of the ones who built the impressive cities in the jungles and mountains. Neither documents nor ethnographic analogy are without pitfalls, but both provide intriguing data often missing from Brown records.

Ethnoastronomers, by contrast, work primarily with non-Western people who are alive and possess functioning systems of science that are not based on Western-derived canons or presuppositions. Also, ethno-astronomers are fortunate in being able to work with people whose astro-nomical systems, while certainly different from what they may have been a hundred or a thousand years ago, are still intact. They work with people whose vision is skyward, into the blue of the celestial canopy; for that reason, Farrer (n.d.) has referred to them as Blue in contrast to the archaeo-astronomical Brown and Green. An archaeoastronomer might well decode the Governor's Palace at the Mayan site of Uxmal in the Yucatán and demonstrate, through alignments and glyphs, that the building functioned as a Venus calendar; an ethnoastronomer would be busy in the Yucatan countryside talking with contemporary Mayan speakers and learning their use of the sky and how Venus relates to the entirety of their perceived ethnoastronomical system and further how that system articulates with everyday life. It is a matter of concentration on separate aspects of the interdiscipline, with ethnoastronomers having the luxury of checking de-ductions and understandings with the people whose astronomy is the sub-ject of investigation. Yet archaeoastronomers and ethnoastronomers work together in the field on each other's teams, whether we wear the uniform of Green, Brown, or Blue. Today, the scholarly field of archaeoastronomy is not only Green and Brown (archaeoastronomy proper) but also it is Blue (ethnoastronomy), as this collection of papers from Native North America demonstrates.

Some consider ethnoastronomy to be a subset of archaeoastronomy, but most prefer to view ethnoastronomy both as allied to and different from archaeoastronomy. The prefix *archaeo-* refers to the past, often the remote past. Ethnoastronomers—whether initially trained in astronomy, anthro-pology, architecture, art history, folklore, geography, linguistics, mythol-ogy, philosophy, poetics, psychology, religious studies, or symbolism—work with living peoples whose astronomy does not duplicate the Western

European, scientific model; therefore, they join their kind of astronomy with the *ethno-* prefix and eschew the use of the prefix *archaeo-*. Ethnoastronomers, in working with living non-Western peoples, usually find that not only do their perceptions of celestial phenomena differ from the Euroamerican canon, but also there are significant differences in how those perceptions are utilized to organize other behavior, from cognitive structure to values.

It may appear that the division between archaeoastronomy and ethnoastronomy is an elegant, clear-cut one. Would that it were. As Hoskinson's chapter demonstrates, the two are often intertwined in interesting ways. Hoskinson uses standard archaeoastronomical data, alignments, and rock art, which he then illuminates through a combination of ethnology and ethnoastronomy: the contemporary practice of the saguaro wine-making event tied to the celestial event of the summer solstice. He demonstrates that while people's contemporary practice may have changed from their past history, it is nonetheless possible to demystify and explain arcane, and silent, structures through careful archaeoastronomy combined with the interview techniques (common to ethnoastronomy) and scholarly library research. His chapter illustrates, first, the importance of always keeping in mind that archaeoastronomy and ethnoastronomy are handmaidens to each other as well as, second, demonstrating the value of adding Blue, whenever possible, to what initially appear to be Green or Brown sites.

Archaeoastronomers usually must *re*-construct astronomical systems and their import from the often scanty data from no longer extant people; ethnoastronomers must learn alternative *con*structions that living people have devised, based upon their own observations and interpretations of the celestial sphere that all humans share. We refer to these constructions as *cosmovision,* a felicitous term introduced into the literature by Broda (1982:81).

Cosmovision incorporates what anthropologists have termed *cosmogony* (accounts of the physical creation and ordering of the universe) and *cosmology* (ideational accounts of the philosophical nature of, and theories about, the universe); thus, our definitions of the two terms differ somewhat from theoretical astronomers, who use cosmogony to reference the physical construction of the universe and cosmology to reference ideas about the functioning of the universe. Both astronomers and anthropologists find benefit in using cosmovision to reference non-Western views that combine cosmogony and cosmology into an integrated whole; for, as our introduction states, non-Western people in general, and Native North Americans in particular, do not see the dichotomies that characterize much of the thinking of Western, Euroamerican-derived civilizations. Where Westerners see black and white, Native Americans are much more likely to see blackandwhite, all of a piece. They see a unity in Earth and Sky that is encapsulated in the term *cosmovision.*

Additionally, cosmovision presupposes an intimate knowledge of the celestial sphere based upon naked-eye observations. It is the observations that underlie the vision of the cosmos that any one people may project, and it is the observations that suggest the unity between Sky and Earth. But it is more as well; cosmovision orders and explains the universe—it also orders and explains everyday life. The two, Earth and Sky, are truly one in most Native North American conceptions and certainly in those presented in this book.

As the foregoing chapters attest, complex philosophical arguments and sophisticated observations of the natural universe underlie both tangible artifacts and material culture; those same philosophical arguments and sophisticated observations also underlie the verbal expressions given voice in the narratives related in the various chapters. These narratives are much more than just-so stories; they, and the behavior they engender, enliven the dynamic interaction established along the vertices of the *axis mundi.*

In most considerations of the *axis mundi,* it is depicted as a pole tying together the above and below or it is conceived of as a tree with roots in the earth and uppermost branches in the sky. The *axis mundi* of our contributors is an ideational channel that allows movement between this surface world and the world above. At some times the movement is one of beings; at other times the movement is of power, of illness or healing, of sustenance or want, of assistance or deprivation. It is not a devolution of all that is good and proper from the above, Sky world to the below, Earth world. Rather, it is movement of reciprocity. Both Earth and Sky require each other to sustain themselves. The universe is composed of Sky and Earth, of there and here, of possibility and reality, of probability and chance, of direction and indirection. Now one aspect is emphasized while previously another was center-stage. Popular literature and belief credit Native North Americans with a mystical association of nature and people; our contributors remove some of the mystery while illuminating more fully the nature of the intimate association of nature and people, universe and world, people and power, Earth and Sky. The Sky speaks to people in the manifold movements of celestial phenomena, just as people, representing Earth's forces, speak to

Sky in belief, behavior, chant, prayer, ritual ceremony, and myth. Sometimes the voice of one being can be heard; at other times the voice is one of conjoint action or the empowering essence of the word or the visual voice of dance, paint, tipi covers, and visual metaphors. The universe speaks to people who provide an answering chorus, now in a Thank-You Prayer, then in a footrace, here in a set of moral precepts, and there in an enabling myth. Sometimes the speech of the universe is visual rather than aural, as when people look skyward and observe the nightly movement of the stars or the monthly convolutions of the moon or the annual movement of the sun on the horizon. Surely, the voice of Creator echoes through the universe and is made manifest in Sun, Moon, and Stars. The channel of the *axis mundi* is alive with voices and images flowing back and forth, then ramifying out into the entirety of the world and the universe.

Earth and Sky are obverse and reverse to each other, connected by an active, vital channel that we chose to term the *axis mundi*. But this *axis mundi* is not just a vertical shaft connecting Earth and Sky; it also has an horizontal aspect, providing a rationale for the behavior of people living in consort with the created and natural universe: a life line to be lived on Earth in consonance with, or in opposition to, the dictates of the wisdom incorporated in the Sky. Daily-life phenomena are played out against the backdrop of the celestial sphere, a backdrop that, for most Native Americans, includes the results of past behavior written forever in the stars.

This multidimensional *axis mundi* finds expression on tipi cover designs, as Kehoe describes, as well as in the geographic (or sacred) environment, according to Conway's data. The active tension is expressed folkloristically in the various accounts of narratives that weave in and out of the chapters. Constant interchanges between Earth beings and Sky beings provide a living tension, a tension brilliantly captured in "the single breath" from Silko's poem. The breath animates both Earth and Sky and forever interlocks them in mutual dependence, as the very substance of living is constantly interchanged.

A breath is a fragile and enigmatic thing: ephemeral but vital, intangible but audible, insubstantial but animating, ethereal but visible. The breath of life is a single breath composed of many cycles; babies being born and eagerly sucking their first lung-filling breaths; old people quietly setting aside the years and cares with their last breaths; the feathery promise of a new day's light with the summer's 4:00 A.M. purple-fading-to-pink sigh that soon becomes a golden crescendo allowing all living things to awaken and draw in again the breath of life; the promise of new days, new nights, new seasons, continuing cycles as the solstice sun moves from its spot on the horizon to swing back into its life-sustaining process of movement so that the universe as we know it can continue its life's breath.

A few years ago one of us (CRF) was priviledged to attend a Deer Dinner held in honor of, and celebration for, the first winter's kill at Paraje, a village on the Laguna Pueblo Reservation. A matrilineal clan, with matrilateral extensions, gathered early in the evening for the feast. As a house guest of one of the clan members, The Anthropologist, as she was invariably introduced, provided the occasion for explanation and reflection with each ritual act that was performed. Upon entering the home, each family member went first to an end table, cradling the horn rack of the deer, fronted by an exquisite bowl, holding prayer meal; four times the hands were passed over the meal, each time being for a different cardinal direction and each time moving from the deer through the meal before the cupped hands came up to the face where breath was inhaled and exhaled forcefully. The deer's breath had been sacrificed to feed the family and to allow each of them to continue their own breathing. Each act with prayer meal acknowledged the gift of the transfer of the breath of life while children, and The Anthropologist, were apprised of the vital importance of properly acknowledging the gift of life through stories that were related.

The continuity of act and story support the view of the world held, in the above case, by Laguna people. Traditional stories stay vital in families and communities as long as they serve life's purposes—whether religious and cosmological or as mundane as sheer entertainment. Stories are not moribund; they change to incorporate changes in life and in culture, with some becoming, in their own time, traditional stories. They are stories that not only sustain through the cosmic breath but also stories that provide moral imperatives—examples of the good and proper life, canons for aesthetic judgment—and limn the consequences of impropriety.

McElwain's chapter concerning Seneca hunting practice illustrates the intimate connection sustained between Sky Beings and Earth Beings through careful monitoring of natural phenomena. Tobacco smoke, visible breath, establishes the channel of communication from Earthbound spirits or beings to Sky-spirit Beings. Communication is also from the natural world. Sun itself, in its presence and in its absence, provides information to people, as does the seasonal appearance in particular places in the sky of specific constellations. Paying proper attention to the injunctions, and boons, allows success or failure to occur here on Earth for people.

The opportunity for success has been removed for some Earth people by others acting, one hopes, in ignorance rather than in malice. The inherent poignancy of Broughton's and Buckskin's chapter becomes almost unbearable when thought about carefully. How can an Ajumawi man possibly be powerful, and potentially successful, if he can no longer race *Simloki*'s shadow because the white man has fenced the land? How wrenching it must be to watch the shadow fly across the land, indicate power places, remember the old stories, and know that avenue is closed yet tantalizingly visible. What courage it must take to live a proper life when one's connection to the eternal and infinite has been disrupted.

But disruption, too, is written in the sky, as Conway shows for the Ojibwa. Once people inhabited what is now only a light in the sky. Once comets scoured the Earth, leaving their visible marks in the very rocks. Once people did not heed those who have wisdom; the consequences are paraded nightly. Now, contemporary life notwithstanding, the shaking lodge is every bit as important as ever it was, yet it seems to be on the verge of extinction. Does this also portend extinction for the Ojibwa? For vital portions of their heritage? Or are there alternative explanations, alternative stories, that will allow life to continue, to allow the breath to continue to animate the up above and the here below?

People must maintain interest in the stories, beliefs, and rituals for them to continue to breathe life into the culture. Even the interest of outsiders is sometimes sufficient for revitalization of an important heritage that was experiencing death throes.

The Young (Zuni), Griffin-Pierce (Navajo), Pinxten and van Dooren (Navajo), and Farrer (Mescalero Apache) chapters share, in common, cultures that are vital with much of their ceremonial life intact. That is not to aver that there is no change—far from it. Rather, it is to note that salvage ethnoastronomy has not been a concern, for the life's breath is still actively exchanged between Earth and Sky for each of the members of those cultures.

Young's discussion of Zuni stories concerning Morning and Evening Stars provides an implicit cautionary note in that our Western perceptions are too often placed atop Native ones, resulting in misapprehensions, at best. Twins, for Westerners, are either identical or fraternal; whichever they are, we expect them to behave in similar manner, to be mystically in touch with each other and to be somehow special and different from their singly born siblings. Zuni people, while acknowledging specialness of twins, see other roles for them, at least for the Twin War Gods who, in two of their many incarnations, are also Evening Star and Morning Star. Twins incorporate not only the principle of duality but also that of balance, being, as she notes, more than complementary yet less than isomorphic: both are of a piece, perceivable as separate but, in truth, inalienable. The Twins share a single breath of life that animates them both separately and together, providing a model for the Zuni in which to cast other perceptions of the natural and created universe as being all of a piece.

Athabascan speakers, by contrast, seem to be more didactic in their perceptions. Farrer's Mescalero Apache chapter states that the stars are in the sky specifically to provide guidance to people. The guidance, however, is not just in physical space but also in metaphysical and moral space, for the lessons of life are encoded in the stars and are interpreted by holy men, or Singers of Ceremonies. It is their breath, in song, that reanimates both the universe and the people who live on the Earth's surface and who watch the stars and who, consequently, know that their actions will allow either the continuation of the exquisite harmony and balance of the universe or will allow chaos to reign supreme. It is no wonder that the sung word is an empowering force, as the breath used to sing returns to the Sky its nurturance while reminding people of their good fortune and responsibilities.

Both Navajo chapters, that of Pinxten and van Dooren and that of Griffin-Pierce, deal with many of the same celestial phenomena and some of the same earthly phenomena, yet in different ways. Again, there is an implicit lesson here. All too often, scholars accord primary credence to those read first or who did their work earlier; there seems to be a notion that early is better. But here we have cases of fieldwork taking place at the same time (during the 1970s and 1980s), assessing some of the same phenomena, and, while sharing some conclusions, still being quite different. The differences are due both to separate emphases in training of the investigators as well as to having worked with various Native consultants. When considered as a whole, rather than looking for truth in one place or the other, the multifaceted character of the animating breath is beautifully illustrated through what Bakhtin (1981) terms *heteroglossia,* the multiplicity of voices, each of which contributes to the whole of understanding.

Griffin-Pierce finds a corollary between the Sky, as house of Celestial Beings and home of Celestial Events, and the *hooghan,* as house of mortals and place of earthly events. Celestial events and constellations serve as visual mnemonics of proper moral behavior for humans, particularly since what Westerners term *events* are perceived as *beings* by many Navajo. Particular constellations are seen as congruent with the structure of the home, the *hooghan.* Essentially, the *hooghan* is modeled on the celestial home. In this view, looking to the night sky provides a reflection of what one should see in looking into the earth-surface home—again providing a balanced unity between Earth and Sky, a balance through which the enlivening breath can be exchanged.

Pinxten and van Dooren also speak of balanced unity; as long as things remain in their proper places, balance ensues. When, however, there is a disruption of properness, as in a solar eclipse, it is taken as a sign of improperness (in this case, too many deaths) that must be restored ritually. Or when death-out-of-proper-time occurs, there is an imbalance in *nítch?i,* the in-dwelling wind or breath. Navajo understand that this animating force moves throughout the universe, inhabits all living beings, and is exchanged between Earth and Sky upon death. It is the most lucid statement in all the chapters of the importance of the universal breath.

Williamson's chapter on the Alabama demonstrates both that not all Native cultures are as intact as the Athabascan ones and that there are important gleanings to be had from combining archaeoastronomy and ethnoastronomy. Just where does archaeoastronomy end and ethnoastronomy begin? Obviously, there can be no pat answer to such a question. Each aspect of the interdiscipline has insights to offer and each has methodologies that are important for understanding the relationships obtaining among Native people and the Earth and Sky. Previous ethnographers who carefully noted what they were being told have provided precious records that allow reconstruction of previous beliefs with specific referents. In this instance, a reference to a "celestial skiff" can fairly certainly be identified as the Big Dipper. This, in turn, allows Williamson to begin to understand the importance of the night sky for the traditional Alabama, a people decimated by centuries of incursions by various Westerners and a people, so far as we know today, who no longer practice their traditional astronomy. Yet through working with the records from prior to cultural collapse, Williamson is able to demonstrate that when the stars were combined with religious ceremonials, and especially the Busk, channels were opened that allowed exchanges between the Earth-dwelling Alabama and the Sky-dwelling Celestial Beings. Smoke, as a kind of visible breath, served as a communication medium between the realms. And, if all went as dictated by the stars and enacted in ritual, the breath of universal life was restored for another year.

Zolbrod's consideration of the Seneca Thank-You Prayer moves to another level of breath, that of humans giving voice in gnomic speech to events that link Earth and Sky. Air, like Navajo Wind, is the breath of life existing between Earth and Sky. Voices giving speech into Air thus communicate not just with Earth people, but also with Sky dwellers—and again, the breath of life flows between the realms of existence. This chapter also illustrates the intimate series of connections in force between the now and the ago, such that speaking now of what was then brings it back into existence. Surely this is living breath, par excellence.

At one time the Cahuilla, whom Bean describes, lived in intimate contact with their deities. Moon, upon whom he focuses, not only lived with her Earth-surface children, but she also showed them how to play, how to behave socially, how to be proper morally; her breath was one of instruction. Now, because of events over which the Cahuilla had no control, Moon is silent, no longer speaking aloud to her children. She is visible but does not communicate. Instead, it is people who must return breath to her through their living and, most importantly, remembering. The breath of life is fragile, as the Cahuilla themselves fully recognize; it can go out and leave only a silent shell where once there had been active animations. Life's breath has already escaped from many former Cahuilla spirit beings and it is a struggle to maintain it in those who remain.

The struggle has been largely lost for Northwest Coast people, as Miller's chapter details. His is truly salvage ethnoastronomy. And as with the Ajumawi, it is painful to consider what has been lost. Not too long ago, there was a vital Earth and Sky connection, whether from one sitting in the astronomer's seat and observing horizon events or from one providing calendrical calibrations. Now, it seems the breath of Northwest Coast Earth and Sky interchanges is in danger of voicing its death rattle.

Immanent death is a key feature of Kehoe's chapter of a Blackfoot narrative that is very long and complex.[1] Improper behavior on the part of a son-in-law threatens death for some and occasions the death of others until the magical Clot-of-Blood intervenes and returns life's breath properly, defeating death with the gift of life through food that, in turn, allows continuation of human breath and hence life. Not only is the narrative's message in the Sky, but also it is represented iconographically on certain tipi covers. Going out of a tipi at night and seeing what Westerners call Orion's Sword allows a Blackfoot person to be reminded of the personal consequences of failure to live up to cultural mandates and the beauty of those who do abide by properness, for there is no greater gift than that of life, symbolized by the breaths we take and immortalized in the stars.

While Clot-of-Blood sustains through proper usage of natural resources combined with appropriate behavior toward categories of social personages, Goodman brings us face to face with sustenance being dependent upon personal sacrifice in his chapter on Lakota stellar directives. Westerners have been fascinated with blood sacrifice, whether in the Lakota Sun Dance or in various Latin American Indian rituals. Seldom, however, have they looked beyond the blood to consider the metaphysical statements being made. These Goodman outlines for us with reference to the Lakota, as he suggests that the willing participation in flesh and blood sacrifice has important consequences in today's world. The disappearance of a constellation is both the signal for a tribal gathering, where sacrifice will occur through the Sun Dance, as well as a reminder of important cultural values of sharing and generosity. As so often happens, the memory is made stronger by reference to the breach of social expectations rather than in upholding them properly.

If breath is the invisible animator, blood is the visible one. Through integration of a narrative of improperness of the selfish Chief, with observations of "the holy breath of God," the stars—the Lakota are seen to behave in consonance with celestial imperatives. In order for the earth to be renewed and its invisible breath sustained, there must be a concomitant sacrifice of visible blood, achieved by the Lakota through the Sun Dance ritual. Of all the chapters, the *axis mundi* is most clearly seen in this one, as the Sun Dance participants pierce themselves and are attached to the very connection between Earth and Sky, living and sacrificing themselves at, and on, the channel between Earth and Sky, exchanging their blood for the breath of the universe that will reanimate the Lakota people.

Life's breath animates more than bodily processes, as Chamberlain describes in his discussion of the Skidi Pawnee use of the Corona Borealis as a visual metaphor and moral template for political practices. Here, the animating force again changes levels and moves to a more abstract level as it concerns processes rather than individuals or even the tribe, as the stars give breath to political life. Just as it is necessary for food and breath to sustain living people, whether resident on Earth or in the Sky, it is also necessary for political life to be sustained so that groups of people can join together rather than remain as small, separate entities of a few weak persons. There is strength in congregation, provided the congregates have ways of behaving that reinforce the group while not denigrating the individual. Could there be a more perfect model for chiefly councils on Earth than the stellar model of the Corona Borealis in the Sky? Here, the Sky provides the breath of insight, allowing social life to exist harmoniously in the political sphere.

Throughout the book, physical and metaphysical life is restored and sustained by cosmic breath. After all the chapters were in hand, we searched

Silko's work for our epigraph, since both of us had a vague memory that she had focused on our topic some time previously. We were struck, when we refound her poem, by her economy of speech that, in a few lines of less than twenty-five words, summed up our book. We like to think that the Universal Breath blew through all our minds as we considered the ways in which Brown and Green archaeoastronomy are informed by Blue ethnoastronomy, for as Silko states, "It is all / a single breath."

## Notes

1. We, as editors, found ourselves in a paradoxical position with Kehoe's data. While most contributors were encouraged to include more of the folklore, or narratives, of the tribes under consideration, we had to ask Kehoe to cut and condense, for the narrative alone, as she first presented it, was longer than most of the chapters. We are hopeful that she will soon do a book-length treatment of the Clot-of-Blood narrative with all of its many ramifications for both Earth and Sky.

## References

Aveni, Anthony F. 1989. Introduction: Whither Archaeoastronomy? In *World Archaeoastronomy*. Cambridge: Cambridge University Press.

Bakhtin, Mikhail M. 1981. *The Dialogic Imagination: Four Essays by M. M. Bakhtin*. ed. Michael Holquist, trans. Caryl Emerson and Michael Holquist. Austin: University of Texas Press.

Broda, Johanna. 1982. Astronomy, *Cosmovision,* and Ideology in Pre-Hispanic Mesoamerica. In *Ethnoastronomy and Archaeoastronomy in the American Tropics*. ed. Anthony F. Aveni and Gary Urton. Annals of the New York Academy of Sciences, vol. 385.

Farrer, Claire R. n.d. *Blue Archaeoastronomy*. Unpublished manuscript.

# Index